Dr Andy Brough has, in a few 100 pages, helped elevate our understanding of leadership for the modern age. He takes us on a well-researched and informative journey with relevant examples and testimonies across a wide range of industries and sectors with a powerful message for all those aspiring to leadership. As an experienced practitioner working inside and alongside organizations, Andy offers us pragmatic advice and a set of tools and approaches to support how we amplify the impact of leadership. In the current context, his approach to amplify leadership as an impact you have in service of others, really resonates. As organizations strive to adapt; becoming flatter, less hierarchical, and more networked – the need for greater leadership from all increases. By connecting how we think about leadership in terms of self, the team and the wider organizational context, Andy has given us an opportunity to think in a more connected way on how to deliver the positive, exponential impact of leadership.

– Robin Lilley
Global Director of Leadership, Learning & Development, The Coca Cola Company, Atlanta, Georgia, USA.

* * *

Meaning and direction are two key concepts occupying the minds of people across the world. This publication succeeds in putting leadership at the centre of creating influence and impact through the meaningful integration of key personal characteristics and effective contextual awareness. Considering the twelve key elements as significant building blocks of relevant leadership, defines it directly into the key role of creating value and direction for people. Dr Andy Brough succeeds in presenting leadership in a practical and useful manner; relevant for both students of leadership and practicing leaders.

– Professor Alwyn Louw
Vice Chancellor, Torrens University and Academic Director, Think Education, Adelaide, Australia.

* * *

"Dr Brough has done a masterful job of explaining the complexity of leadership in a clear and straightforth manner. Professor Einstein is often quoted as saying, 'If you cannot explain something simply then you don't understand it,' and it is clear that Andrew understands leadership. He not only presents the complex elements of leadership but provides exercises to help readers gain deeper insight into the concepts. From leading yourself to leading others, whether in stable or chaotic environments, Dr Brough's book can help you understand the what, why, and how of leadership. This is a must read for anyone interested in understanding the deeper concepts of leadership."

– Bruce E. Winston, PhD
Professor, School of Business & Leadership, Regent University, Virginia Beach, USA.

* * *

"This not just another book on Leadership. It is a guide, template and coach for all of us to reflect on the leaders we aspire to be and the impact we want to make on others and the world around us. At its heart is a simple, yet powerful set of propositions, brought vividly to life, that capture a new paradigm for exponential effectiveness in leadership. This book has the potential to not only transform the way we think about leadership but, through application, to also provide the possibilities for real personal change and discovery."

– Chris Crosby
CEO TMA World & Country Navigator, London, UK.

"A great book filled with leadership wisdom and practical exercises to help in personal, team and organizational leadership. We need this kind of effort in a world where perhaps the greatest challenge is our leadership crisis. Andy's book will help us expedite the emergence of authentic leaders and leadership. Thank you Andy. This is especially needed in a world that will likely offer bigger and more dangerous leadership challenges."

– Adriaan Groenewald
CEO of Leadership Platform, founder of Thinklead, author of '*Seamless Leadership: Universal Lessons from South Africa*'.

* * *

A post-lockdown (I'm cautious about 'post-Covid') organisational context is going to require effective leadership that could pivot organisations to greatness, quickly; The type of leadership that will have an exponential effect. The twelve leadership principles are skilfully explicated through theory-infused practices, ranging from stories from Andrew Brough's extensive leadership practice, vignettes from real executive experiences, and questions at the end of each chapter to guide your own reflective practice. Ambitiously comprehensive in its reach, a highly useful companion for leaders to radically transform their game.

– Dr Andrew J. Johnson
Action Scientist and Chief Learning Officer, co-editor (and contributor) of '*Leadership: Perspectives From The Frontline*', Johannesburg, South Africa.

* * *

Without any doubt a must-read book for all leaders, those in managerial positions and proud South Africans. The reflections provided, the contextual interpretation and rich insights on important conversations in business, the words of wisdom from Dr Brough on leadership are a real inspiration. The book takes a novel approach and opens new avenues for further discussion and research on the underlying principles supporting effective and efficient leaders. It provides a valuable framework for daily use to inform and guide decision-making while simultaneously also deepening the current discourse amongst passionate scholars on the topic.

– Prof HB Klopper
Executive Dean: Research and Institutional Partnerships, Da Vinci Institute, Modderfontein, South Africa.

LEADERSHIP
THE EXPONENTIAL EFFECT

ANDREW J. BROUGH

LEADERSHIP
THE EXPONENTIAL EFFECT

PRINCIPLES FOR SIGNIFICANT PERSONAL, INTERPERSONAL,
TEAM AND ORGANISATIONAL IMPACT

Published by Quickfox Publishing
on behalf of the Brough Leadership Institute
PO Box 50660, West Beach, 7449
Cape Town, South Africa
www.quickfox.co.za | info@quickfox.co.za

Leadership: The Exponential Effect
ISBN Print: 978-0-620-89474-6

First edition 2021

Edited by Michelle Bovey-Wood
Book design and typesetting by Vanessa Wilson
Cover concept by www.bookcoverzone.com
Printed by Digital Action SA, Cape Town, South Africa

To Cor, Kirsty and Matt, for teaching me the
greatest leadership lessons.

ACKNOWLEDGEMENTS

A project like this is the result of a lifetime of formal and informal conversations; road trips; fireside chats; coaching sessions; lectures; break-out groups; virtual classes and webinars.
Thank you to my family. Without you, this book would never have come to fruition.

Thank you to Michelle Bovey-Wood for editing the manuscript and to Vanessa Wilson and Adele Wilson, the team at Quickfox Publishing, for the final product.

I need to acknowledge the support and input of my colleagues and friends, including Keith du Plessis; Russell Delmar; Dr Mark Manley; Dr Gustav Puth; Dr Fred Otten; Craig Rowe; James Mpele; Llewellyn Thorne; Karl Trusler and Prof. H.B. Klopper.

Thanks to all of those who agreed to have their stories included in the book, or who were interviewed for my Leadership Insights podcasts. Steve Barnett; Dr Cathy Bollaert; Colin Coleman; Prof. David Block; Murray Burger; Prof. Eugene Cloete; Jean du Plessis; Peter du Toit; Dr Dennis Farrell; Andrew Greeff; Julie Hollely; Gert Jonker; Prof. Nicola Kleyn; Riaan Manser; Seipati Mokhuoa; Maria Moralo-Sebate; Nokwazi Mzobe; Alex MacPhail; Gary Lee Price and Leesa Clark-Price; Brand Pretorius; Daniel Silke; Prof. Herman Singh; Captain Nicholas Sloane; Christo van der Westhuizen and Michele Wucker: Thank you so much for sharing your wisdom and insights.

Thanks to Michael Puffett for working with me on the initial concept and structure.

Then, to all of my clients and students from around the world with whom I have interacted, either in a coaching context or in short courses, in-house leadership or executive education programmes: You have taught me so much.

CONTENTS

PART TWO: LEADING THEM (DEVELOPING OTHERS)

PART THREE: LEADING US (DEVELOPING TEAMS)

FOREWORD

I find myself still processing the deep truths found within the pages of this book. Herein lie new ideas, new constructs and models, and above all, new applications in leadership – an area which, up until now, has felt over-subscribed.

Leaders determine so much of what we judge to be a success or a failure. They make the significant difference between the progress of humanity and the retardation of our development towards better things. So, as a society, we are at once desperate for good leadership, but saturated with so many leadership ideas, poor leadership, and wanna-be leaders that distract the world from its historical progress.

What a pleasure to have in my hands a book that concisely plots a way that is research- and evidence-based, logical, and instructional in the quest for better leadership.

Dr Andrew Brough has succeeded in making a substantial contribution to our understanding of leadership in a way that is engaging while still containing academic breadth and depth.

From interviews and stories with a wide range of leaders, Andrew extracts powerful principles and lessons that clearly illustrate his core theme of exponential effectiveness. The wide scope of references give authority to his message, and he has astutely drawn together a diverse range of leadership approaches into one approach that all leaders, at any level, will be able to use, either in part or in full.

The timing of this book is excellent. In the wake of the Covid-19 epidemic, leaders and organisations are resetting their thinking, models and strategies. It's an opportune time to shed old leadership approaches and adopt a more effective framework.

Being devoted to the development of leadership myself, I particularly appreciated the use of challenging and revealing questions, which apply Andrew's ideas in everyday leadership life.

I believe that in the future, we will come to cherish Andrew's integration of seemingly disparate dimensions of leadership into an approach that is grounded in goodness, practical in application, and aspirational in the hope that we can help establish leaders who follow his principles.

Now get on with reading the book and changing the world!

Dr Mark Manley
International Strategy and Leadership Consultant
Author of *The Leadership*

INTRODUCTION

A LEADERSHIP CRISIS

We needed a leadership reset. In a survey undertaken by the World Economic Forum in 2015 (Outlook on the Global Agenda[1]), 86% of respondents agreed that there was a leadership crisis at that time. Those interviewed referenced a failure to address global issues and noted that dishonesty and corruption had tainted global leadership.[2]

The survey revealed that one of the top three trends impacting the world (along with deepening income inequality and a growth in joblessness) was a lack of leadership. The other trends: rising geostrategic competition; a weakening of representative democracy; rising pollution in the developing world; intensifying nationalism; and the growing importance of health in the economy, also underpinned the need for robust and effective leadership.

Leaders, the survey showed, needed to negotiate the complexity of the increasing occurrence of severe weather events and resource-constrained water stress. The world required effective leaders and effective leadership. A leadership vacuum was not sustainable.

Although some leaders had anticipated the possibility of a global flu pandemic, no one could have estimated the sheer scale of the Covid-19 outbreak or the toll it would take on both human life and the world economy five years later. Now, as we look to emerge from the midst of an extended pandemic-induced lockdown, one could argue that the term 'leadership vacuum' is an oxymoron.

> **Vacuum**: "A void, a place in which there is no matter, where the pressure is so low that any particles in the space do not affect the processes being carried on there."[3] An environment where humans lose consciousness and die of hypoxia.

'Leadership' has hundreds of definitions, but if we mean: "*One or more people who influence one or more followers to achieve specific objectives*," then a vacuum seems contradictory. That, however, is precisely the point.

When leaders fail to lead themselves; when they fall at the bar of character and when they do not follow through with their commitments, unintended consequences may result. The initiatives they were designated to lead often end up failing. The 'particles' (the leader) no longer positively affect the 'processes'.

Many argue that nothing happens in a leadership vacuum. If only that were true. A better way of putting it might be: "Everything you don't want to happen, happens in a leadership vacuum." The system breaks down and followers become disgruntled, frustrated, and even disheartened.

In a leadership vacuum, trust, irrevocably eroded, reaches an all-time low. The 2015 Edelman Trust Barometer[4] indicted that only 42% of the general public trusted the government to do what was right.[5] Five years later, the 2020 global survey showed that while some institutions are trusted as 'competent', and others as 'ethical', the general public does not regard any single institution as both competent and ethical.[6]

Historians attribute Aristotle with the notion of "*horror vacui*", or "nature abhors a vacuum". Although Aristotle was referring to the natural world, he may well have been describing the world of leadership, too! Although scientists went on to prove him wrong, (we now know that vacuums are evident throughout the universe), we repeatedly see a lack of ethical leadership in different spheres of society: A lack of accountability and follow-through; blame-shifting; overpromising and under-delivering are all characteristics of a leadership vacuum.

If the leader does not positively affect the processes, this can directly impact the followers, resulting in higher volatility, uncertainty, complexity and ambiguity.

- Have leaders become impervious to the needs of their followers?
- Have we, as followers, lost consciousness?
- Have we become numb to the inaction of our leaders?
- Have we become 'heady' from living 'well below normal pressure'?

Leadership is the subject of countless books. Between all of those written pages are some excellent insights, principles, and practical advice. There is plenty of evidence to suggest that while some people are more naturally predisposed to leadership, others can – and do – learn how to lead. Leadership skills can be developed and improved through a process of systematic equipping. I write from the belief that leaders are born to be made.

Some of the enduring questions asked by leadership specialists are:

- What does effective leadership look like?
- What is the relationship between self-leadership, leading others, leading teams and leading for results?
- What do organisations need to do to create a sustainable, high-quality leadership development pipeline?

"Leadership is one of the most observed and least understood phenomena on earth."

J.M. Burns
Historian and political scientist

This book attempts to answer these questions. *Leadership: The Exponential Effect* is a cumulative expression of 25 years' experience working in the areas of leadership development in more than 80 countries. The individuals with whom I work are organisational leaders committed to personal and professional development. The leadership principles examined in this book apply equally in the business context, government and the not-for-profit sectors.

"What is leadership to me? How to be, not to do."

Francis Hesselbein
Former CEO of Girl Scouts of the USA and leadership author

Why 'The Exponential Effect'?

The exploration of leadership has many different facets. It is worth examining what we mean by "exponential".

> **Exponential**: *adjective \ˌek-spə-'nen-chəl*
> 1. Characterised by an extremely rapid increase (as in size or extent).
> 2. Mathematics: Including or using an exponent.
> 3. Involving a variable in an exponent <10x is an exponential expression>[7]

This book aims to highlight the relationship between widely-accepted leadership principles: Although you may possess the correct separate, individual, leadership elements, you will only see their power – their true impact – when you combine them; when you catalyse. It takes:

- The right elements.
- In the right place.
- At the right time.

Together, these elements unlock a chain reaction, creating an exponential effect. Some writers have focused on the attributes of leadership, and others have focused on the impact of good leadership. This book, however, explores a systems approach.

Leaders are committed to creating a systems approach for success. This systems approach means understanding both the effective leader and the impact of that leadership.

Leadership can be quite an abstract concept, so to illustrate the exponential effect and to help clarify my thinking, I have looked for examples in nature and in the world around us. Mathematics; chemistry; chaos theory; fire; dominoes; physical distancing and fractals are just some of the instances in which this exponential effect becomes apparent.

Mathematics

Number sequences are probably the most practical example of the exponential effect. By taking only one number and continually doubling it, what is known as a geometric progression is produced.

In this example, there is a factor of two between each number. This progression quickly generates exceptionally high numbers.

> **An example of exponential effect is the number sequence:**
>
> 1, 2, 4, 8, 16, 32, 64, 128, 256, 512, 1 024, 2 048, 8 096,
>
> expressed in the function $f(x) = 2x$

When you unlock leadership principles and see them applied in some form of sequence, the results are often exponential.

Fire

Fire requires a heat source, fuel, and oxygen. Separately, these elements do extraordinarily little. However, when combined, they produce a chain reaction that has the exponential effect of creating light, heat, and energy. Left unchecked, the combination of these three elements can do exponential damage.

In 2017, a raging bushfire ravaged my hometown of Knysna, on the Garden Route of South Africa. Thousands of hectares of forest were destroyed, many people lost their homes and some businesses never recovered. Tragically, seven people lost their lives in the fires. Years later, the cause of the fires is still being probed.

> - Does leadership have a 'heat source', 'fuel' and 'oxygen'?
> - If so, what happens when you combine them?
> - Can leadership get out of control?

Mentos and Coke

"If you're a fan of YouTube, you've probably encountered the explosive Mentos-Coke clips: If you drop a tube of Mentos into a bottle of Coke, the carbon dioxide escapes very quickly. The rapid expulsion forces the gas out of the bottle in a shower of foam.

In 2014, a Guinness World Record of 4 344 simultaneous 'Coke and candy geysers' was set at the Festival Internaçional del Globo in León, Guanajuato, Mexico.

The Mentos and Coke experiment epitomises the exponential effect. In a leadership situation, leaders seek to identify the leverage points in their teams and organisations in order to create the maximum impact.

> What are the leadership 'geysers' that you need to create and release in order to see meaningful results?

Dominoes

Professor Stephen Morris of the University of Toronto showed the power of the exponential effect through the use of dominoes.[8]

Intricate, record-breaking domino set-ups require endless patience and endurance, before simply tipping the first one over. Previous world records include the longest domino chain; the biggest domino fall; the most extended domino spiral and the tallest domino structure built.

Here is where Prof Morris's demonstration was so powerful: Starting with a domino just five millimetres high and one millimetre thick, he showed how each domino has the potential to knock down not only another similar-sized domino, but also one that it is one-and-a-half times its size. He used 13 dominos – the largest of which weighed almost 50kg and stood over a metre tall. As unbelievable as it sounds, that tiny, first domino can knock over the huge 13th domino.

Prof Morris showed that if you were to keep proportionally increasing the domino size, it would take only 29 progressively larger dominoes for the five-millimetre domino to topple one the size of the Empire State Building. What a remarkable exponential effect!

So, for leaders, the exponential effect is a crucial one to understand. Even if you are starting small and have limited influence, you can still have a dramatic impact.

There is a big difference between influence and positional authority. You do not need to rely on hierarchy to get things done. In fact, in the new world of work (which is matrixed, remote and characterised by virtual teams), understanding how to create small wins through leverage will become an increasingly important leadership ability.

The Butterfly Effect

Edward Lorenz used chaos theory to question the relationship between a butterfly flapping its wings and the potential direct impact that would have on the formation of a hurricane. A negligible change in one part of a system could have a significant, sometimes indirect, impact on another.

A minor change in the initial condition of one part of the system, seen over time, can produce a dramatic result – a chain reaction leading to the large-scale alterations of events. From a leadership perspective, this makes the exponential principle even more significant. The responsible leader understands the interconnectedness of what he or she does; and the accountable leader has a deep appreciation for his or her actions.

Physical Distancing

About three weeks into my local lockdown, in an attempt to address the person-to-person transmission of the Covid-19 virus, the Ohio State Department of Public Health in the US released a video on the power of physical distancing. The video went viral because it graphically captured the multiplier effect of a single ping pong ball dropped on to other balls positioned over mouse traps. The ball was released twice: Once, when the other balls were close together, and then again when they were further apart. The difference was dramatic. In the first instance, that single ball directly impacted almost every other mouse trap and every other ping pong ball. In the second demonstration, when the mouse traps were spaced out, there was almost no impact either on the other balls or the traps. The message was clear: Physical distancing can slow the spread of the virus.

Fractals

One of nature's most compelling examples of the exponential effect is fractals. A simple Internet search for 'fractal images' reveals a kaleidoscope of colours and shapes presenting in fascinating patterns. Without getting into the mathematics of fractals, simply put: Fractals are self-replicating patterns that are identical at all scales. Under a microscope, non-fractals reveals all different kinds of shapes, angles and patterns. A fractal is different. Fractals are infinitely complex and are created by repeating an uncomplicated design process. When you divide a fractal pattern into its parts, you achieve a nearly identical, reduced-size copy of the whole.

Fractals are abundant in the natural world. Some of the most dramatic examples include the structure of the human lungs; seashells; spiral galaxies and even, unbelievably, certain kinds of broccoli. They are fitting examples of the exponential effect. Their structure and design mean that you can zoom in exponentially to see their self-replicating patterns repeated over and over again.

Fractals, along with all of the previous examples, create powerful leadership and organisational metaphors. Whatever you want your organisation to look like, you need to ensure that it is replicated repeatedly at smaller and smaller levels – be it a business unit, department, or a team – right down to the individual member.

An ideal situation for a leader would involve every follower embracing the mission, vision, and values of the organisation (as represented by the leader, or leaders). Fractal leadership is usually evident in instances where everyone understands, buys into, and embodies that for which the organisation stands.

This is not to suggest that we should be aspiring to create 'cardboard cutouts' of leaders, or that everybody should be a replica of the leader, either. Effective leadership reflects the values, ethos, and DNA of the leader in the followers in a way that is authentic and consistent.

Four key priorities

The aim of this book is to help equip leaders: To be a resource to enable leaders to realise the exponential effect of transformation at personal, team and organisational levels.

I want to move this 'exponential' idea from a leadership metaphor into a leadership reality. To achieve this, it is worth clarifying my priorities in authoring the book:

1. Strengthening leadership understanding, aptitude, and skills.
2. Supporting leaders who have some responsibility for teaching organisational values.
3. Equipping senior leaders with the tools to analyse, impart and apply core leadership principles.
4. Illustrating the relationship between elements of self-leadership; the development of followers; team building; and the delivery of results.

Building on the idea of fractals, consider the relationship between:

- Individual elements of leadership.
- Those elements that enable leaders to engage with others.
- Those elements that underpin broader team and organisation-wide capability.

FIGURE 1: THE FRACTAL SPIRAL AS A METAPHOR FOR LEADERSHIP

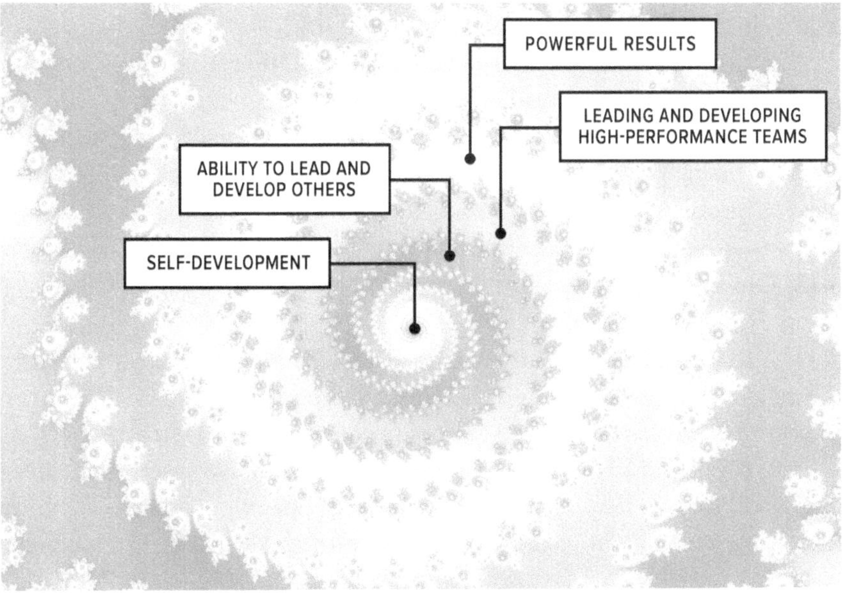

- In the centre is the reference to **self-leadership**.
- As the spiral opens outwards, the next loop represents the **ability to lead and develop others**.
- As followers develop and grow, this ever-increasing multiplier effect expands into **leading and developing high-performance teams** and eventually into **powerful results**.

Effective self-leadership exponentially replicates at all four levels of the leadership dynamic. Of course, the exponential effect works in reverse, too. When leaders fail to lead themselves, there is a direct knock-on effect to those they lead, the teams of which they are a part, and to the broader stakeholder community with whom they interact – often with disastrous consequences.

I believe that leadership begins with the individual – the basis of self-leadership.

When I first sought feedback on the initial structure of my book from certain individuals, I was asked several times why I had chosen to start Part One of the book with **Leading Me (Developing Self).**

"Isn't leadership about others?" I was asked.

Indeed, this is true, especially when one looks at principles of both followership and servant leadership. However, when it comes to explaining the exponential effect, it is critical to acknowledge the importance of being able to lead yourself before you can lead others.

Part Two, **Leading Them (Developing Others)**, focuses on the relationship between the leader and the follower. Having established vital elements of self-leadership at a personal level, it then becomes easier to begin to focus on building these elements with those you lead. You also need to be able to influence others before you can ever lead a whole team.

Part Three, **Leading Us (Developing Teams)**, focuses specifically on team leadership and some of the critical components of high-performing teams.

In Part Four, **Leading for Results (Delivering Solutions)**, we explore the relationship between the other three leadership components and the impact they have on creating a catalysing environment to enable results.

Some Agile leadership thinkers propose that we move away from 'directive' leadership, which focuses on results, to a 'catalysing' approach, which focuses on creating an enabling environment. I believe that if the correct environment is created, the solutions will emerge. If the solutions are correct, the results will follow.

Although we move between the ideas of 'self', 'others', 'teams', and 'results', it is not always possible to separate these ideas from one another.

It's also worth mentioning that there is no single 'ideal' leadership skill set. However, leadership involves getting things done. Different contexts and situations require varied leadership approaches.

Twelve Key Leadership Elements

Numerous texts explore the 12 key leadership ideas that make up this book. My research involved comparing a series of leadership competency models that were developed by some of the world's top leadership thinkers and writers. Once I had found the commonalities in those models, I then compared the competencies to my own experience of what makes an effective leader.

FIGURE 2: INTEGRATION OF THE LEADERSHIP ELEMENTS

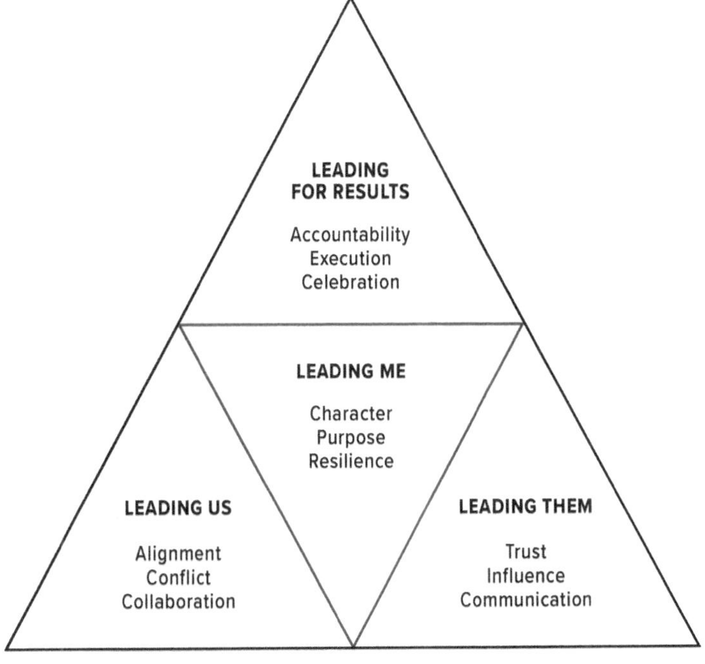

I then compared that list of leadership elements with those identified by some of the top international talent management consultancies as crucial competencies for leadership effectiveness. The content covered in *The Exponential Effect* is by no means unique, exhaustive, or even necessarily sequential. However, there is sufficient evidence to show that these 12 leadership elements will go some way to supporting competency frameworks that enable more effective leadership.

While different organisations may indeed require more specific skill sets, this book covers a set of universal core leadership elements placed in a simple leadership matrix. Each of these elements will be explored in detail, while sharing some of the insights of leaders from their own specific experiences with these leadership elements.

At the end of each chapter, you will find a series of questions relating to the content that has been covered. These questions will help you to work either on a personal level or with your team, while facilitating discussion and debate. They will also support you in the compilation and execution of an action plan, ensuring that the principles apply within your specific leadership context.

Finally, these elements will culminate in the compilation of 12 principles of a proposed Personal Leadership Charter.

Leadership: A Definition

Among the many definitions of leadership, I defer to my colleague, work psychologist Prof Theo Veldsman, who describes leadership as: *"Acts of persuasive influence exercised by a collectivity of individuals (shared leadership), engaging a set of stakeholders (mobilised followers), in enabling and empowering ways, concerning a joint course of action and, intended to bring about a shared, desirable, future-referenced outcome (dream) with the desired effect (legacy) within a specific context, past, present and future referenced."*[9]

With this definition as an overarching and framing context, I would like to add:

> **Leadership**: Moving a network of stakeholders in a direction towards achieving a specific goal.

Leadership Results and Impact

At the end of the 20th century, the authors of the book *Results-based Leadership* highlighted the importance of connecting leadership attributes to results. One of the key points made in the book was: "*When exploring leadership and leadership development, we often stop at the point of talking about leadership attributes, rather than putting greater emphasis on the measurement of results.*"[10]

Leaders do need to be able to both set and realise objectives, and to develop practical solutions by creating an enabling environment. Current research supports the findings of previous studies, which suggest that effective leadership has an impact both within and outside of an organisation.

Inside the Organisation

Several key leadership researchers have highlighted the fact that effective leadership has a direct impact on the organisation's ability to attract and retain the right talent. Leaders also have a significant effect on employee engagement, satisfaction and commitment. A review of US Gallup studies over the past 18 years reveal that average workforce engagement tracks around 30%.[11] Leadership effectiveness also has a significant bearing on sales force effectiveness and workplace productivity.

Outside the Organisation

Over the past 10 years, my specific research has focused on the impact of leadership on the broadest range of stakeholders, from the perspective of corporate reputation. There is now sufficient evidence to prove the correlation between effective leadership and customer satisfaction, corporate image, and corporate reputation.

How a leader defines success is essential. During my interactions with leaders around the world, I've seen that many are focused on a legacy of entrepreneurship, job creation, market capitalisation, profitability, and even sustainable development goals. These are critical results, for which all leaders must take responsibility.

Effective leaders need to consider a distinct set of leadership questions:

- Did I make a difference?
- Did I develop people?
- Did people's work lives have meaning?
- Did I get people to the point where they realised their potential or self-worth?
- Did I make a difference in society through my involvement?
- Did I leave people with memories to treasure?
- Did I show respect?
- Did I show compassion?

Join us as we consider these questions in the context of the leadership journey.

PART ONE

LEADING ME
(DEVELOPING MYSELF)

1 / CHARACTER

LET THE EVIDENCE SPEAK FOR ITSELF

Determining the non-negotiable, core drivers that constitute who you are, what you stand for, and the mental and moral qualities that make you a unique, distinctive leader.

Costa Concordia

At 4pm on the evening of 13 January 2012, the Costa Concordia, a cruise liner almost twice the size of the Titanic, set sail from Rome, Italy, for a seven-day cruise – as it did every week. The ship was scheduled to arrive in Savona, Italy, the following day. Around 9.15pm, the ship took a five-mile detour to pass closer to the picturesque Tuscan Island of Giglio.

Captain Schettino appeared to have misjudged the manoeuvre. At 9.30pm the vessel collided with a rocky reef known as Le Scole. The collision ripped a 36m-long gash in the hull of the ship and the Concordia lost power. Captain Schettino's order to abandon ship exposed passengers to, what can only be described as, absolute chaos.

As the leader of the vessel, the captain was simply not available. Under maritime safety regulations, his job was to assist passengers and crew members in times of distress. However, reports revealed that Captain Schettino left his command and sailed to safety in a lifeboat before the evacuation of his ship was complete.

While the Costa Concordia was sinking, Capt Schettino had a heated exchange with Capt Gregorio De Falco of the Italian Coast Guard in Livorno. Captain De Falco repeatedly ordered Schettino to return to the ship to oversee the evacuation. The captain resisted, making excuses that it was dark, and the vessel was listing.

A complete, translated transcript of their conversation follows:

SCHETTINO: It's Capt Schettino.

DE FALCO: Schettino, listen to me. There are people trapped aboard, now you go back, you will go with your rescue boat under the stern of the ship. There are some steps, you climb those steps, and you get on board. You get back to me, letting me know how many people are on board. Is that clear to you? I am recording this conversation, captain.

DE FALCO: Speak in a louder voice.

SCHETTINO: So, the ship right now... [inaudible]

DE FALCO: Speak in a loud voice! Put your hand by the microphone to cover it and speak up! Is that clear?

SCHETTINO: So, right now the ship is tilted.

DE FALCO: I understand that. Listen to me, some people are off using the rope ladder on the stern side. You go back there, and you go up that ladder the opposite way. You go on board the ship, and you tell me how many people [are there] and what they need. You tell me if there are children, women or people that need assistance and you give me a number for each one of these categories. Is that clear? Look, Schettino, you may have saved yourself from the sea, but this will put you through a lot of trouble. It will be very bad for you! Get back on board for [expletive]'s sake!

SCHETTINO: Officer, please.

DE FALCO: There are no "pleases"! Get back on board! Please assure me that you are going back on board.

SCHETTINO: I am here on the rescue boat. I'm right here. I didn't go anywhere else. I'm here.

DE FALCO: What are you doing, Captain?

SCHETTINO: I'm here to co-ordinate rescue operations.

DE FALCO: What are you co-ordinating? Get back on board and co-ordinate rescue operations from onboard the ship.

SCHETTINO: [inaudible]

DE FALCO: Do you refuse to do that?

SCHETTINO: No, I'm not refusing to do that.

DE FALCO: What? Are you refusing to get back on board?

SCHETTINO: No, I am not refusing to go back. I am not going because the other rescue boat stopped.

DE FALCO: Get back on board! This is an order! You don't need to make any other assessment. You have declared that you have abandoned ship, therefore I'm in command. Get back on board right now. Is that clear?

SCHETTINO: Officer…

DE FALCO: Can you hear me?

SCHETTINO: Yes, I am getting back on board.

DE FALCO: Then go! And call me right away when you are on board. There's my rescuer there.

SCHETTINO: Where is your rescuer?

DE FALCO: My rescuer is on the stern side, go! There are already bodies, Schettino! Go!

SCHETTINO: Officer, how many bodies are there?

DE FALCO: I don't know. I know about one. I have heard about one, but you must tell me [expletive]!

SCHETTINO: Do you realise it's dark out here and we can't see anything?

DE FALCO: What do you want to do? Do you want to go home? It's dark, so you want to go home? Get on the stern of that ship, climb the ladder and tell me what can be done, how many people there are, and what they need. Right now!

SCHETTINO: I'm here with my second officer.

DE FALCO: You and your second officer must get back on board right now. Is that clear?

SCHETTINO: I just wanted to tell you that the other rescue boat here with other rescuers stopped. It's just stopped. Now I've called the other rescuers.

DE FALCO: You've been telling me the same thing for an hour, now get back on board! On board! And you get back to me right away, telling me how many people are there.

SCHETTINO: It's fine, officer. I'm going.

DE FALCO: Then go. Right now!

SCHETTINO: I have spoken to the company, and there seem to be some people still on board, possibly about 100.

DE FALCO: And you can't even give me a precise number? You say: "There seem to be?"

SCHETTINO: Well, we were carrying out evacuation procedures, but now all the officers have gathered on the rescue boat with me."

DE FALCO: Where are you guys? All on the rescue boat? Excuse me, earlier you told me you were with one colleague only – now all the officers are there?

SCHETTINO: Yes, there's me, my second officer and…

DE FALCO: If the officers were able to get down there, it means they were still able to move.

SCHETTINO: Indeed, now.

DE FALCO: Then why are they not going back on board to see what the situation is like and then tell us about it, thank you? Send them on board! Send someone on board to co-ordinate!

SCHETTINO: Now it's not…

DE FALCO: Send someone back on board!

SCHETTINO: I am trying to co-ordinate that.

DE FALCO: I am giving you an order. You must send someone on board now!

SCHETTINO: We are going on board to co-ordinate ourselves…

DE FALCO: Exactly! You must go on board to co-ordinate the disembarking! Is that clear?

SCHETTINO: We can no longer get on board now. The ship has sunk completely.

DE FALCO: Why did you allow them to get off, captain?

SCHETTINO: I didn't. We just abandoned ship.

DE FALCO: With 100 people still on board, you abandoned ship?

SCHETTINO: I didn't abandon any ship… because the ship turned on its side quickly and we were catapulted into the water.

DE FALCO: We'll clarify later what actually happened. For now, tell me everything that goes on. Everything! Place yourself under the ship with your rescue boat and don't leave.

SCHETTINO: We're here. We're here.

(Ends).[12]

Thirty-two passengers and crew lost their lives in the disaster. A Spanish salvage diver died after cutting his leg on a metal sheet while preparing the vessel for removal. In the aftermath of the incident, prosecutors charged Schettino on two counts: Manslaughter and causing a maritime disaster. They used footage from a video shot by Italian firefighters to show the captain standing at the ready, preparing to climb into a lifeboat.

Schettino still claims that he fell overboard; that, as the ship rolled on to its side, he was thrown into the water and then into a lifeboat. Five other crew members who were initially charged, secured plea bargains. The court sentenced Schettino to an effective 16 years in prison: 10 years for multiple manslaughters, five years for causing the shipwreck, one year for abandoning the passengers, and one month for providing false information to port authorities.

How will the world remember Captain Schettino?

- For his poor judgment in sailing too close to the reef?
- For his poor decision-making?
- For his apparent cowardice because he 'jumped' ship?
- For his profound crisis of personal ethics and values?

Only time will tell.

The judges held Schettino responsible for not just causing a maritime disaster, but also for his lack of response once the ship ran aground. Schettino admitted to the court that his reason for sailing close to Giglio was to "impress the passengers". From the available facts, events surrounding the demise of the Concordia were as much a tragedy of personal values as it was the product of poor decision-making. The sheer size of the vessel and the scale of the impact, combined with the almost non-stop media coverage, made it hard to ignore.

In the aftermath of the disaster, some commentators argued that Schettino's employers made him a scapegoat. Further investigation revealed that one could not wholly absolve the shipping company of responsibility for the technical failings of the vessel; for an incomplete evacuation plan; and for the disastrous communication between authorities and the ship.

In a letter written from jail in 2018, Schettino argued: "*Any officer, part of a bridge team, is expected to be able to reckon and detect the peril in order to be in a position to offer his contribution to the whole team.*"

The reality is that leaders at all levels of society, in both financial and non-commercial organisations, struggle daily with values-based decisions. Some enjoy the 'anonymity' of leading small, medium or micro-enterprise businesses, believing that 'mistakes' in values-based judgments might be more easily overlooked. Many are leaders of multinational empires or even entire nations, overseeing often 'hidden' errors of judgment. Either way, decisions based on values, or the lack of them, have repercussions.

> But, this begs the question:
> - How do leaders develop character?
> - Why is character so important when it comes to leadership?"

"We live in an age of transparency. People are going to know your values, whether you announce them or not."

Lisa Earle Mcleod
Sales leadership expert

Although many organisations are realising the increasing importance of character when it comes to developing leaders, others have tried to argue that leadership character is purely situational. Surely you can't even begin to consider self-leadership without considering individual character.

Forevermark Diamonds

The Jewel of Capricorn; The Eternal Sky; The Song of Lyra and The Atacama Sky are all names of exquisite Forevermark diamonds. The De Beers Group is both the world's leading diamond company and the largest diamond producer by value. Of more than 140 million carats of diamonds produced annually, less than one per cent achieve this highly-coveted status.

Based on stringent criteria, these gemstones are hand-selected and then inscribed with both an icon and a unique identification number (the inscription is $1/20^{th}$ of a micron deep – $1/5\ 000^{th}$ the depth of a human hair). These diamonds are exceptional; unparalleled and recognised for their intrinsic qualities and characteristics.

"A diamond's character cannot always be explained and is often likened to chemistry – a person may be drawn to it without having tangible reasons why. It is something that speaks to the heart and is often felt at first glance."

Shimansky

Diamond experts refer to the '4Cs' of a diamond's character: Cut, colour, clarity and carat. The 'cut' of the diamond refers to how the polished finish produces fire (flashes of colour), brilliance (how white light reflects internally and externally), and scintillation (flashes of light produced as the diamond moves). The cut also determines the diamond's strength, symmetry, and durability. The diamond's proportions and finish determine the final assessment.

The 'colour' of the diamond describes its transparency, or hue. The rarest diamonds in nature are colourless, although 'fancy colour', 'pink' and 'blue' diamonds, have a higher value.

The 'clarity' of the diamond refers to the measure of the intrinsic features, the purity, and the degree to which it is free of very tiny blemishes or inclusions (sometimes referred to as the unique fingerprint of the diamond).

The 'carat' weight of the diamond is such that, the larger the carat, the higher the rarity and value. These four: Cut, colour, clarity and carat, create the 5th 'C' – a sense of confidence in the intrinsic worth of the diamond.

"There are three things that are extremely hard: Steel, a diamond, and to know one's self."

Benjamin Franklin

The traditional (and somewhat stereotyped) image of a leader is one of an individual who has excellent vision, looking out into the future, gazing through a telescope, taking a long-term view. While vision is, and remains, a critical part of leadership, none of that forward-looking is sustainable without also undertaking some extremely focused introspection. Practical, authentic leadership starts with self-reflection and self-discovery.

Otto Scharmer, Senior Lecturer at the Sloan School of Management (MIT) and founder of the Presencing Institute, describes the process in this way:

> *Galileo transformed science by encouraging us to use our eyes, our senses, to gather external data. Now we are asked to broaden and deepen that method by gathering a much more subtle set of data and experiences from within. To do that, we have to invent another type of telescope: Not one that helps us to observe only what is far out – the moons of Jupiter – but one that enables us to observe the observer's blind spot by bending the beam of observation back upon its source: the self that is performing the scientific activity. The instruments that we need to utilize to bend the beam of observation back upon its source include not only an open mind (part of the normal mode of inquiry and investigation) but also an open heart and open will.*[13]

This "bending of the observation beam back upon its source", with an open mind, heart and will, brings us to the next question:

- What is character?

Just as diamond experts have identified the four or five elements of a diamond's character, I want to explore the five primary aspects of a leader's character; shaped significantly by the leader's moral attributes and qualities.

Five Cardinal Facets

Character refers to one's distinct values, traits, or virtues, while **personality** refers to the collection of abilities; behaviours; beliefs; ideologies or attitudes.

In this chapter, I examine what I view as five distinct facets of character, linked to identity, integrity, insight, intent, and initiative.

"It can be argued that our moral character is the sum total of our values, virtues, and vices."[14]

Al Gini and **Ronald M. Green**
Leadership authors

Character as Identity

At some point or another, every leader will struggle with questions of identity, and every leader needs to make peace with the virtue of humanity. Although they may never bring themselves to verbalise them, leaders who are honest in the process of self-reflection need to come to terms with the following questions:

- Who am I?

This first question is the basis of identity. A leader's identity links directly to who they perceive themselves to be, long before they are defined by what they do. Other questions of identity are:

- Who do I fear I am?
- Who do I fear I am not?
- Who do I feel tempted to pretend to be?
- Where am I leading from?

These four questions reveal something of the potential 'imposter thinking' that arrests leaders, preventing them from developing the full range of their leadership abilities.

Leading from a basis of fear is paralysing, and leading from a foundation of fear is limiting. Leading from the grounds of suspicion produces second-guessing, misgivings, apprehension and mistrust, both in the leader and those they lead.

Fear-based leaders alienate followers, resist self-disclosure and feel compelled to be something that they are not. This temptation to pretend is not only inauthentic, but also exhausting.

Answers to the question: "Where am I leading from?" provide clarity about identity. This clarity enables an individual to arrive at the place of leadership where personal ego enhances, rather than gets in the way of, effective leadership. We have tended to think of effective leaders as being devoid of ego, but maybe we need to reframe that approach. What is clear is that we need to make sure that we don't conflate ego (a clear sense of personal identity) and egocentrism (an inability to appreciate that others may have a different point of view).

Leadership with positive ego produces positive shared results – results that benefit both leaders and followers.[15] Egocentric leadership, on the other hand, is hampered by self-centredness and by the need for ongoing approval from others – a temptation that should be resisted at all costs.

Leaders who lead from the basis of threat; insecurity; inadequacy; scarcity and insufficiency will always be looking over their shoulders. These leaders' apparent sense of lack tempts them to overcompensate. They tend to respond from a basis of defensiveness whenever their competency or judgment is challenged.

Leadership without egocentrism means that you can get out of the way of your own leading. One of South Africa's great business leaders, Brand Pretorius, who headed up Toyota South Africa and later the McCarthy Group, has his own perspective on the ego question:

"Ego is a source of energy and inspiration, because you want to prove yourself, be an achiever and be recognised upfront. Don't be obsessed with "ME INC" and then become arrogant and insensitive. Your willingness to serve diminishes, and you start creating distance between yourself and your people.

"To be a dedicated or a devoted servant leader, you almost have no option but to disintegrate your ego, otherwise the willingness to serve and the capacity to care will not be authentic. If you use it as a technique, then to be authentic and genuine, you have to acknowledge that 'without my people, I'm nothing'.

"I needed their help, intelligence, energy, advice, loyalty and contribution. I needed to touch their hearts. I had to sacrifice my ego, get off my pedestal and become one of them, all without abandoning the critical leadership function of giving direction and going first.

"The crux of my answer is that if you want to be an authentic servant leader, you need to suppress your ego, put the interests of your people and the organisation first. Emphasise for the good of all, without abandoning the need to give direction, and instil confidence and hope. Be humble without being timid."

Brand then reflected specifically on his move from Toyota to McCarthy:

"Had I remained with Toyota; I wouldn't have realised what I am telling you now. The dark days of McCarthy brought me down to earth. I tried to impose a culture because my frame of reference was different, and I came horribly short.

"It was quite humbling because I was parachuted in to lead the organisation. I arrived with a reasonable reputation, and I thought people would acknowledge that, but they didn't. I discovered that after a couple of months, I had limited influence and (realised) that to influence, you have to engage the minds and you also need to touch the hearts. In addition to caring and serving, you also have to show respect. Imposing a different culture was interpreted as a lack of respect for what they had, so it was a valuable lesson. The people get the impression that if you don't acknowledge and respect) them. They just isolate you, and then you end up on your own and without influence.

"If you are a new leader, you have to 'infiltrate' in the most constructive manner possible. You cannot demand trust, respect and confidence. Position means little. At face value, people will support you, but to get into their hearts, you have to do the proper thing, the right thing.

"I did my best and achieved some success. When I assess my behaviour, I deliberately refer back to the principles I believe in, my 'code of personal conduct', as the reference point. I am tough on myself, and ask: 'Am I behaving consistently, with integrity; am I honouring the principle of fairness? Am I demonstrating my compassion?'

"I do these assessments often… sometimes in the middle of the night. Sometimes, I don't sleep because I talk about being transparent and open and the acceptance of responsibility. I use the power of reflection quite often to do self-assessment. One has to work extremely hard on one's emotional, moral and spiritual intelligence. The toughest taskmaster should be your conscience.

"I am far from the complete leader. I fall short, but I am very blessed. I have a wife who is the most principled person I know. When I am in doubt, I check that there is alignment between the principles I have committed to and what I am doing."

Brand is very clear that he embraced the *"disintegrating, suppressing and sacrificing"* of his ego in order to be effective as a servant leader. But, as students of leadership, we are now starting to think slightly differently about this idea. Rather than shrinking back and sacrificing ego, effective leaders need to step into who they are but still ensure that their leadership focus is on developing and improving others. The question is how can leaders both serve and care for others in an authentic way without feeling the need to underrate how they see themselves? An understanding of the difference between ego and egocentrism is paramount.

> How do you respond to these questions around identity?

Stop. Pause. Reflect.

> This time, reread each question, slowly, carefully and reflectively. Dig deep before you answer. Try and respond as honestly as you can. Allow that "beam of observation to be bent back upon its source."

Here are the questions again:

> 1. Who am I?
> **Your answer:** "I am ..."

Notice how we often resort to position, title or our track record of accomplishments in an attempt to answer this one.

> 2. Who do I fear I am?
> **Your answer:** "I fear I am ..."

This answer often seems to focus on insufficiencies, inadequacies, failures and shortcomings.

> 3. Who do I fear I am not?
> **Your answer:** "I fear I am not ..."

Answers in this section may seem to focus on issues of self-worth ("I fear I am not worthy"), or confidence, competence, or experience ("I fear I am not qualified, or not skilled; I fear I'm not a good speaker").

Sometimes the answers reveal deep-seated beliefs about age, race, sex, or nationality. ("I fear I am not old enough, young enough"; "I'm not male"; "I fear I am not a specific nationality", etc.) Each of these answers is a way to try to legitimise our own, often-negative view of our place in the world.

> Now try to answer the question, this way:
>
> "Because I am not ... I can't ..."

Now ask yourself if the answers are true, or if there is merely a mindset that you have held. Notice how it frames your identity and, therefore, your leadership from a scarcity mindset. Over many years of executive coaching, I've seen how people will use this lens as a reason for feeling that they could never lead others.

> 4. Who do I feel tempted to pretend to be?
> **Your answer:** "I often feel tempted to pretend to be ..."

Often answers here seem to focus on others and involve some degree of comparison. We tend to become hung up on the talents, sufficiencies, adequacies, accomplishments, track records and successes of others.

> 5. Where am I leading from?
> **Your answer:** "I am leading from hope/strength/naivety/fear/despair/ obligation."

I am not sure how you would try and resolve these questions of identity, but let me suggest that they compel us to address issues not just of personal emotional security, but also of deep purpose and destiny.

The worldview that I hold enables me to reason my identity within the context of my leadership; my marriage; my family; my business and my community from the following points of departure:

> **I am confident that:**
>
> **My identity is based on who God has called me to be.**
> **My identity is not determined by what I do, but rather, by the deep-seated sense of acceptance of my uniqueness and gifting from God.**
> **My security is based on who God has called Himself.**
> **My destiny is based on what God has called me to do.**

This confidence does not mean that I have not struggled, or that I do not ever struggle with the question of identity. Each time I start to sense a challenge to these foundations, I find myself going back, time and again, and reaffirming these answers.

"The true measure of leadership is in its redundancy. So, lose your ego and gain engaged, passionate people, gain a thriving business, make the world a better place."

Prof Isaac Getz
ESCP Business School

Once 'character' has been addressed at the level of 'identity', leaders need to be willing to answer the questions of 'integrity'.

Character as Integrity

Although widely regarded as a city of many contradictions, I always find Florence to be a delight. It is even more magnificent in the summer. One of my most potent memories on my first trip to Italy is walking through the Galleria dell' Accademia di Firenze. As you walk through the Hall of Prisoners, past the 'Slaves', you are confronted by the magnificence of, what is probably Michelangelo's best-known work, *La Tribuna del David*, more commonly known as the statue of David.

But, what many tourists fail to realise is that much of the city's renaissance roots trace back to the work of Giotto, born 200 years earlier. History records that he was appointed the Director of Cathedral Works in 1334, and the *Campanile*, named after him (adjacent to the postcard-famous Brunelleschi's Dome), was completed three years after his death.

Giotto was renowned for transporting Gothic art to a more nuanced place by exploring perspective, and showing the human figure in a way that captured the 'psychology' of the subject. He was also one of the first artists to personify the virtues. One of his classical works is the painting of the stone statues of *Seven Vices-Seven Virtues*.

Prudentius was a classical scholar who believed that the human character develops through a series of choices we make throughout our lives. These choices lay down habitual styles of responding that become increasingly ingrained as we mature. Prudentius based his model on Giotto's paintings of the stone statues.

Leaders of character are leaders of integrity. In almost all character assessments, integrity is the number one leadership attribute. But, like so many of the ideas associated with leadership, we need to explain what we mean.

> **Integrity**: The Latin word for integrity bases its meaning on the idea of 'wholeness' – the same root word for 'integer'. Integrity is *"a leader's consistency in values, word, actions, principles, methods, measures, expectations, and outcomes."*[16]

Simply put, a leader with integrity stands up for what he or she believes.

When you discuss integrity with ethicists, they argue that without the 'moral' qualifier, integrity is simply about consistency of beliefs with actions.

Imagine my initial shock when, early on in my leadership development career, one of my mentors, Dr Mark Manley, challenged me to think of leaders who, throughout history, had acted atrociously. It did not take me long to rattle off a list that included infamous people known more for their acts of genocide and global oppression than anything else.

Mark's next question floored me: "You would agree that these were leaders of integrity?"

"Well of course not!" I began.

"But, based on the definition of integrity as 'consistency in values, word, and actions', then you have to conclude that they demonstrated integrity," Mark replied. "They acted on their values and did what they said they were going to do."

After thinking about it for a moment, I had to concede that, using that definition, even a person who promises to do great harm and then follows through with that promise, would have to be regarded as demonstrating integrity.

That conclusion about integrity seemed insufficient and fundamentally flawed in terms of what I was trying to articulate at a leadership level. It was lacking the completeness of the picture of integrity that I wanted to portray. Of course, it is possible to be a leader with integrity without being moral. So, when we talk about leaders of integrity, we mean leaders who demonstrate steadfast adherence to agreed principles within a well-established moral code.

> We refer to integrity as a leader's moral consistency in word
> and action, irrespective of circumstances.

HR professionals and recruitment specialists have devised ways to assess potential candidates' integrity as part of their total employability profile. However, it seems (certainly at first glance) that the majority of these tests are primarily concerned with an individual's likelihood to conform to the rules. The general approach to integrity in the workplace seems positioned from the "let's-catch-the-crooks" perspective – a plan that's certainly not without merit.

PwC publishes an annual *Global Economic Crime* survey. Their 2020 report revealed that reported global fraud amounted to $42 billion in asset misappropriation; procurement fraud; bribery and corruption; cybercrime; and accounting fraud.[17] This fraud demonstrate the tension between making a profit on the one hand, and the need for business compliance on the other. Those interviewed identified bribery and corruption as the most significant future economic threat to business.

While it is relatively easy to calculate the financial implications of this fraud, what is not as easy to quantify is the impact that this lack of integrity has on share price; relations with regulators; stakeholder relations; employee morale and, ultimately, brand reputation.

Over the years, psychologists have devised several integrity tests. Two of the most well-known ones are the Perceived Leader Integrity Scale (PLIS)[18] and the Behavioural Integrity scale.[19]

Perceived Leader Integrity Scale (PLIS)

The PLIS Scale asks questions of direct reports to indicate how well each item describes their immediate supervisor.

Would he/she:

1. Use my mistakes to attack me personally?
2. Always get even?
3. Give special favours to certain 'pet' employees, but not to me?
4. Lie to me?
5. Risk me to protect himself/herself in work matters?
6. Deliberately fuel conflict among employees?
7. Be considered evil?
8. Use my performance appraisal to criticise me as a person?
9. Have it in for me?
10. Allow me to be blamed for his/her mistake?
11. Falsify records if it would help his/her work situation?
12. Lack high morals?
13. Make fun of my mistakes instead of coaching me to do my job better?
14. Deliberately exaggerate my mistakes to make me look bad when describing my performance to his/her superiors?
15. Be vindictive?
16. Blame me for his/her own mistake?
17. Avoid coaching me because (s)he wants me to fail?
18. Treat me better if I belonged to a different ethnic group?
19. Deliberately distort what I say?
20. Deliberately makes employees angry with one another?
21. Be a hypocrite?
22. Limit my training opportunities to prevent me from advancing?
23. Blackmail an employee if (s)he thought (s)he could get away with it?
24. Enjoy turning down my requests?
25. Make trouble for me if I got on his/her bad side?

26. Take credit for my ideas?
27. Steal from the organisation?
28. Risk me to get back at someone else?
29. Engage in sabotage against the organisation?
30. Fire people just because (s)he does not like them, if (s)he could get away with it?
31. Do things that violate the organisational policy and then expect his/her subordinates to cover for him/her?

One of the criticisms of this instrument was that although it certainly helped to identify non-ethical behaviour, it was not particularly good at identifying ethical behaviour.

"I believe leadership is not about power or status, but that it has to do with influencing. It has to be earned by leaders that have integrity. It is not what you say, it's what you do. It's about character, not charisma."

Brand Pretorius

The Behavioural Integrity Scale tried to address this gap by reframing what is meant by ethical behaviour in the context of everyday situations. Participants respond to questions on a five point scale.

The Behavioural Integrity Scale (BIS)

1. There is a match between my manager's words and actions.
2. My manager delivers on promises.
3. My manager practices what he/she preaches.
4. My manager does what he/she says he/she will do.
5. My manager conducts himself/herself by the same values he/she talks about.
6. My manager shows the same priorities that he/she describes.
7. When my manager promises something, I can be certain that it will happen.
8. If my manager says he/she is going to do something, he/she will do it.

9. I would be willing to let my manager have complete control over my future in this company.
10. I would not mind putting my wellbeing in my manager's hands.
11. I would feel good about letting my manager make decisions that seriously affect my life.

The Giotto Integrity Scale (GIS)

The third addition to these integrity tests is the Giotto Integrity Scale.[20] The GIS is a work-based assessment that uses seven scales based on the Prudentius model of personality. While it is clear that character and personality are not the same, it is beyond the scope of this book to explore these differences in detail. Suffice to say, the focus of character is much more on a sense of moral worth and responsibility.

- **Prudence.** (Proficiency vs. carelessness.) Assesses the degree of care that is likely to be taken in carrying out a task.
- **Fortitude.** (Work orientation vs. absenteeism.) Assesses the work ethic.
- **Temperance.** (Patience vs. hostility.) Assesses the ability to control aggression, in whatever form.
- **Justice.** (Fair-mindedness – balanced and impartial in decision-making – vs. subversion – tends to be suspicious of the intentions of others.) Assesses fairness in judging the actions of others.
- **Faith.** (Loyalty – shows obedience to authority and a sense of duty – vs. disloyalty – might ignore the advice of those who know better.) Assesses the sense of obedience to company policy.
- **Charity.** (Generosity – open and honest in dealings with others – vs. covetousness – occasionally known to elaborate or distort the truth.) Assesses social desirability items.
- **Hope.** (Initiative – resourceful and enthusiastic about the future vs. inertia – somewhat pessimistic about the future.) Assesses a sense of purpose and a forward-looking approach.

To what extent have you developed the habit of either:

* Being prudent, or careless in carrying out our task?
* Working hard, or only as necessary?
* Being prone to settle disputes by reconciliation, or by aggression?
* Being trusting, or suspicious in your dealings with your colleagues?
* Having faith in your employers, or only in yourself?
* Being open, or scheming in your dealings with others?
* Being welcoming of, or resistant to change at work?

When we refer to integrity and character, it is the leader's ability to consistently self-govern, with or without external constraints.

> You cannot have brand integrity without employee integrity.
> You cannot have employee integrity without leadership integrity.
> You cannot have leadership integrity without personal integrity.

You cannot talk about 'character as integrity' without referencing the fundamental beliefs that people hold about what is valuable, worthwhile, and non-negotiable. Character and values are integral. There is a sense in which 'character as integrity' relates closely to the virtue of transcendence. As a virtue, these are strengths that tie to coherent beliefs and actions about a higher purpose and the meaning of life.

Character as Intent

Leaders of character are leaders of intent. A leader's intent is as important as a leader's actions. Where 'intent' is the concentration of the will, intention is the action that follows.

> **Intent** suggests deliberate planning, or the active application of the will to make an action happen.

When we talk about 'character as intent', we refer to the leader's desire that those with whom they interact be the best that they can be. Leaders of intent have no alternative agenda and feel no need to manipulate others to achieve their own goals.

> **Malintent:** The opposite of intent, it suggests the intention to harm someone or engage in wrongdoing.

Intentional leaders consider not just what needs to be done (the task), but also why it needs to be done (the purpose). In considering *why* something needs to be done, intentional leaders also need to consider the eventual outcome (intended and unintended), should this goal be achieved or not.

Leaders of intent display character values, traits and behaviours that are also concerned with reassuring followers that: "I am not out to get you!"

When Chairman and CEO of PepsiCo Indra Nooyi was asked by *Fortune* magazine for the most important leadership advice she had ever received, she said: *"Whatever anybody says or does, assume positive intent."*[21]

The four-phase framework that underpins this book (culminating in effective execution) might create the illusion that leadership is purely about getting something done through others. Leaders of intent understand that while results are a priority, 'being' always precedes 'doing'. This 'being' brings us to the question of character as insight.

Character as insight

This element requires being self-aware, socially aware, and situationally aware. I am attempting to integrate, if not collapse, character and elements of emotional intelligence (EI) into one set of ideas. Moral character and EI are distinct concepts, but there is an interrelationship between the elements that enhance ethical behaviour, (identity; intent; integrity; insight and initiative) and the self and social awareness that gives expression to these traits.

As Vicki Zakrzewski, Education Director of the Greater Good Science Centre (GGSC) at University of California Berkeley puts it: *"Emotional intelligence still needs a moral rudder."*[22]

Author Daniel Goleman notes: *"We don't want to be in a situation where we are valuing a calculating intellect but ignoring the virtues of a warm heart."*[23]

We need to focus on both performance character (perseverance, optimism, and creativity – what I call 'character as initiative') and moral character ('character as intent'). To do this requires insight.

Insight as self-awareness

If the beginning of leadership development is emotional intelligence, then the beginning of emotional intelligence is self-awareness.

"Emotional self-awareness refers to an individual's perception of their own ability to identify and 'read' their own emotions and recognize their impact. Self-awareness involves knowing one's strengths, weaknesses, drives, values, and impact on others."[24]

Daniel Goleman
Psychologist, author and science journalist

Once self-awareness is in place, it becomes possible to regulate our emotional responses, both within ourselves and in the way that we interact with others. Organisational psychologist Tasha Eurich conducted several surveys and found that most respondents were far less self-aware than they thought.

Her research showed that there are two types of self-awareness: Internal self-awareness (the extent to which we can identify our values, passions, and aspirations), countered by external self-awareness (understanding how other people view us).

One of Eurich's key findings was that having a high internal self-awareness does not necessarily mean an individual will have high external self-awareness, and vice versa.[25]

This idea of character as insight helps us to make ethical decisions.

"This above all: to thine own self be true,
And it must follow, as the night the day,
Thou canst not then be false to any man.
Farewell, my blessing season this in thee!"[26]

Polonius to Laertes, *Hamlet*
William Shakespeare

Insight as social awareness

Socially aware leaders consciously manage their relationships with others. They are 'socially intelligent'.

"The socially intelligent leader focuses on demonstrating empathy (feeling with others and sensing non-verbal), attunement, (listening with full receptivity), empathic accuracy (understanding another person's thoughts, feelings, and intentions), and social cognition (knowing how the world works)."[27]

Daniel Goleman

If one of the virtues of character is humanity, then this insight underpins a leader's ability to 'tend and befriend' others. In so doing, leaders of intent demonstrate that they are leaders who care. Leaders of intent are also leaders of empathy. Historically, however, one does not typically think of the words 'leadership' and 'care' in the same sentence.

The traditional command-and-control styles have groomed many of today's C-suite leaders. In commenting on how work will look different in a post-Covid-19 world, Dr Roze Phillips, a Group Executive of People and Culture, noted: *"Business models will change. Those companies that have flattened bureaucracy and removed the hierarchy will benefit from the agility this creates. Command-and-control companies will struggle."*

For many organisations, the focus was on leading from a place of authority and position. Their key objective was on primarily meeting the needs of shareholders. What a privilege it has been for me to work with senior leaders of multinational companies, and to have them consider what 'caring deeply' means to them. Some of their answers (among others) have included:

- "Doing the right thing and doing things right."
- "Commitment to people and the environment."
- "Being mentally present with the team, not just physically."
- "Doing the right thing for your team members and the communities in which you work."
- "Operating safely and delivering projects on time."
- "Thinking of others first."
- "Do no harm."

In discussions and interviews with successful leaders, the recurring themes of **transparency** and **openness** emerge. It strikes me how 'character as insight' also links closely to the virtues of temperance and justice. The question of leadership intent has moved front and centre with the emergence of more significant accountability mechanisms, along with the quest for businesses to deliver stakeholder value as much shareholder value. Insight requires leaders to be far more situationally aware.

Insight as situational awareness

Leaders of insight are people of sound judgment. They take a systems approach to the interconnected world. Their discernment means that they are astutely aware of their worldview. These leaders read events through the lens of that worldview, conscious of the impact of the decisions they take, based on their understanding of the context in which they live.

Situational awareness comprises at least three elements:

1. Firstly, there is the question of context. Leaders with high situational awareness can place events (planned or unexpected), current information (facts or opinions) or even people, in context. This kind of insight means that leaders do not just take things at face value. They are able to examine something from all sides because they have developed situational awareness as 'perspective'. Sometimes this even means holding contradictory views at the same time.
2. By applying critical thinking skills, leaders do not only see things in context, but they also develop a way of understanding what they see. This thinking is situational awareness as 'comprehension'.
3. Having used perception and comprehension, these leaders are then able to foresee not just a 'probable' future, but also a 'possible' future. This final element of insight is called 'projection'.

This interplay between perspective, comprehension and projection is not always a linear process. Leaders of insight are happy to test their initial assumptions about their perceptions; to test how they have comprehended what they have seen and even, where necessary, to test and retest previous projections. Leaders of insight are also happy to admit when they are wrong. Leaders of insight are also leaders of humility.

Character as Initiative

Leaders of character are leaders of 'initiative'. Even in the face of opposition, they have the courage of their convictions to accomplish results. These leaders put steps into action, even before being asked to do so. Initiative is what motivates leaders to 'put legs' on to feelings of empathy, to give life to compassion and, where necessary, to even deal with unresolved conflict.

If we go back to Giotto, these leaders are people of fortitude. At the same time, they are resourceful and enthusiastic about the future. So, character as initiative comprises at least three parts:

First, 'initiative' requires acts of courage, even in the face of pain (some might refer to this as bravery or persistence). Chapter 3 explores what happens when circumstances, or even other people, challenge our character. We will consider this under the topic of Leadership Resilience.

Secondly, leaders of initiative are resourceful. This simply means that they can identify ways to overcome opposition.

Thirdly, they have a favourable view of the future. The situational awareness we identified earlier seems to tie into the ability to take the initiative, too.

Character is a foundational element of the exponential effect. In a positive sense, character provides the anchor to much of what makes up good leadership. Conversely, failures in leadership character have untold repercussions – both for the leaders concerned and for those whom they lead. At the same time, I am more convinced than ever that leaders of character are also leaders of purpose.

1 / EXERCISE

CHARACTER QUESTIONS

For you to consider:

- Have you listed your non-negotiables (values that define you and that will define your work)?
- How do your values guide you in the kind of leader you are becoming?
- Consider moments in your life in which you have cut across or compromised your values. How did these moments impact you?
- Who would you hold up as a value-based leader? Why do you think this way?
- How does character influence your recruiting decisions?
- What, in your opinion, are the hallmarks of good character?
- Can you think of instances in your life in which a lack of character has jeopardised a leadership opportunity?

2 / PURPOSE

SEEING THE UNSEEN

> Clarifying the essential reasons for your existence and
> shaping your intentions and objectives as a leader.

"Those who have a 'why' to live can bear
almost any 'how'."

Victor E. Frankl
Man's Search for Meaning

Resolution to Act

In the early part of the 1780s, the English abolitionists met at Barham Court, the home of Charles Middelton, to discuss a national campaign to end slavery. One of the men attending those meetings was the MP for Kingston-Upon-Hull, William Wilberforce. He described slavery as "*so wicked, a trade founded in iniquity*", that he could not justify how "*one part of the world could make its success dependent on the depopulation and devastation of another*".

When you read Wilberforce's speech to the House of Commons, you can see how a keen sense of purpose determined his course of action.

"... As soon as ever I had arrived thus far in my investigation of the slave trade, I confess to you, sir, so enormous, so dreadful, so irremediable did its wickedness appear that my own mind was completely made up for the abolition. A trade founded in iniquity, and carried on as this was, must be abolished, let the policy be what it might, let the consequences be what they would, I from this time determined that I would never rest till I had effected its abolition.

"Such enormities as these, having once come within my knowledge, I should not have been faithful to the sight of my eyes, the use of my senses and my reason, if I had shrunk from attempting the abolition: it is true, indeed, my mind was harassed beyond measure; for when West-India planters and merchants retorted it upon me that it was the British parliament had authorised this trade; when they said to me: "It is your acts of parliament, it is your encouragement, it is faith in your laws, in your protection, that had tempted us into this trade, and has now made it necessary to us."

"It has become difficult, indeed, what to answer; if the ruin of the West Indies threatened us on the one hand, while this load of wickedness pressed upon us the other, the alternative, indeed, was awful. It naturally suggested itself to me, how strange it was that providence, however mysterious in its ways, should so have constituted the world, as to make one part of it depend for its existence on the depopulation and devastation of another.

"I could not, therefore, help, distrusting the arguments of those, who insisted that the plundering of Africa was necessary for the cultivation of the West Indies. I could not believe that the same Being who forbids rapine and bloodshed, had made rapine and bloodshed necessary to the wellbeing of any part of his universe. I felt a confidence in this principle, and took the resolution to act upon it: soon, indeed, the light broke in upon me... Having heard all of this you may choose to look the other way, but you can never again say that you did not know."[28]

William Wilberforce
House of Commons
Tuesday, 12 May 1789

Wilberforce started with a concern for social conscience. His *"confidence in this principle of wellbeing in any part of the universe"* made him resolute in his purpose. But it was not as if things changed immediately. After his speech, parliament agreed to introduce a series of resolutions on slavery, but it would take a further 18 years for them to promulgate the Slave Trade Act, in 1807.

In their classic book, *Good to Great* Jim Collins and Jerry Porras noted that one of the stand-out reasons for individual companies outperforming others was what they called *"an enduring sense of purpose"*.[29]

I have spent many days consulting with leaders and helping them to define organisational missions, visions, goals, and objectives. Only a few of their companies had initially taken the time to equip followers to define and describe their individual purpose within the context of that specific organisational focus.

I don't believe that you can have purposeful leadership if you don't have purpose-filled leaders. If you trace the evolution of leadership thinking over the last 50 years or so, you will see how the 'purpose principle' has also evolved and matured.

The Purpose Principle

Purpose as servant leadership

> **Servant leadership**, first developed by Robert Greenleaf, was defined as: *"standing for what is good and right, even when it is not in the financial interest of the organisation. Meaningful work for employees is as important as providing a quality product or service for the customer."*[30]

A robust underlying principle of servant leadership is the idea that leaders put followers first. They have to make their personal development a priority in order to help them understand the 'larger purpose' of their work. For Greenleaf, leadership meant making a choice; a choice to serve, motivated strongly by a belief in a purpose that was always going to be significantly more worthwhile than merely making more money (a higher purpose).

"Servant leadership is not a contradiction to achieving organisational objectives. The two form such a powerful partnership. Because of your servant leadership approach, the probability that you will get people to volunteer their intelligence, energy, expertise and commitment goes up exponentially."

Brand Pretorius

Purpose as transformational leadership

Transformational leadership came to the fore in the mid-1970s. This approach saw leadership as a *"process of leaders and followers raising one another through autonomy and purpose to higher levels of morality and motivation."*[31]

This 'process' brings about change in individuals and social systems. A transformational leader who has a sense of purpose in life (as opposed to a transactional manager) displays a strong emotional involvement with the ideals and vision of the organisation. The work and personal life of this leader are not that distinguishable. Transformational leaders achieve commitment through inspiration. They hold people accountable to an agreed purpose, and place a strong emphasis on the end state. These leaders are not necessarily looking for conformity. Their deep sense of purpose engenders powerful feelings (positively or negatively) in followers.[32]

Purpose as responsible leadership

As leadership thinking has evolved, the context of leadership has changed from focusing solely on the leader-follower relationship to more of a 'stakeholder view'. Organisations and their leaders have become far more aware of the need to develop social capital. To achieve that, leaders have to adopt responsible decision-making.

> **Responsible leadership**, as described by Thomas Maak and Nicola Pless, is a *"relational and ethical phenomenon, which occurs in social processes of interaction with those who affect, or are affected by, leadership, and who have a stake in the purpose and vision of the leadership relationship."*[33] So, the purpose of responsible leadership is to take *"responsibility, through an acknowledgement of purpose, principles, respect and power. The result is the creation of both value and social capital."*[34]

Chapter 11 will cover the importance of responsibility in further detail.

Purpose as authentic leadership

In the late 1930s, business executive and author Chester Barnard first proposed that authentic leadership was the litmus test for what he called "*executive quality*". But we forget that the ancient Greek stoics also used this notion of authenticity as a robust moral reply to what they saw as declining civic and religious values at the time.[35] Society seems to have come full circle.

It is only in the last 20 years, since authors like Bill George began writing about authentic leadership, that we have sat up and taken note. George's description (particularly as it relates to purpose) is daunting, provocative, and inspiring.

> **Authentic leaders** are: *"People of the highest integrity committed to building enduring organisations, who have a deep sense of purpose and are true to their core values who have the courage to build their companies to meet the needs of all their stakeholders, and who recognise the importance of their service to society."*[36]

George notes that since 2003, when he authored his first book, there has been what he calls a 'sea change' in the general view on leadership. Authentic leadership is now widely regarded as the gold standard.

Many of my students, upon seeing this definition for the first time, ask: "Who are these leaders?" or: "Do these leaders even exist?" The combination of high integrity; commitment; a deep sense of purpose; of being true to core values; and of serving stakeholders and broader society, make this kind of leader an exceedingly rare breed.

Looking across the global political spectrum, my students have also highlighted a vast gap in credibility between the leaders occupying positions of power and the 'authentic leader' that George described. I believe that we should not allow any individual leader's short-term 'success' to nullify the fact that, over time, authentic leadership is what matters most. Those leaders who are short on integrity and operate with no real concern for servicing society at large, will eventually be exposed.

Many leadership thinkers and authors equate leadership, purpose and calling. I do not use 'calling' in a religious sense but, rather, as the extent to which one can clarify 'meaning' in life.

In my work with leaders, I witness a dynamic interplay between purpose, meaning, calling and wellbeing. People with a higher sense of purpose display improved physical and mental health. Professor of Medicine at the Icahn School at Mount Sinai, Alan Rozanski, says that when it comes to wellbeing, *the need for meaning and purpose is number one. It's the deepest driver of wellbeing there is.*[37]

Defining purpose

But how exactly do aspirant leaders discover and articulate 'purpose in life'?

Author, speaker and leadership coach Kristi Hedges poses five questions to support clarity around purpose:[38]
- What are you good at doing?
- What do you enjoy doing?
- What feels most useful?
- What creates a sense of forward momentum?
- How do you relate to others?

In their article, *From Purpose to Impact*, Nick Craig and Scott A. Snook pinpointed the following three questions as helpful:[39]
- What did you especially love doing when you were a child, before the world told you what you should or shouldn't enjoy doing? Describe a moment and how it made you feel.
- Tell us about two of your most challenging life experiences. How have they shaped you?
- What do you enjoy doing in your life now that helps you sing your song?

Penny Law, who has a PhD in Spiritual Leadership, proposes these four questions:[40]
- If money were no concern, how would you spend your time?
- What is your *raison d'etre*, your reason for existing?
- What are your key strengths and talents, as identified by you and others?
- What deeply motivates and inspires you?

A leader who is purposeful and purpose-filled is committed to finding answers to these critical questions.

> I would add:
> - What makes you come alive?
> - What breathes life into you?
> - How will you measure your life?
> - How will you move from success to significance?

Research on 'purpose in life' concludes that among other questions, purpose starts with identifying the absence or presence of clear life goals. These goals help to clarify the degree to which life is meaningful or not. Whether or not we attain those life goals goes a long way to explaining life purpose.[41]

Prof Bill George calls this quest for personal purpose: "*Discovering your True North*".[42] I have used his books and approach to personal and authentic leadership as the seminal texts in an online MBA programme, in a unit called *Leading in a Dynamic Era*. What a delight it is to see postgraduate, working professionals challenged, often for the first time, about their life purpose. Each student is required to write a Personal Leadership Development Plan (PLDP). This is not just an academic exercise: My PLDP, written in my postgraduate years, two decades ago, is something to which I refer back frequently.

Here are some the short extracts and reflections on 'purpose' from my students:

"My past does not define me. Where I come from does not define who I am. I can reframe my story. My story creates purpose and empowerment; it represents small monuments of conquering."

"I must learn not to be influenced by power and money (which) compromise my integrity. I must not be distracted from my True North and learn to frame and transform my crucibles from wound to pearl. Knowing that I cannot bury my past, given that my memories will always be with me, the other key insight is to avoid seeing myself as a victim of my past and to begin to embrace it."

"My values are essential. I must not let others distract me from doing what I believe is right."

"I also view my failure to prioritise my tertiary education as a stepping stone to my success. I had a strong desire to self-correct, and I pursued it."

"My vision is to be empathic and honest. I aim for recognition as an impactful leader in my industry of expertise. I will stay committed to growing as a leader and sharing value-added input towards my followers, for them to be successful. My vision is to contribute to their full potential to make my community a better place, so that our descendants can live peacefully."

"The purpose of my leadership is to mentor and coach ethical leaders of tomorrow, empowering them to transform the world positively. My purpose statement is as follows: E to the passion of 3 = Empower, Encourage, Establish (body, soul and mind)."

To determine your leadership purpose, it is essential to identify and clarify your strengths. Purpose links positively to strengths.

Dr Courtney McCashland co-developed the Standout Strengths Assessment with Marcus Buckingham. At the age of 26, Courtney's brother took his life. In the technical report on this global strengths test, she reflects:

"In life, we find ourselves cursed and blessed with things we can't control. Yet we have choices, and we have time. What we choose to do with our time is up to us. A witness to my brother's struggle and tragic death, I felt then, and feel to this day, tremendous accountability. Curt's death inspired my life's mission: To invest my own gifts to help others find theirs.[43]

My friend, Gert Jonker's life might help to illustrate this notion of purpose as a life mission.

From Concern to Cause

In 1981, at the height of apartheid, and immediately after his final year of high school, 17-year-old Gert joined the Uniform branch of the South African Police Force. During his time at Police College, he was one of 75 of the youngest students promoted to the rank of sergeant in the history of the South African Police. After four years, (including two counter-terrorism deployments to the Angolan and Botswana borders), Gert resigned to study Law and Political Science.

The Police Security Branch recruited Gert as a Strategic Communications Specialist in Crime Intelligence at John Vorster Square (now Johannesburg

Central Police Station), which was a primary location for interrogations and detentions during the apartheid era. Gert joined the Media Analysis Unit, but refused to participate in illegal operations. The Security Branch questioned his loyalty. They even suspected him of being a double agent.

"To get rid of me, they sent me to the Hillbrow Police Station," Gert says.

In the late 1980s, this move was widely regarded by members of the force as a career-ender. There, Gert spent his time working in the position of Detective Sergeant in the Internal Investigation Unit, which focused mainly on police impropriety. His role led to a changed view of policing and to serving the community – all at a time when Hillbrow was undergoing notable change and urban decay.

But then, as Gert describes it, what came next was a significant, eventually life-changing, transfer. In 1992, the Family Violence, Child Protection and Sexual Offences Unit assigned Gert as a Detective Warrant Officer.

Talking to Gert, it is clear that, of everything he had seen on the street up to that point, his seven years in that unit had a profound effect on his perspective and outlook on life. Gert was confronted daily with brutal, horrific crimes committed both against children and by children.

As one of a few national specialists concerned with looking for missing children and investigating child abuse, child pornography and paedophilia, there was also a sharp focus on occult-related crimes involving children at this time.

Gert describes that period in his career as one of *"real satisfaction"*. He recalled a sense of *"real-time measurable impact"*; *"a sense of results"* and even, in some cases, *"an overwhelming sense of gratitude from the children that we helped"*. Probed a little further, Gert said: *"I felt appreciated because we had a made a small difference in a child's life. I felt as if I was able to serve the community."*

At the same time, Gert became very aware of what he calls: *"my limitations in my role as a police officer"*, and of the *"limitations of the system"*.

"As more cases came my way, I realised I was not a social worker, I was not a youth worker, and in fact, I had an extremely limited mandate."

As Gert interacted with various parts of the community, including places of safety and children's homes, he could not ignore the challenges and deficiencies in the system. The often-fragmented handling of children's cases meant that, as far as Gert could see, children were not enjoying the full benefits of the child abuse management system.

Gert began to work on different forums, looking to enhance the integration between the police department, the justice department, and the health department. Gert recalls that although things did improve, he realised that he could not ignore the gaps in the management of child and youth cases.

"I recognised that I had some 'unique requirements', and a sense of discontentment in wanting to make the system better for the children. I also realised that as a police officer, I had a skills deficit, a capacity deficit and even a financial deficit."

Gert eventually left the police force to work in executive protection for a six-year period. There, he had the opportunity to interact with some prominent business leaders, including the CEO of a South African bank, the chairman of the national power supplier, and a business leader who went on to become the SA Minister of Finance. But, he never forgot the children.

"I needed to cross the divide and develop my skills and capacity outside of the police force. Listening and learning from these men; being informally mentored; as well as having access to the senior staff of 650 branches of the bank across the country, meant I was taking steps closer to realising my dream."

At the age of 33, Gert, and his wife, Antoinette, launched the Induduzo Foundation, a social transformation organisation geared towards service delivery for poor and marginalised juvenile communities. They also started two children's homes: Bethany House Child and Youth Care Centre, and the IKUSASA Child and Youth Care Centre.

The Bethany House Trust, a Child Protection Organisation, as envisaged by the Children's Act (Act 35/2005), renders specialised services to child victims of abuse, neglect, and abandonment. However, it certainly did not happen overnight.

Twenty-three years later, the foundation and the children's homes have impacted more than 10 000 children. Gert has also had the opportunity to influence government thinking and policy and to improve case management. He has also held executive positions on national, provincial and local child welfare forums.

"It is a calling. The only outcome I want is for the best interests of the child to be served. But it is also often a heartbreaking journey. Unless it's a calling, you simply won't make it.

"Our purpose is simply to take kids away from places of harm and to place them in better environments. But there is no checklist for success. Each child is unique, and not every situation has a happy ending. Foremost, in my mind are the cases that didn't work out. They spur me on to look at where we went wrong

and what we would do differently to minimise the chances of failed cases in the future."

Walking into Bethany House always floods me with emotions. It is now not just one building, but an interconnected set-up with a central kitchen and dining area, surrounded by separate homes for children of various ages.

I am never left unmoved when I visit the baby home at the bottom of the garden. I am always struck by the sheer dependence of these young lives, often rescued from unbelievably awful situations. What society might cruelly regard as 'statistics', are real people, confronted at the start of their lives with the horror of abuse, neglect and even abandonment.

Over the years, many HIV-positive babies have arrived at the home. Sadly, quite a few have died as a result of the ineffective HIV/AIDS policy of previous national administrations.

"*These children often struggle to connect emotionally. Even at such an early age, it is challenging for them to attach to caregivers,*" Gert says.

"*Because they arrive so lacking in human interaction, so emotionally detached, we need to make physical contact a high priority. We are talking about a relationship that has a starting point, but no end. A child is not a 'project'. We are on a journey, with many relationships. For many of our children, even when they leave home and go out into the world as adults, we have the privilege of being substitute parents.*"

When I pressed Gert a little more on 'purpose' and 'meaning' in what he does, he replied: "*This all comes at (the cost of) a huge personal sacrifice. There is no difference between our personal lives and our professional lives. We have had to bring everything to the table and remove the limitations and start giving. When we do, the reserves never seem to run dry. There is no exit strategy and no retirement plan. I will die doing this.*"

We are not all going to be a William Wilberforce or a Gert Jonker. We should not even try. Identity and purpose are intrinsically linked. If we each have a unique identity, it follows that we each have a unique purpose.

These examples might create the impression that purpose is only borne out of pain (your own, or the pain of others). From conversations with many leaders, there is an apparent strong correlation between personal struggle and defined purpose. Discovering that purpose involves identifying what the world needs and then clarifying what you love.

The Japanese have a beautiful way of reframing purpose as the intersection of what you love and what you are good at – (**your passion**). Then you can identify the intersection of what you are good at and what the world needs (**your mission**).

You can then look for any overlap between what the world needs and what you can be paid to do (**your vocation**). Finally, you need to identify the point where how you can earn you money intersects with what you are good at (**your profession**). The centre point of your **mission, passion, vocation**, and **profession** will bring clarity and focus to your purpose – giving you a reason to jump out of bed each morning![44]

"Purpose means focusing on things that matter most.
Ironically, things that matter most are rarely things."

Margie Warrel
Keynote speaker and author

The first three chapters of this book focus on self-leadership. To realise the exponential effect, you need to be clear about your purpose. You can never successfully lead others without a powerful sense of personal meaning. Purpose involves a sense of understanding the end at the beginning. You develop purpose when you develop the ability to ask: "Why?"

Life purpose is not about deciding whether you will become a doctor or a taxi driver. Purpose is about who you are at your very core. Understanding your purpose makes you secure in yourself. Someone walking in their purpose learns from both their choices and the consequences of those choices. Often this is simply about choosing to walk from the mundane towards a place of curiosity. Momentum develops as you stretch towards your purpose.

A 2016 Deloitte survey revealed how millennials tend to prioritise the sense of individual purpose over company growth or profit maximisation.[45] While I coach and work with leaders, I'm learning that you can't bring about organisational purpose if you are not working from the basis of a personal mission.

Leaders lead on purpose. They have clarity and a keen sense of how what they are doing contributes to the big picture. They identify reasons for leading, whatever the cost. When we lead from a place of purpose, the result is a multiplier – an exponential effect.

> Purpose is linked as much to who you are as to what
> you do: A clear purpose is the lifeblood of clear vision.

An individual may feel that they don't have the capacity, skills, or even the opportunity to give expression to their purpose, but here's an exciting thought: Research indicates that purpose is derived much more from internal motivation than from external factors.

Previous research has shown that people who do the same work can view it as a job, a career, or a calling, and that people who see their work as a calling find more satisfaction and do better than people with the other two orientations. Callings denote a focus on the fulfilment experienced from work itself, often accompanied by a sense that the work contributes to others in a meaningful way.[46]

If this is true, then doing what you love (combined with what you are good at) is vitally important in determining purpose. Internal motives are far more critical than the external drivers of what the world needs, or where you earn a pay cheque.

Chris Underwood, MD of an executive search and talent advisory firm, suggests:

"A sense of purpose is a meaningful, mental model that provides a reason for being, and a guiding set of personal goals and objectives. A sense of purpose provides clarity of direction, unifying people to operate beyond their business objectives. A sense of purpose evokes passion and commitment; it makes sense of the world and the person's role within it."[47]

As you work back through the 'purpose' questions, I trust that you will draw closer to discovering and articulating your purpose in life. See this as an opportunity to bring purpose to your leadership, and to create the link between your leadership character (Chapter 1) and your resilience (Chapter 3). Leaders of purpose can, and do, have an exponential effect.

2 / EXERCISE

PURPOSE QUESTIONS

For you to consider:

- Consider the original purpose of why you entered your particular field or industry. Write your thoughts down. To what extent have you been faithful to this purpose?
- Why do you do what you do?
- What are you good at doing?
- What do you enjoy doing?
- What activity feels most useful?
- What activity creates a sense of forward momentum?
- How do you relate to others?
- What did you especially love doing when you were a child, before the world told you what you should or shouldn't like or do? Describe a moment and how it made you feel.
- Tell us about two of your most challenging life experiences. How have they shaped you?
- What do you enjoy doing in your life now that helps you sing your song?
- If money were no concern in your life, how would you spend your time?
- What is your *raison d'etre*, your reason for existing?
- What are your key strengths and talents, identified by you and others?
- What deeply motivates you and inspires you?[48]
- What makes me come alive?
- What breathes life into you?
- How will you measure your life?
- How will you move from success to significance?

3 / RESILIENCE

BOUNCING BACK, BREAKING THROUGH

Resilience: The ability and capability to endure, and even thrive, in the face of opposition, by remaining true to one's identity and purpose.

"Do not judge me by my successes, judge me by how many times I fell down and got back up again."

Nelson Mandela

Pioneering Explorers

In his first expedition in 2003, Riaan Manser cycled some 36 000km around the coastline of the continent of Africa. This journey took him two years, two months and 15 days. His adventure through 32 countries involved 808 days of cycling. At the end of his book, *Around Africa on my Bicycle*, Manser concludes:

> *"This journey told me to back myself, even when there was an imminent possibility of failure. Failure is part of success, as long as you pick yourself up and keep going. Your greatest reward is that you personally discover your true value, regardless of what any of those around you might think, realising that you are worthy of more than you think you are worthy of, that you are better than you think you are. The foundation of all your unwillingness to*

attempt what you dream of, but never believed to be possible, is the fear of failure."[49]

Manser describes himself as a 'pioneering explorer'. This seemingly grand title accurately represents who he is and what he does: Pioneering and exploring. As a pioneer, Riaan has set up and completed at least four one-of-a-kind expeditions. As an explorer, he has travelled thousands of kilometres along routes few people will ever even attempt, never mind complete.

Manser took the notion of the 'fear of failure' to heart. In 2009, his second expedition involved an 11-month, 5 000km solo kayak around the island of Madagascar.

In 2011, Riaan and colleague, Dan Skinstad, paddled 2 300km and circumnavigated Iceland in 147 days.

In 2013, Riaan, together with his partner, Vasti, rowed 10 400 km in a seven-metre boat for over 150 days, from Agadir, Morocco, to New York, United States of America (USA). They had no back-up crew and no rescue boat. They estimated that between them, they rowed about 1.8 million oar strokes. Between all of those adventures, Riaan has also summited Mt Kilimanjaro (the highest peak in Africa) and plunged the depths of Lake Assal, in Djibouti (the lowest point on the African continent).

When I interviewed him, Riaan spoke candidly about the physical and emotional challenges associated with endurance events, and of the effect of extended periods of isolation on the psyche. Many would agree that Riaan has redefined tenacity and has become the epitome of courage, determination and resilience within the context of extreme expeditions. It's also worth noting that I interviewed him way before the pandemic.

When I planned this book, I had already identified that the subject of leadership and resilience would need an entire chapter. But what is so fascinating is how, in this Covid/post-Covid-19 world, resilience has taken on a whole new level of importance.

People have had to endure an indeterminate lockdown. Weeks spent self-isolating, dealing with the strict conditions of staying indoors (other than shopping for essentials) requires self-discipline. Then there is the relentless 24-hour news cycle of ever-increasing infection rates, deaths and the reality that the virus is all-prevalent. It is here, and it is here now. When friends and family started getting infected and people began losing loved ones to the virus, the pandemic took on a whole new reality.

I am also arrested by the news of the less fortunate in our communities who cannot self-isolate because they live in informal settlements. Many share a single pit latrine with 15 or 20 other people. Many have to walk long distances simply to access clean drinking water. Physical distancing, handwashing and basic personal hygiene present untold, even impossible, challenges.

Practically, there is the question of what this means for children's education, and how they and their fellow students will always be known as The Corona Year. Those who can, have needed to suddenly shift to remote learning and navigate all of the logistical challenges of connectivity and online interactions.

As a business consultant, I am also well aware that advisors have been inundated with queries about labour legislation ("How do we go about retrenching staff?"), and about who to approach about their business's future.

"How do we apply for business rescue?"

"What are the steps for business liquidation?"

Many businesses, particularly small, single-owner entities, will probably never reopen. Even if they never encountered the virus directly, no business owner has been immune to the consequences of not trading for months on end. They are calling the post-Covid 19 world, 'the new normal'.

One theme emerges repeatedly: The impact that the events of 2020 have had on people's mental state and their psychological wellness and wellbeing. We have all been affected – if not physically, then financially, and certainly emotionally. We need resilience.

Leadership literature contains numerous references to the fact that resilience is key to effective leadership. The research is overwhelming: The way leaders deal with adversity, and learn from, what some have called 'crucibles', directly impacts on their future outlook, their choices and their leadership efficacy.[50]

What is resilience?

Dr George Everly from Johns Hopkins Bloomberg School of Public Health and the Resiliency Science Institute, explains: Leaders who realise the exponential effect, display a remarkable *"ability to withstand, adapt to, or rebound from, extreme challenges or adversity"*.[51]

"Men are disturbed, not by things, but the views that they take of them."

Epictetus

Post-traumatic Growth

Neuroscience provides us with a deeper understanding of the way the brain responds to perceived threats. A low-stress situation requires low coping skills and we are said to be in a state of calm. We might also find ourselves in a place of strength when we are in a low-stress situation, but have high coping skills.

However, the moment a situation of imminent danger arises, a chain reaction of brain activity is set in motion, all within nanoseconds. The amygdala is programmed to release an incredibly powerful stress hormone, cortisol, which produces both an increased heart rate and blood flow. If we are in a situation of high stress where we display low, or lowered, coping skills, then this can exacerbate the situation.

The challenge comes when we find ourselves in a permanent, extended period of stress and feel unable to cope. Ideally, what we are looking to develop in leaders is a combination of elevated coping levels – specifically during periods of high stress. There is overwhelming evidence that long-term exposure to stressful situations can, and does, impact negatively on people with low resilience.

Leadership resilience is not just a brain chemistry issue. It seems to be a matter of perspective and curiosity; as well mental, physical and emotional congruence.

> Resilience focuses on our positive qualities and strengths, so that we can live life with purpose, despite the difficulties.

Researchers have examined the question of resilience, specifically within the context of the effect of war on soldiers. People with low resilience seemed to struggle more to avoid negative thoughts and emotions both during and after a crisis.

Another group of people seemed to come through disaster on what they called a *"resilience trajectory"*. An individual faced with adversity shows a *"temporary reduction in adjustment, but returns to normal when the threat diminishes. They bend, but they do not break."* [52]

The third group of people displayed noticeable signs of thriving (almost despite the crisis) – a kind of 'post-traumatic growth'.

Whichever group an individual may find themselves in, the critical idea is that resilience is a learned behaviour. During my discussions with counselling psychologists, they all seemed to agree that resilience is an ability to confront the stressors and challenges of life and to then negotiate, resolve and even grow in the face of adversity. Even when people feel like they are not coping, experienced counsellors will direct them to the 'evidence': Evidence that people are still present; that they are functioning; and that even though they may not be happy about a situation, they are still getting things done.

Manser agreed to chat with me about some of his experiences. I asked him if there were any lessons to learn from his story about personal resilience as a component of self-leadership.

Q **Before we discuss resilience, can you please tell us how you decide on these seemingly outrageous goals for your expeditions?**

A There was not one person who believed we could do it. It is as definitive as that. There was not one person who said to me: "Listen, great, wonderful idea. You are a super-intelligent guy, let us back you; let us assist you!" Everybody told me that what I was attempting, or even just considering, was outrageous. I had to start in that vacuum – that support vacuum where I did not have a support base. I had to continually remind myself that this was a personal expedition and a personal goal that I was trying to achieve.

I had an honest conversation with myself. I sat on the proverbial rock, weekend after weekend after weekend, but I had been kidding myself about the fact that I was going to make a change. One particular Sunday was the most honest conversation I had ever had. I realised that I was a loser by doing a lot of talk but no action. It all started with the decision to be honest with myself. When I then made the decision that I was going to try to do something, the word that kept sticking in my mind was 'extraordinary'.

What is 'extraordinary'? Is it doing something subjective and led by opinion? Do people come and tell you: "That is extraordinary!" Do you tell yourself: "That is extraordinary!"? Or are you going to do something where there is no debate?

I decided that doing something that no human being had ever done in history (which is an exceptionally long time, I thought), to make history – that would be extraordinary. That is where it started for me. That was the process.

Q Your expeditions seem to be characterised by persistence and tenacity. How did you develop this quality?

A By not overemphasising problems. If I have a problem, my mind immediately jumps to what the solution could be. I don't know where I learned that, but I do know that when it comes to problem-solving, my mind has only one gear.

I could probably take that back to my childhood. I did not grow up with the luxury of an environment that others had. I did not grow up in a traditional family with the sort of guidance that other children received. I was a kid without a family. I had to find solutions for everything – moving from school to school; from town to town; making new friends; finding solutions for the sports I wanted to play; getting things that I needed; being happy. All of those things were my problem. There was nobody around to solve them for me. So, what I initially, as a teenager, believed was a negative for me, absolutely created that character of not accepting the negatives.

Q You seem to have a positive outlook on life. Does that come naturally?

A Now, when I look back, I realise that I was given a gift. What some would have considered to be difficulties created what I now regard as a talent.

Q What have been some of your lowest points and biggest frustrations? At those points, how do you keep going? How are you able to continually bounce back from adversity?

A When I did the Africa trip, I was super-immature and super-naïve. That was an asset I needed. The naivety was what I needed on the bicycle trip… Coming out of the Liberia situation, when I had passed the French military that was in Côte d'Ivoire, and when their colonel tried to stop me near the border of Liberia, trying to convince me not to continue on this little dirt road that was running into the jungle… I can remember only one thought going through my mind while I was standing in front of him. I was not listening to him, I was just asking myself, or thinking to myself: "I hope this guy doesn't have the authority to make me turn around. I hope he can't take my bicycle away. I hope he can't force me to get off the road."

It turned out that he couldn't, so I cycled past him, on into Liberia. The next day, the rebels captured me. You can imagine what my mind was trying to digest that evening: "How intelligent am I?"; "What am I willing to offer up here?"; "Is there going to be a reward for the sacrifice that I am putting in?"

I could easily have given negative answers to those three questions, but my mind did not see those negatives. I felt that I needed to believe in what I had set out to achieve. I had to believe in it. I had no other choice.

Q How is the need for resilience different when you do expeditions with someone else? I'm thinking of with Dan Skinstad, and then later, Vasti.

A The situation with Dan in Iceland was one for which I was not prepared. Emotionally, I was still immature in managing tough situations with another person. But what I did learn there (and on my subsequent journey with Vasti) was that if you are planning to take on a challenge with someone else, you have to be evenly yoked. So, if I said to you: "Come on, let's go and climb Everest," and I know nothing about your personality or your willingness to suffer, we are going to be unevenly yoked.

With Vasti, I knew what I was in for. I knew that she was more determined than me. I knew that she was willing to offer up her life, if it came down to it. In the situation with Dan, I was too emotionally immature to understand that concept. After a little bit of bumping my head here and there and a couple of tears, I learned that lesson.

Q The emotional, physical, financial investment relative to the reward is incredible. What is the prize? What are the motivators?

A They are not the traditional motivators. When I started out, I didn't have the razzmatazz and television and media coverage in mind. To bring it down to the nuts and bolts of what makes you mentally resilient: Your attitude at the beginning of what you are taking on needs to be sincere. Your goal, or the reward that you are hoping for, has to be absolutely sincere.

If I had set off on the bicycle trip with the plan to be famous, I would never have made it to Angola. I had been through hell already. I wanted to return from that journey around the continent with remarkable stories for my grandchildren. That was what I told myself. That did not change two years, two months later. I still had that goal.

I could not pay rent that month (I returned). We had R48 in our bank account. I always believed that I did not want the traditional rewards, like money and fame. I wanted to have great stories for my grandchildren. The honesty and sincerity of what you want the reward to be are really important.

Q Where is the intersection between physical toughness and mental/ emotional toughness?

A On all four of the big journeys, I would say (that intersection) was essential. I remember cycling out of Cape Town and looking back at Table Mountain and seeing the cloud coming over it. (It was a very misty morning.) I remember having a sharp vision in my mind of cycling back to that exact spot where I started (I was planning for the journey to take about a year). I remember that vision being so clear – of cycling back to the Waterfront. But it's amazing; minute after minute, day after day, month after month, the tougher it got, the more that vision became blurred. Eventually, that became non-existent.

When your body is going through too much, you run the risk of losing sight of the vision. It was the same on the 'row' that Vasti and I had. We spoke so much for that first month about what it was going to be like to row into New York City Harbour, row right alongside the Statue of Liberty.

You can imagine the excitement for Vasti, as it was something she had only ever seen on TV: The legendary city of New York and she was planning to row there! That vision for Vasti became blurred when the physical toughness took over. Your mind has to become tough when that initial vision blurs.

Q **Does that mean you continually do a lot of visualisation? Are you creating those images of the final part of the journey in your mind?**

A Oh absolutely. Resilience doesn't mean that you are powerful and robust and just keep bulldozing everything in front of you. It just means that when you fall, you get back on your feet and keep going. To get up, you need incredible visualisation of the success of the last day, or the finished project. That is so important.

"When surprises are the new normal,
resilience is the new skill."

Rosabeth Moss Kanter
Director and Chair
Harvard University Advanced Leadership Initiative

I realise that one stark difference between Manser's situation and the global crisis we have faced is that his journey is somewhat self-inflicted. Riaan gets to choose his adventure and to set the bar; to determine (to some extent) how arduous the expedition will be, and then go for it. Life, however, is not as compartmentalised. But, if we can take anything away from Riaan's reflections, it is the idea that the clearer your sense of purpose and the more well defined your meaning, the more resilience you will display. The sharper your focus of what success looks like, of what the end goal is, the better.

A Sense of Coherence

A resilience perspective approaches the world from the basis of health rather than from pathology. When we are in a place of stress or tension, we either manage that stress successfully or unsuccessfully. We are all somewhere on a health ease/disease continuum. The field of executive coaching places a strong emphasis on two foundational resilience ideas:

First, resilience links to the idea that life experiences shape our sense of coherence. A resilient world view means that life is more or less comprehensible; more or less meaningful; and more or less manageable.[53]

Secondly, there are resources that we use to develop resilience. These resources can be internal (within an individual's attitude, self-efficacy, beliefs and hope) or in our immediate environment (our immediate circle of social support).[54]

When we struggle to make sense of a situation; when we are unable to link cause and effect; and when faced with sudden, unpredictable tragedies; one of our first natural responses is to ask: "Why?"; "Why me?" or "How could this have happened?" Our ability to make sense of an event, to create order out of chaos, or to look towards that preferred future, all impact on our sense of 'comprehending' events. People with a keen sense of coherence (perception) cope better in the face of everyday life stressors.

Finding meaning in the face of adversity is a choice. Resilient leaders who display this quality feel compelled to view problems or setbacks as 'energy-investing opportunities'. When we can't seem to make sense, or feel unable to create meaning out of a situation, we find resilience more challenging. The experience of a 'meaningful life' enhances people's resilience and protects them against the damaging effects of significant life changes.[54]

In response to the pandemic, a number of my mentors would say things like: "I don't know why this has happened. No one could have predicted it, but it's as if we are in a reset. Let's pause, let's reflect; let's slow down. What can we learn from this?"

I found this to be poignant advice, particularly during extended periods of physical distancing and social isolation.

As an aside, this search for meaning might explain the abundance of conspiracy theories that have sparked over such a brief period. In the absence of credible data and advice, and often faced with contradictory findings, people feel compelled to grasp at anything that will answer the "Why?" question – even if the source of their advice and the conclusions they draw are completely outlandish.

The manageability question is about a sense of control.

Resilient leaders ask:

- What part of this situation is out of my control?
- What part of this situation is within my control?
- What internal and external resources are at my disposal to manage this situation?

The first two questions help create the sense of an ability to cope. It's no use worrying about things that are out of your control. Identify the overlap between the circle of concern and the sphere of influence. It is liberating to come to the place of release; to the position of surrender, in the areas over which you do not have control.

Sometimes accepting the limits of what you can change in a situation is the hardest part of the resilience journey. Resilient leaders have a wide circle of concern, but a focused circle of influence. Acknowledging that you have no control over exchange rates, weather patterns and virus mutation is critical.

These 'resistance resources' are tools that are developed to facilitate bouncing back in the face of adversity. Internal resources, such as vision, perspective, and meaning, correlate with research on the quality of life. People who have a clear identity and purpose also have more robust physical and mental health, as well as higher resilience.

We should not underestimate the role that hope plays in enabling us to bounce back from disappointment, trauma, and tragedy. There are numerous instances of individuals who, in the middle of seemingly impossible situations, keep going (way beyond their apparent physical and emotional limits), as long as they still have hope.

As far as external resources are concerned, relationships are critical. I watched with fascination as, faced with an indefinite period of isolation during the pandemic, those who were able, upgraded their communication platforms. People jumped on to video chat-enabled applications and reached out to loved ones – including those who, in some cases, they had not seen or spoken to in years. Some people then even began describing the challenge of video-conferencing fatigue. There is no doubt that as social creatures, we need support in times of adversity.

Emily Werner, a developmental psychologist, studied 698 Hawaiian children from the time of their birth, over a 32-year period.[55] Although one-third of the group was from an 'at-risk' background (not all successful, stable or happy), they did not all respond to stress in the same way. By the end of the study, Werner was able to show how one-third of the at-risk group had grown into competent, confident, caring adults.

The stand-out difference in this group was that they displayed a significantly higher locus of control. At the same time, Werner showed how resilience is not a fixed output. There is an ongoing balancing act that people perform between resilience and external stressors. Individuals displaying high resilience believe they can 'control the controllables'.

Neuroscientists and psychologists propose that one's ability to reframe adversity plays a significant role in resilience development.[56]

Lack of blame (this is not my fault), **specificity** (this doesn't mean everything in my life is terrible), and **permanence** (I can do something about this; this will not last forever) are all critical perspectives.

In my work as a leadership development specialist and coach, I want to see my clients grow and develop – not just in their specific skill sets in, for instance, IT, engineering, sales, strategy or project management, but also in their interactions with others.

Chapter 1 introduced the importance of EQ (emotional intelligence). Another area of intelligence that is critical for leaders in the world of work is cultural intelligence – your cultural quotient (CQ). This focuses on developing the ability to engage, adapt, interact, relate and work with individuals and groups from diverse cultures. In the field of resilience, Dr Paul Stoltz developed what he calls the leader's AQ (the adversity quotient).[57]

"Resilience is not simply about bouncing back from adversity, it's your capacity to be strengthened and improved by it."

Dr Paul G. Stoltz

Simply put, the adversity quotient measures the extent to which:

- The individual perceives they can influence whatever happens next (**control**).
- The likelihood that the individual will do something to improve their situation, regardless of their formal responsibilities (**ownership**).
- The extent to which someone perceives that adversity will affect other aspects of the situation, or beyond (**reach**).

- Someone will display **endurance** (the length of time the individual lasts or endures the situation/adversity).

> The adversity quotient is said to be at the **CORE**:
> Control
> Ownership
> Reach
> Endurance
> of our resilience.

Dealing with Rejection

"Your pigs are far more intelligent than the other animals; and therefore, the best qualified to run the farm – in fact, there couldn't have been an Animal Farm without them: so, what was needed was not more communism but more public-spirited pigs."[58]

The above quote was from a rejection letter by T.S. Elliot, then-editor of a worldwide publisher, of George Orwell's now-famous novel, *Animal Farm*, sent in 1945. A second, unnamed editor, reinforced this rejection: *"It is impossible to sell animal stories in the US."*

Recently, author Robert Galbraith posted two rejection letters on Twitter. One response from a publisher noted that *"they could not publish the book with commercial success"*. Another suggested that the author considered *"double-checking in a helpful bookshop"* or *"in the twice-yearly buyer's guide"*. Both publishers no doubt regretted that they passed up an opportunity to publish J.K. Rowling's work, which was written under a pseudonym. Her work, in her name, has sold over 400 million copies.

"I have applied for multiple jobs but with no response."

I increasingly see this message on my timeline. As the global economy shrinks, I think it is likely we will see more such predicaments. In thinking more broadly about resilience beyond just general adversity, it's worth considering how we successfully handle rejection. The relationship between rejection and resilience is an important one.

Walt Disney was told he lacked imagination. Steven Spielberg was rejected multiple times from film school. Thomas Edison was told he was too stupid to learn. Albert Einstein initially struggled to communicate. Theodore Seuss Geisel saw his work rejected by 27 publishers. Jeff Bezos, the founder of Amazon, launched ZShops, an online auction site, which failed. Peter Thiel lost more than $6 billion in assets before starting PayPal. We also tend to forget that Apple fired Steve Jobs in 1985, before later rehiring him.

"I didn't see it then, but it turned out that getting fired from Apple was the best thing that could have ever happened to me. The heaviness of being successful was replaced by the lightness of being a beginner again."[59]

Steve Jobs

When you are in sales, and you get that fourth or fifth "no", you need resilience. As a team member whose ideas are not acknowledged, you need resilience. When your application for university entrance or a research grant is rejected, you need resilience. When you fail that board exam, you need resilience. When your family relationships are at risk because of rejection, you need resilience.

> **Resilience** *is the ability and the capability to endure and even thrive in the face of opposition by remaining true to one's identity and purpose.*

The **VUCA** environment describes a world of:[60]

- Volatility.
- Uncertainty.
- Complexity.
- Ambiguity.

Recent events compel me to add one more – **R**ecurrency. In the aftermath of the pandemic, we are learning that the VUCA world is repeatedly volatile, uncertain, complex and ambiguous. Many are asking, "How long? How long must we hold on? How long must we wait?' The unknowns in terms of timescales are often really hard to navigate. In many ways, the situation can seem relentless.

Leadership thinkers have recommended that we need a VUCA-positive mindset that displays vision in the face of the volatility; understanding in the uncertainty; clarity to make sense of the complexity; and agility as a countermeasure to ambiguity.[61] I propose that 'VUCA positive' be reframed as 'VUCAR positive', with **Resilience** as a determining quality and countermeasure to the often relentless nature of external challenges.

In 2020, Dr Jack Zenger and Dr Joseph Folkman conducted a leadership study of more than 20 000 leaders. The study highlighted how resilience was one of the key characteristics that differentiated the most effective leaders from the rest.[62] Covid-19 has, understandably, caused a decline in resilience levels. Not only does positive resilience help individual leaders, but their resilience seems to be contagious, producing an exponential effect in those around them.

3 / EXERCISE

RESILIENCE QUESTIONS

For you to consider:

- What are you currently facing that may require you to find a fresh perspective?
- How would you describe your state of resilience right now? Low, medium or high? Why do you describe your current state this way?
- What could you do to improve your resilience?
- What is your outlook on your current situation or circumstances?
- What is in your circle of concern? What is in your circle of influence? Where do these two spheres overlap?
- What can you do to find a fresh perspective on your current reality?
- Can you make sense of adversity? How do you make sense of difficulty?
- On what internal resources can you draw to help you cope?
- On what external resources can you draw to help you cope?

SELF-LEADERSHIP

Having considered some of the critical elements of self-leadership, it is worth stopping to reflect on our journey so far.

- Do you have a clear set of personal values?
- How would you describe your character? Are you able to see through your character flaws and embrace your identity, intent and integrity?
- Do you have a clear sense of personal vision and purpose?
- What is your level of personal and professional resilience?

The focus of Part One of this book was self-leadership and developing oneself as a leader. Self-leadership and 'Leading Me' are critical elements to help create the exponential effect in practice. Without self-leadership and a clear set of values – shaped by a clearly defined purpose, an energising passion and wholeness of character – leadership will be ineffective.

The second part of this book is about leading others, about 'Leading Them' – developing those around you as followers. Leading others involves identifying those who embrace your leadership, so that you can see them move and grow to the next level.

LEADING THEM
(DEVELOPING OTHERS)

4 / TRUST

BUILDING THE BEDROCK

Trust the currency of relationships; the currency
of leadership

Footage of Erin Langworthy's bungee jump off the Victoria Falls Bridge, between Zimbabwe and Zambia, went viral for all the wrong reasons. On the video, Erin could be seen leaping off the top of the bridge, 110m above the water. Moments later, the gasps of those watching from the bridge are clearly audible as the bungee cord snaps.

Freefalling, Erin hits the water. She is dragged down the Zambezi River, her legs still tied together, about 20m of bungee cord flailing behind her. She initially blacks out from the impact and then, comes to. Still groggy, she fights to keep her head above water. Conscious of the roar of the rapids further downstream, after what seems an eternity, she manages to make her way safely to the riverbank.

Erin miraculously survived, having suffered only cuts, bruises and a broken collarbone. The severity of the accident, and the impact of hitting the water with such force, meant doctors recommended that she not fly out of the country immediately. They were concerned about the state of her lungs.

In an interview conducted after a full week's observation in hospital, Erin recounted her death-defying experience. All she remembered before hitting the water was instinctively placing her hands over her head. Understandably, both Erin and her friend, (who filmed the incident), were

"

at pains to point out that they would be not going anywhere near a bungee cord anytime soon.

The power of social media spread the news of Erin's accident around the world almost instantly. Both Zambia and Zimbabwe rely heavily on tourism, and the Victoria Falls Bridge jump is a major attraction, particularly for international tourists. After very graphic reports of Langworthy's accident, fears about safety, or lack thereof, soon spread like wildfire.

But, what of the next bungee jumper? Who would be brave (crazy) enough to get back into the harness after such a dramatic incident? To quell concerns and restore some level of faith in the attraction, Zambia Tourism Minister Given Lubinda offered to be the first person to bungee jump after Langworthy's ordeal. As head of tourism, he believed it was his responsibility to prove that it was perfectly safe to jump. He was adamant. It was the first time in 17 years, after more than 150 000 jumps, that the system had failed.

Despite those very public reassurances, we can only guess what went through Lubinda's mind as he stood on precisely the same spot Erin had stood. Asked how he felt, Lubinda reflected: *"Looking down and seeing nothing but water and rocks and knowing that the only thing that holds you is a bungee rope – is extremely fearful."*

Once safely back on top of the bridge, Lubinda quipped: *"I decided that the world could use me as a guinea pig, and if I wanted to risk my life, it means that it is safe. Let everyone come and jump."*[63]

There are dozens of research papers on, and descriptions of, trust as a foundation of leadership. Most would agree that trust includes *"an expectation or belief that the other party will act benevolently"*.[64] A *"willingness to be vulnerable"*,[65] involving *"some level of dependency on the other party while recognising the very real possibility that the other party may not fulfil expectations"*.[66]

> **Trust:** A willingness to accept vulnerability or risk, based on expectations regarding another person's behaviour.[67]

If trust is foundational to leadership, what are the elements of interpersonal trust? To answer this question, we need to reflect on Part One. Here is where we start to see the exponential effect in action. Trust links strongly to the individual character (on all levels: Identity, integrity, intent, insight, and initiative).

- I am more likely to trust someone authentic.
- I am more likely to trust someone who has no hidden agenda.
- I am more likely to trust someone who has a self, social, and situational awareness (insight).
- I am also more likely to trust someone who takes the initiative in the relationship and shows care and empathy.
- I am more likely to trust someone who is competent.

Trust links strongly to capability. As an aside, research shows that this is not a blanket, all-embracing trust. Capability trust relates to specific situations with exact requirements. As a global keynote speaker or facilitator, you might trust me to address your board, but you might not necessarily trust me to take care of your elderly grandmother. People do not follow those they don't trust. You can force people to follow you out of fear, but that's something different. With every decision a leader makes, the question has to be asked:

> "Am I building trust, or am I undermining trust?"

The Psychology of Trust

Social, cognitive neuroscience has given us an unprecedented view of the brain. We now know that humans have an automated, quick-working, slow-learning neural system that does not do well in unfamiliar situations. The brain combines this with a controlled, slower-response, quick-learning system that is adapted and shaped through formal reasoning.

We also know that brain chemicals (oxytocin-neuropeptide hormone, dopamine, and vasopressins) all play a part in decisions related to trust.[68]

Oxytocin has been specifically touted as the star of the show, as levels increase in breastfeeding mothers and other instances of social attachment. But it's not that the higher oxytocin levels mean higher trust. Human beings are complex; human interaction is complex; and context is vital to understanding the psychology of trust-building. The interplay between brain activity and brain chemistry, and the 'CODES' of influence will be explained in more detail in Chapter 5.

Psychologist Robert Plutchik developed a 'psycho-evolutionary' theory that takes the traditional fight-or-flight emotional response model to the next level. His 'wheel' approach identified four basic positive emotions: Joy, fear, surprise and trust.

Plutchik showed that where the opposite of joy is sadness; the opposite of fear is anger; and the opposite of surprise is anticipation. What is most interesting is that he proposed that the opposite emotion of trust was not mistrust, as many might have thought, but rather, disgust.[69] On an intensity scale, if the consequence of trust is acceptance, then, according to Plutchik, the net result of disgust is loathing.

The bottom line is that while trust is incredibly fragile, the consequences of strong trust are powerful. The adverse effects of broken trust are equally dramatic. The fragility of trust means that once broken; it is incredibly difficult to restore.

Broken trust produces incredibly intense, primal emotions. Leaders need to acknowledge and identify the importance of trust. They also need to understand how trust is built, and to take cognisance of the full impact of breaking it.

Social capital is an increasingly important consideration. In this world of online media and soundbites, we are at the mercy of the keyboard warriors who will not hesitate to post, blog, and vlog and let the world know their thoughts on a range of topics and experiences. Ironically, this increased access to independent information does not appear to make us more trusting of one another.

The General Social Survey in the USA gathers information each year on interpersonal dynamics. In answer to the question: "*Generally speaking, do you believe that most people can be trusted, or that you can't be too careful in dealing with people?*" the survey shows that trust has been in decline for the past 40 years.[70]

But what is driving this general reluctance to give others the benefit of the doubt? Professor Tim Levine provides some exciting answers through his work on what he calls Truth Default Theory.[71] Levine suggests that we tend to operate in a truth-default mindset. We usually accept most messages we receive as honest. He concludes that "*we are perceptually blind to deception. We are hard-wired to being duped. We are not as good at detecting lies as we thought.*"

From a trust point of view, could this suggest a paradox between the fact that although we are generally suspicious of the messenger, we tend to assume the best when receiving unfamiliar information?

I don't think it's that simple. One thing is clear: We are gullible. It's possible that our inherent self-awareness that we are prone to deception makes us less trusting of others. The result is that truth-tellers are often second-guessed, and we tend to believe liars.

Since the year 2000, PR company, Edelman, has taken a particular interest in gauging stakeholder perceptions. The focus has been on understanding how leaders and organisations' leaders develop both trust and corporate reputation. The Edelman Trust Barometer, as discussed earlier, has become an annual global benchmark to gauge the level of trust at a company, in an industry, sector, or at country level.

The 2020 survey reveals important discrepancies between the informed public and the mass population (where no single institution is trusted to be both competent and ethical). More than 80% earned higher scores on competence than they did on ethics. Here, trust is a question that centres on purpose, vision, honesty, and fairness. Edelman shows that ethical attributes drive 76% of the trust capital of organisations.[72]

There is a growing pessimism in economic prospects. Fewer people believe they will be better off in five years' time. People worry about losing respect and dignity, and they struggle with a sense of injustice. Many are concerned about job losses; that technology is 'out of control', and about the quality of information provided by news media.

Societal leaders did not escape this growing mistrust in answers to the statement: *"I do not have confidence that our current leaders will be able to address our country's challenges successfully."*

Before the pandemic, scientists (80%) and people in local communities (69%) were regarded as far more trustworthy than religious leaders (46%) and government leaders (42%). As the pandemic started, it was the scientific community to whom people looked for answers. But even this sector of society is not united. Within this community, we witnessed the presentation of data, followed by contradictions, personal attacks, and accusations of conspiracy theories.

"Trust – the mental state of expecting fairness
from the trusted."[73]

Dr Tara Swart, Kitty Chisholm and Paul Brown
Neuroscientists and researchers

As Warren Buffett famously said: *"It can take more than 20 years to build a reputation and five minutes to ruin it. If you think about that, you'll do things differently."*

The 2012 London Interbank Offered Rate (LIBOR) scandal is a case in point. Without going into all of the detail, the LIBOR is a benchmark that many of the world's leading finance houses charge each other for short-term loans. These interest rates are the key indicator for the average rate at which banks can obtain loans.

More than six years after the monetary crisis swept through the banking system, it became apparent that banks were manipulating these rates to advantage specific individual traders and their respective finance houses. A rate-fixing scandal uncovered the extent of the fraud and how banks were falsely adjusting their rates to profit from individual trades. In some cases, these rate adjustments created the impression that the banks were more creditworthy than they actually were.

The *Financial Times* published an article revealing that this kind of manipulation had been going on for more than 30 years. Once uncovered, it resulted in a number of the finance houses (including an acknowledgement by Barclays Bank in mid-2012) that the LIBOR scandal had decimated *"trust in banks"*.[74]

An international company based in sub-Saharan Africa needed to form a new team from three separate regions and two business divisions. The MD of the operation approached me to facilitate a strategic planning exercise for the 12 months to come. When I looked at this team, it became glaringly apparent that the relational dynamics needed to be addressed.

I shared with them the importance of trust in a team and asked the participants to define trust. We then discussed the importance of trust in a team. Next, I brought things closer to home and asked them to comment on the level of trust within the new team. I knew I had hit a nerve when my question was met by a deathly silence.

Eventually, one brave team member spoke up and explained that things were not just bad, they were toxic. On cue, as if the others were just waiting for someone to speak first, people unleashed an avalanche of accusations against one another.

I realised that I needed to step in and offer some direction. I asked the team to break up into smaller groups and consider what specific behaviours had led to the damaged trust. In what must have been the most straightforward group exercise they had ever completed, their list included:

- Backstabbing.
- Defamation of character.
- Broken promises.
- Lack of discipline.
- Lack of passion.
- Inconsistency.
- Self-centredness.
- Lack of acknowledgement.
- Lack of respect.
- Dishonesty.

If there was no trust in place, there was no point trying to facilitate a session on shared goals and how to execute those goals. We spent an exceedingly difficult morning engaging in some very frank and open conversations about why the trust level had declined and what it would take to try to get those team members to begin to trust each other. Leaders would do well to understand the actions that develop and destroy trust. The more we delved into matters with that team, the more apparent it became that the lack of trust was not an isolated occurrence.

Transparency, Vulnerability and Risk

Transparency is an important driver of trust. In this world of increased scrutiny, leaders who are serious about building trust need to learn to be both transparent and vulnerable. Transparency is the key to trust.

> How do the concepts of transparency and vulnerability differ?

The first thing to note is that although transparency does not hide the facts, it is still relatively emotionally safe. In a leader-follower relationship, it is possible to be transparent, open and honest without ever revealing deeper emotions.

The second dynamic then comes into play. Vulnerability is a willingness to take a risk to reveal one's deeper emotions. One can be transparent but emotionally risk-averse. However, when you are genuinely vulnerable, you open yourself up in a way that makes you far more emotionally defenceless.

If you think about the dynamic between trust and vulnerability then, as a leader, the question is:

> "If we are going to build meaningful relationships, are we prepared to move from simply being forthright to taking the risk of being vulnerable?"

Trust and risk go hand in hand. Every time someone commits to meet with you, you run the risk of a late start or them being a no-show. Every time you delegate a task, you run the risk that the job will not be done to your standards, not done on time, or completely overlooked. Every time you share your thoughts, feelings, apprehensions, excitements or misgivings, you run the risk of a betrayed confidence. Every time you draw close to someone, you run the risk that they might have sinister, ulterior motives. Every day we make trust choices that are risk-based vulnerabilities.

- You can't have a real relationship without vulnerability.
- You can't have vulnerability without emotional exposure.
- You can't have emotional exposure without being prepared to take an emotional risk.

"Vulnerability is simply defined as uncertainty, risk, and emotional exposure. And if you are alive and in a relationship, you do vulnerability. If you are alive and in a relationship and in business, you do it hourly."

Brené Brown
Research professor, University of Houston

Leaders who want to build real trust need to be willing to explore the risks of being vulnerable. When it comes to relational dynamics, we are learning is that the more vulnerable the leader, the higher the chances of developing trust through meaningful relationships.

"To love at all is to be vulnerable. Love anything, and your heart will be wrung and possibly broken. If you want to make sure of keeping it intact, you must give it to no one, not even an animal. Wrap it carefully round with hobbies and little luxuries; avoid all entanglements. Lock it up safe in the casket or coffin of your selfishness. But in that casket – safe, dark, motionless, airless – it will change. It will not be broken; it will become unbreakable, impenetrable, irredeemable. The alternative to tragedy, or at least to the risk of tragedy, is damnation. The only place outside of Heaven where you can be perfectly safe from all the dangers and perturbations of love is Hell."

C.S. Lewis
The Four Loves

Vulnerability is not weakness. You have to choose to be vulnerable because you believe that you are worthy of healthy relationships. A leader who is serious about building trust, gives timely, honest and vulnerable responses. You need to be wise in your vulnerability. You cannot simply blurt things out. Recognise the value of building relationships with an identified group of leaders.

In trying to understand something of the dynamics of trust and vulnerability, I chatted to Alex MacPhail, who flew Falcon Three for the Silver Falcons, a South Africa aerobatic team.

Alex explained: *"Trust is critical. It's the bedrock of it all. Trust also allows you to free up your processes. By trusting your teammates, you free up your thinking and your abilities. You are not worried about what's happening. The person you're following and your wingman next to you are all in the same skin-in-the-game type of operation. You know that if anything goes wrong, we all go down, which is not what you want.*

"Because you have the level of trust, it frees you up to be in the moment and to take in everything. You are on your controls; you stay in position; you know whatever inputs are required of you to stay there. You do it knowing that you have a stable platform in the front; quite literally a 'follow-my-leader' approach.

"The leader provides a stable platform. You don't question what the leader is doing – his job to make sure that this is a safe and a good-looking show. My job is to follow the leader. I have supreme trust in him that he's not going to take me into the ground. He's taking me into the loop or the manoeuvre, and my job is to stay in position.

"I have to know my standard references on the aeroplane: An up and down reference, a forward and back reference and an in/out reference. I look after my position on the team. I can do that because I know my leader is going to look after me. If I am sitting there in number three, four or five (positions in the formation) wondering: 'Am I safe?' or 'Is this or that going to happen?' or 'I wonder what's going to happen now with this leader?' then my concentration isn't on staying in position anymore. Now I am jeopardising my safety and the safety of the entire team. I have to rule out any nagging doubts and say: 'Well, I trust you. We're going to be safe. Now I'll do my job to make it look good!'"

Raising the Trust Quotient

One of the activities included in our leadership development programme is a trust-factor ranking exercise. Given a list of 15–20 trust-building elements, participants are asked to rank them in order of importance. While, in many cases, the individual drivers of trust (what makes one person more likely to trust another) may be different, time after time these are the factors that rank the highest:

- **Shared expectations** – the degree to which the other person's behaviour is consistent with your norms and values.
- **Understanding** – reassurance that the other party knows and understands your needs and priorities.

- **Competence** – the other person has the skills and resources to do the job.
- **History** – experiences you have over time around someone's trustworthiness.
- **Self-control** – the other person is disciplined enough to control their behaviour.
- **Awareness of impact and consequence of actions** – the other person is aware that their decision and actions do not happen in isolation and can, and do, have a significant effect on those around them.

Maybe this list goes some way to explaining why such a notable emphasis has been placed on 'the responsible leader'.

Respondents to the Survey on the Global Agenda[75] proposed that to win back trust, leaders would need to demonstrate a global interdisciplinary perspective and long-term, empirical planning. Leaders required strong communication skills; a prioritisation of social justice and wellbeing over financial growth; empathy; courage; morality; and a collaborative approach.

In *The Speed of Trust*, S.M. Covey proposes that a leader's ability to build trust is a matter of character and competence – a combination of who you are and what you do.[76]

Author Jim Harter describes a high-trust environment in which employee engagement increases in line with trust. Outcomes and specific responsibilities are clear, and leaders are *"put in an optimal position to use their strengths to achieve those results"*.[77]

Paul Zak from the Centre for Neuro Economic Studies found that in high-trust environments, productivity was 19% higher than in low-trust workplaces.[78]

"To be trusted is a greater compliment than being loved."

George Macdonald

In her book, *The Truth About Trust in Business*, Vanessa Hall analyses trust in the context of three dimensions: Expectations, needs, and promises.[79] She then illustrates how these dimensions anchor any trust relationship. One party has needs and expectations of the other fulfilled (or unfulfilled) through either implicit or explicit promises. Trust-building is challenging.

Elevating expectations from implicit to explicit provides clear understanding and expectations of all concerned. It is then far less likely that trust is damaged.

Many of the principles that we have yet to discuss (including effective communication, accountability and conflict handling) all have a role to play in the trust-building process. Leaders who are serious about trust-building look to deliver results and to confront reality. They are upfront and honest when they are unable to deliver on commitments they have made.

The Tandem Jump

At the age of 12, my daughter, Kirsty, decided she wanted to go skydiving. Being the persistent go-getter that she is, I knew she was serious. We were told that there was a minimum age to jump and managed to convince her to wait until she was 16. I think I was secretly hoping that the idea would dissipate. Of course, it did not.

On her 16th birthday, Kirsty and her friend, Kate, presented us with all of the details. The costs and requirements were investigated, and we secured a booking for later in the year.

I remember driving out west early on a spring morning to the Johannesburg Skydiving Club at the Carletonville Aerodrome. The sun glistening behind us, we made our way past the old mine dumps and around the area above the world's deepest gold mine. It was barren. Dusty and barren. Dusty, barren and remote. I had too much time to think, and the longer we drove, the more my mind wandered.

What dad could realistically wait on *terra firma* while his first-born bounced around the sky in a plane with no door? What father in his right mind would allow his daughter to be strapped to some random stranger, only to watch her flung out of a small tube at 11 000 feet above ground level?

What responsible parent would stand by while his child went into 40 seconds of freefall somewhere above his head? What would it be like, peering through the sky, as she hurtled at 200 km/h down to 5 000 feet? Would the nylon canopy do its job and slow her down? Would she land safely? Questions bombarded me.

As I listened to the giggles of excitement from the back of the car, I kept my thoughts to myself. Her jump was going to be the longest eight minutes of my life! Once we arrived, my signatures on the indemnity and consent forms brought home the reality of what was about to happen.

Kitted out in jumpsuits, the tandem masters introduced themselves to the girls. Chris Grosch was cool. Trim and fully geared out, he oozed confidence. As he helped Kirsty into her harness, he began the pre-jump briefing drill. He started by creating a mental picture of what would happen in the sky. Chris was animated but precise; excited but collected. He stood behind Kirsty and held her arms up.

"So, let's practice. Imagine we are now in the plane. Shuffle into the doorway, feet hanging outside, arms crossed, and smile for the camera! Thumbs up, and then the exit is forward, back, forward and roll out of the aircraft. As we go out, I want you to go into your freefall position. Arms open, head back, hips forward… nice and chilled. I'll do a little barrel roll on the way out and literally, within four seconds, you are going to have the cameraman drifting up in front of you. But, because he's also falling, it's going to feel as if he is stationary, almost like we're all floating. This is your chance to perform. You have to interact with him for 40 seconds. If you don't smile, your cheeks are going to flap! You can wave and you can blow kisses. You can say: 'I love you, Mom!'

"Then we are going to spin around. When it's time to open, I'm going to give you a little warning. You will feel a tap on your shoulder, and it will feel like five seconds of deceleration, like we are putting on brakes, because we are going from 200km an hour to zero in five seconds. Once the parachute is open, it will be dead quiet, and we can chat to each other. Then we are going to fly the parachute around for about seven or eight minutes and then come and land in front here."

All of this time, I was watching proudly, but quietly panicked. Then I heard Chris ask: "Any questions?"

Kirsty's broad-faced grin showed her readiness.

I couldn't help myself. Thinking back, I wonder how it must have sounded. "Yes, Chris," I heard myself say. "Why should we trust you?"

My question was delivered casually, in an off-handed kind of way, but my meaning was clear.

"Andy," he replied with a wry smile, "I've been skydiving for more than 30 years. I have done over 10 000 jumps and more than 7 000 tandem jumps. This is jump number …" (he rattled off an exact figure).

I don't remember the specifics, but it was impressive.

"Oh, and by the way," Chris paused, "I also jumped with my young son when he was three-and-a-half!"

He went on: "Tandem jumping is a way for me to keep my jump frequency consistent. I love giving other people the experience."

Chris probably didn't realise it, but at that moment, he had displayed competency, self-disclosure and intent. It was a triple-trust effect in action, and I was suddenly far more at ease. The jump went off perfectly, and we still watch the video with fond memories. The experience has spurred Kirsty on to try other extreme sports.

In the various contexts in which we work, one typical pattern seems to emerge, providing us with some insights:

- Trust involves vulnerability and risk.
- Leaders need to focus on trust-building.

"Trust is the residue of promises fulfilled."

Frank Navran
Ethics and compliance management consultant

Developing Trust Remotely

The pandemic meant that, for those employees who could, working from home became the status quo. Although many companies had the tools and the technology to make it happen, it was apparent that not every leader was comfortable operating in a 'results-only' environment. Supervisors and leaders found themselves wondering, if not overtly asking: "What will my people do all day? How do I know where they will be focused?"

The psychology of virtual or remote working is that the further away we are, the more we need to trust each other. Conversely, the bigger the physical distance, the lower the trust level.

Many of our clients have been faced with a larger percentage of their workforce being distributed everywhere. There was little or no prospect of meeting face to face in the immediate future. In my coaching, leaders shared how this new way of working only served to highlight existing interpersonal strains. Working remotely often exposes existing deficits in the working relationship between colleagues.

As people hurried to online conferencing to increase social contact, instances of 'meeting hijacking' and 'zoom bombing' increased. Reports of data breaches and some 530 000 email addresses and passwords being sold on hacker forums set alarm bells ringing.

The challenge with building trust remotely is that it requires a counter-intuitive mindset. Rather than going into a meeting with someone for the first time, thinking: "Give me a reason to trust you," that approach needs to be swung around 180 degrees. It's a far more vulnerable approach – a far riskier approach. Now the mindset has to be: "Give me a reason not to trust you!"

Ironically, a remote working context may just require a **truth-default** approach. With such a mindset, showing up enhances trust. It's too easy to just not be there on the other side of a remote meeting. I also believe that showing up punctually, regardless of your cultural view on time, is deeply respectful. Building in some leeway for connection, plugins and updates might also be necessary – particularly if you are meeting on an unfamiliar platform.

Trust grows when we deliver results and keep our promises. I think the most critical remote relationship-building principle is being **fully present**. The temptation, with multiple windows and apps on our computers and smartphones, is to allow ourselves to drift off.

Astute remote leaders focus on **social cohesion** in virtual relationships as much as **task cohesion**. Team dynamics, particularly in virtual teams, will be explored in Chapters 7–9.

"Your ability to cultivate quality relationships is a critical success factor. That provides with you the platform to influence constructively. If you have a relationship built on trust and respect, then you earn their commitment. But this is a time-intensive exercise."

Brand Pretorius

"The way to manage an organisation is to put your cards on the table, then you get buy-in, you get ownership and people follow. When you keep information away from people, it is a natural way of eroding trust."[80]

Prof Eugene Cloete

Trust is one of the most valuable business and leadership commodities. Just as tricky as it may be to gain trust, it can disappear in a moment. Trust is the currency of leadership, and it develops more naturally when parties understand each other's motives. A track record tested over time goes a long way to building trust. Trust breeds confidence and underpins an individual's willingness to take calculated risks. Leaders who break trust sow the seeds of disgust in their followers.

The benefits of building trust with those you lead are relatively self-evident. When leaders become more vulnerable, those around them are likely to reciprocate, resulting in a higher level of affinity. Feelings of mutuality produce higher commitment, recommendations and a 'licence to operate'.

4 / EXERCISE

TRUST QUESTIONS

For you to consider:

- Do you consider yourself to be trustworthy?
- Do your followers consider you trustworthy?
- How do you feel when someone places their trust in you? Why do you feel this way?
- How do you feel when you sense someone is reluctant to trust you? Why do you feel this way?
- Are you comfortable being vulnerable with those you trust? Why, or why not?
- What specific steps can you take to raise your level of trustworthiness?
- How will you focus on building trust in the new world of work?

5 / INFLUENCE

PERSUADING WITHOUT POSITION

Impacting the behaviours, thoughts, opinions, attitudes and choices of others.

It was always going to be a tall order. Would it even work? We were embarking on an international programme to convince all customer-facing staff working for a premium brand to think and behave in a consistently professional manner. Would they buy into the idea? It was an idea based not just on teaching brand theory, but on creating a tangible brand experience. Would staff embrace the learning opportunity? Would they show their commitment as brand ambassadors? I couldn't decide whether it was a stroke of genius or just an incredibly bold social experiment. All of those questions ran through my mind as the plane touched down in Munich for what was to be a whirlwind three-day trip.

A few years ago, I attended the BMW Brand Academy as a member of a select group of leadership and marketing specialists. Years before the establishment of BMW World (The Welt), the Academy had started in a nondescript office complex on the outskirts of the city. Upon entering the building, we found ourselves transported to a completely different world. It was, in short, a multisensory experience of brand immersion. Each room had been set-up to communicate the unique brand attributes of BMW, MINI and Rolls Royce, respectively. The design of the rooms; the décor; music and activities had all been carefully selected to convey particular brand messages.

In the BMW room, we felt a sense of innovation, dynamism and of challenging the status quo. The brand messaging in the white, minimalist design played off against technological advancement and a sense of speed and culture.

Conversely, in the MINI room, the combination of brightly-coloured luminescence on black backdrops, along with funky music, created a playful, even somewhat daring and cheeky mood.

In the Rolls Royce room, the sheer scale and sophistication of the brand – "inspiring greatness" – reinforced the signature craftsmanship.

The philosophy behind Goodwood, the home of the brand, was conveyed in bespoke luxury, interior trim and the exquisite design of the champagne chest. The attention to detail was demonstrated in how the centre caps on the wheels of the Rolls Royce do not rotate. The 'RR' logo attaches to bearings, keeping it in an upright position, even when the wheels turn. Designers provided great detail on interior trim, describing the carefully crafted, premium leather seats. The hides for these seats come from prize stock that is nurtured and fed in open pastures (with no barbed wire fences, thus reducing the chance of cuts or scuffs on the leather). The Spirit of Ecstasy statuette at the front of the bonnet retracts automatically.

There we were, presented with three hugely different brands with three vastly different brand messages. Each one was based on the philosophy of premium branding. The science behind this approach to branding was simple yet profound: Identify the emotional core of your brand; find multiple ways to communicate this in your brand messaging; and then be very explicit in the brand behaviours that you want your staff to adopt in order to reinforce that message.

Brand exposure should lead to the brand experience. If your brand core is joy, then deliver that in the vehicle design, the quality of the finish and the engine performance. Then make sure that this experience replicates at every touchpoint in the customer value chain. At the end of the process, we provided staff with realistic customer scenarios and asked them to come up with best practices to address the issues, reasoning from the basis of the brand values.

The training involved was not about enforcing compliance. Rather, it was an attempt to appeal to intuition and common sense. Instead of telling staff how to behave, we wanted them to arrive at best practices through the brand values. It made no sense for the vehicle to offer "sheer driving pleasure" if the service or after-sales experience was one of frustration and anger. What was needed was consistency, predictability and reassurance in every interaction.

BMW's Brand Academy concept, as a House of Brands, incorporated a combination of colours; texture; sound; video and lighting, which translated into an unparalleled user experience. But could this exposure to the psychology of branding influence, or even change behaviour? At the end of the training, I sensed the project stood a chance. Rather than just talking about customer service, we were taking the principles of brand behaviour and cascading them into the forefront of the minds of our customer-facing staff.

On my return to South Africa, I realised that we faced some unique challenges of our own. The Brand Academy incorporated lessons from other premium brands around the world. Trainers had regaled us with accounts of excellent customer service, and of staff going out of their way to exceed guest expectations. These success stories included the luxury of other premium brands including high-end hotels, like the Ritz Carlton, whose brand slogan is: "We are ladies and gentlemen serving ladies and gentlemen".

While the stories were inspirational and great for illustrative purposes, the problem we faced was dealing with a target population of sales and customer relationship teams who wouldn't necessarily relate to the brands. Most of those customer-facing staff were never going to be able to afford a night in a five-star hotel. We were asking them to role-model a customer mindset and approach that they had never experienced. How do you influence a group of people to deliver on a highly sophisticated, very targeted level of customer service when that same group has had little, or no exposure, to that target market, or any experience of interacting with a premium brand? It was a challenge!

The solution: Take them through the two-day Brand Academy, and on the night in between, book them in as guests of a luxury hotel for a premium experience. The results were astounding! The brand identity approach on day one, followed by a premium brand service experience that night, meant that they arrived on day two with a heightened awareness. Suddenly, it was easy for them to link their knowledge back to all of the touchpoints in their customer service. When we measured a year later, we saw that many customer-facing staff were now more aware of their role in determining both customer service levels and professional brand behaviour. The project successfully influenced staff on a rational, emotional and personal level and brought about noticeable change as far as customer experience and satisfaction were concerned.

Influencing Currencies

I've had the privilege of teaching *'Leadership, Negotiation and Influencing'* to audiences in more than 80 countries. In our programmes, we approach influencing as *"the art of using various sources of power and persuasion to achieve the desired result within a given context"*. Because the intersection between leadership and influence is so close, some leadership thinkers conclude that leadership is influence.

As the world of work changes (particularly post-pandemic), the way we think about influence also needs to change. Historically, in more classically-built organisations, the command-and-control, top-down influence through authority was the order of the day.

Authors describe 'influence' and 'influencing' in several ways. Different analogies are used to explain these sources of power and persuasion. One approach to look at influencing is from the basis of a toolbox – choosing the appropriate tool for each influencing context. You won't have much success using a screwdriver as a hammer, or a chainsaw to build a brick wall. Choosing the appropriate influencing approach means identifying **what** you want to achieve and **who** you need support from in order to achieve that specific goal.

Another way of thinking about influencing is the idea of 'currencies'.[81] The South African Rand is not a recognised currency in Europe. As a South African, I need to convert my money into Euros. In the same way, influencers need to identify their available currencies and then select the best approach, depending on the target audience.

Robert Cialdini identified six major influencing principles:[82]

1. Reciprocity.
2. Commitment.
3. Social proof.
4. Authority.
5. Liking.
6. Scarcity.

Cialdini argued that to be effective at influencing, one needed to understand how to incorporate these principles into one's approach. In extending the metaphor of currencies, I suggest that influencing someone else is similar to choosing a mode of payment.

Modes of payment

In South Africa, few merchants still accept cheques as legal tender. I don't remember when I last paid using a cheque. Locally, banks have placed a limit on the maximum value of a cheque, which has encouraged businesses to migrate to electronic forms of payment. At least one major South African bank has announced it will stop issuing cheques altogether by the end of 2020. In the US, though, cheques are still widely used and accepted.

Here's the first principle of influence. You have to choose an approach, 'a mode of payment' that is going to work for the specific audience you are trying to reach. What might work well and be widely accepted for one audience, may not be effective with another. Where historically you might have relied on seniority or length of service to convince others of a need for change (more traditional 'push' styles of influence), now you might need to think about a 'pull' approach, by appealing to a broader network, or creating more envisioning messages.

While using data is an especially important part of influencing, just like cheques, your influencing approach might need to be updated or adapted to include a more comprehensive and more up-to-date way of getting your message across.

Imagine that you need to convince a board to decide on cost reductions based on well-supported data around market research. If you have only relied on the data to influence, but have not done so with a clear understanding of the source of your data; as well as the context of your audience; their specific frame of reference; their concerns and their past experiences, then your message might well be rejected – even with the hard facts in front of them.

Cheques, when they are accepted, are only valid for a limited period of time. In the same way, data credibility (does this reflect the current reality?), data reliability (is there consistency of measurement under similar conditions?) and data validity (is there accuracy of measurement?) are important.

Cheques also require authentication. When presenting data, it's just as important to confirm and validate the source. Banks will look for changes in handwriting, for spelling mistakes and for anything that might suggest that the bearer of the cheque is not who they say they are, or that the cheque has been altered. In the same way, we will all need to become more astute at not taking data at face value. We need to make the effort to investigate and confirm its accuracy and reliability. The source of the data is as critical as the data itself.

Professor Tali Sharot argues that: *"paradoxically, the wealth of available information makes us more resistant to change because it is so easy to find data that supports our vision. The net result is that groups are moving to extremes. Confirmation bias means that we take in data that fits our worldview, but then tend to assess counterevidence with a critical eye. The brain assesses new evidence in the light of existing information."*[83]

This is not to suggest that data is not a valuable source of influence, but rather, that it is essential to understand how, as Sharot puts it, *"the brain shuts down when faced with contradictory information. It's as if the brain rewards ignorance and shuts down when confronted with information that will highlight loss or decline."*

It is not that data cannot influence; rather, it's how we position that data and the context supporting it. To be effective, the presentation of the information needs to emphasise gain, progress and opportunity. **The 'payment mode' needs to be correctly applied**.

Let's take another example of a well-known 'payment mode': An auction, selling an item to the highest bidder. There is usually a third party (the auctioneer) tasked with working from an agreed opening value, who then uses the relative scarcity of the product, the current demand of other buyers (the social proof, that this item must be worth something if everyone else wants it), and the speed and rhythm of the auction chant to drive up the price.

In many instances, influencing means appealing on a rational and emotional level to persuade people of the intrinsic value of your point of view, your product, service or idea. Auctions seem to appeal to both the head and the heart. I once attended an auction with a friend who was more than happy to pay a small fortune for a vehicle that he had not even test-driven beforehand. A few years ago, a well-known auctioneer used bid-rigging and ghost-bidding tactics to artificially create demand and inflate prices. He essentially held mock auctions. Even when all of the elements of the payment mode line up, we still run the risk of being duped.

Electronic funds transfers have been championed as quick, safe and convenient. My experiences confirmed this – until recently, when I sold a property. The conveyancing attorneys required a stamped letter from the bank confirming my account details. They also needed confirmation that all of the property rates were up to date. Any shortfall would need to be settled directly with them, held in trust, and then paid over to the creditor. I provided them with all of the required documentation and waited for the transfer of the property to be processed.

Imagine my surprise when I received a telephone call, followed by an email from the attorneys to *"please note that we will never change our banking details while this transaction is current, Should you not follow the abovementioned recommendations and should you pay funds into a fraudster's account, then you will unfortunately not be credited in respect of such payment, and accordingly the risk of payment into other accounts vests solely in yourself. We apologise for having to make this statement so clear but have been forced to do so by the large incidents of fraud which have been perpetrated on attorneys in recent times."*

We then discovered that scamsters were tracing pending transfers in the deeds office; intercepting the email correspondence; getting people to amend the beneficiary details and then diverting funds due either to the sellers or to the attorneys and illegally channelling those funds into their illicit accounts. The move to online payments has opened up a whole new set of transaction implications.

Influence occurs on a continuum, from the ethical to the unethical. Leaders who influence ethically do so from the basis of mutuality and collaboration. Unethical influencing is one-sided, and opaque in its intent. It involves some degree of deception or misinformation. There is a word for this approach: Manipulation.

> **Manipulation** involves exerting devious influence over a person for your advantage.[84]

When others try to influence us, we often implement checks and balances, as a means of self-protection. I like to compare influence to going through a toll gate.

With influencing, just as with travelling through on a toll road, I need to get to the other side. With influencing, this 'other side' means conveying my ideas, requests and point of view in a way that is acceptable to the recipient.

Tunnels and Toll Booths

If I drive to Cape Town, I can choose to travel on the N2, which is a more southerly route, or I can go along the N1 and through the Huguenot (Abdullah M. Omar) Tunnel. This road traverses the DuToitskloof Mountains along a four-kilometre stretch. On the other side is a toll booth. On our national, tolled highways, there are signs before toll booths stating the toll fee, relative to the size of the vehicle and its number of axles. The sign explaining the toll fees payable is accompanied by an explanation of acceptable payment methods (cash and certain types of credit cards). To pass through a toll gate, not only do you need the correct amount of money, but you also need to use the specified payment mode assigned to a specific lane. Failure to meet these requirements and the boom stays closed.

Some lanes only allow for payment with an e-tag. These lanes are cashless, and there is no one managing the booth. In the e-tag-only lane, you need the correct amount credited to your e-tag account before you get to the toll booth; you need a valid e-tag on your windscreen; and you also need to enter through the right channel. Line up all of those elements and you will sail straight through. It's quick, seamless and hassle-free. My e-tag also has a sound notification to confirm that a transaction has been successfully processed.

However, if you have the correct amount of cash, but no valid e-tag, the boom will stay down. You will need to find a lane that accepts cash or cards. I can't even count the number of times I have seen solitary vehicles backing up into hundreds of oncoming cars as they reverse out of the e-tag lane and into a cash- or card-only lane.

Another critical aspect of a toll booth is that the larger the load or vehicle, the more money you pay. The tunnel road also has a height restriction, so only vehicles of a specific size are allowed on that stretch of road.

Much like at the BMW Brand Academy, there are multiple elements to the influencing process. We need to ensure that the right channels and the correct modes of influence are used. The bigger the ideas, the more demand you are placing on the recipients, and the more you have to invest in influencing successfully. In the case of significant emotional, physical and even financial decisions, the influencer needs to ensure the correct mode, the exact amount, and the appropriate channel. Any break in this influencing approach will block access to 'the other side'.

Timing is another critical component. If a driver gets to the tunnel entrance after an accident and the road is closed, they will have to take a considerable detour over the mountains. Everything could be lined up in terms of influence, but if the timing is off, you may find yourself having to work that much harder to get your message across, to 'the other side'.

The toll booth analogy is a constructive way to think about influencing. You need to know your audience; identify their currency; choose the correct, appropriate transaction or payment method; consider the 'load' or demand you are placing on them, and then enter the correct lane at the right time. Line all of those up and you will 'get through' and influence effectively.

Meaningful behaviour changes require accessing neural pathways for effective influence.

Similarity Bias

Many electronic payment gateways are based on principles of similarity (QR codes payment systems are an excellent example of merely scanning a bar code on your smartphone to effect a payment). It's quick, convenient and eliminates the need for a card in the transaction.

In the world of influencing, similarity is an important principle. We are definitely more easily influenced and inclined to accept people and their ideas when they look and think as we do. On the one hand, this is extremely useful, but just because something looks familiar doesn't necessarily mean that it is authentic, or even true. With the move towards deep fakes (synthetic media in which likenesses are artificially created), we face the real challenge of not falling into the trap of accepting a message at face value – simply because it comes from a source who looks like someone we have seen before.

Similarity bias cuts both ways. Conversely, we also need to be careful not to reject people or ideas simply because they look or sound unfamiliar, or present the world in a different way. Leaders continue to be challenged in the areas of diversity and inclusion when this means hiring and working with people who don't look, think or work as they do.

The Power of Networks

The power of alliances and networks should not be underestimated. Let's extend the 'mode of payment' metaphor a little further. One quick way to raise money is through crowdfunding. By tapping into a wide range of social media platforms, fundraisers rely on the collective, community efforts of friends, family and colleagues to widen their reach and to target potential investors or donors.

In the new world of work, purely relying on position or expertise is not enough. As we begin to work more remotely and in more matrixed set-ups, the ability to work at the nexus of process and function is paramount.

Identifying stakeholders is the first part of this influencing process. A visual map of the relationships you hold both internally and externally is a quick way to view the concentrations of decision-making and resources. Tracking those networks of relationships and understanding the dynamics of 'who-knows-who' is becoming critical to accessing key leaders and decision-makers.

Social proof, in the form of approval, validation or introductions from mutual third parties, is one way to expand your network and develop strong alliances, strategic relationships and partnerships. In the new world of work, 'network intelligence' and ability to nurture these dynamic connections will be crucial for leadership success.

Cracking the 'CODES'

As leaders, we need to be aware of how barriers to influence create challenges for us. Heightened suspicions from previous negative experiences; a perceived lack of credibility; inconsistency; and even feeling under pressure, will all need mitigation. Leading from the basis of authenticity and trust go some way towards establishing credible influence.

At a neuroscientific level, scientists are providing invaluable insight into these influencing enablers and barriers. Simon Sinek and Drs Tara Swart and Paul Zak (among others) have all written about what I call the 'CODES' of influence. Modern leaders have a deeper awareness of the interplay between brain activity and brain chemistry, based on the research available on 'CODES'.

Let's consider each of these components in more detail:

- Cortisol
- Oxytocin
- Dopamine
- Endorphins
- Serotonin.

Cortisol

Cortisol is a small, highly lipid-soluble molecule; a glucocorticoid hormone released by the adrenal gland cortex and triggered by physical or psychological stress. Cortisol prepares the body for action, increases blood pressure and blood sugar levels, while suppressing the immune system. In typically stressful situations, cortisol provides additional energy to the brain and seems to act as a defence, or even coping mechanism, in challenging circumstances.

Neuroscientists recorded significantly increased cortisol levels in people before serious surgery, during public speaking and even when they were solving complex mathematical problems.[85]

As a stress marker, saliva tests measure cortisol levels. The challenge with cortisol is that while it provides significant short-term benefits, in the long term, raised cortisol levels can have severely deleterious effects. People in a depressed state, or those who experience irregular sleep patterns, tend to record higher cortisol levels. Over time, elevated cortisol levels can be a case of 'too much of a good thing'. Elevated blood pressure and constricted arteries cannot be good for the heart over an extended period of time.

Without even understanding the neuroscience, leaders who rely purely on their position, title or seniority could be tempted to use a command-and-control approach. Although, in a crisis, relying on stress to get results might not be a bad thing, using it as a default influencing style produces adverse effects in followers. Systems theory tells us that the more you try to shut down a system, the more the elements in that system react.

A study published in the *Psychological and Cognitive Sciences Journal*[86] found that leaders have lower cortisol levels than non-leaders. This result could have something to do with leaders having a greater sense of control in any given situation. Whatever the reason, it does seem that the way you assign tasks to followers, coupled with your delegation style, positively influence cortisol levels and ultimately, performance. Over time, there is also a negative correlation between cortisol levels and trust.

Oxytocin

Oxytocin is a nonapeptide strongly associated with social bonding, generosity, mood and reduced psychological disturbances.[87] Simply put, the emotions that mothers and babies experience during breastfeeding can have the same effect on oxytocin levels as when people feel trusted, respected and acknowledged in a relationship. Oxytocin also seems to reduce our fear of trusting strangers. High stress is an oxytocin inhibitor, too. Conversely, higher levels of oxytocin produce higher levels of empathy.

According to Dr Zak, there are several practical steps leaders can take to influence at an interpersonal level. Recognising individual effort; regular progress updates; creating a sense of achievement; giving people a choice of project; and frequent, timeous information updates all go a long way to positively impacting oxytocin levels.[88]

Dopamine

We feel good on dopamine. The brain produces these neurotransmitters, which lead to all forms of habit-forming addiction. The reason for this is how closely dopamine links to pleasurable emotions and general reward systems. As a chemical messenger, the challenge with substance abuse is that the more substances you ingest, the more you will need for the dopamine to keep working.

Frequent phone-checking, regular exercise, and listening to music all help to raise dopamine levels. However, dopamine also supports alertness and is also useful for achieving clarity and developing working memory. Positively higher dopamine levels also relate to higher levels of personal motivation. The brain has a network of dopamine pathways linked to feedback loops – feedback that responds to recognition and reward, anticipating the action and releasing dopamine just at the thought of doing something pleasurable.

This 'seeking-reward' loop means that the brain starts to expect the outcome of an action even before the act itself. As leaders, if we tap into the positive emotions associated with task completion or successful execution, then we start to rely more on the dopamine effect than on the adverse, inhibiting effects of long-term, stressful, cortisol-inducing situations.

Endorphins

Once again, it's worth highlighting the interconnectedness of everything we have discussed so far. As we have said, the leader's ability to bounce back, particularly in a crisis, is vital.

To explain the idea of a natural morphine from within the body, doctors have illustrated how the words 'endogenous' and 'morphine' are the root words of 'endorphin'.[89]

In stressful situations, endorphins perform in a different way from cortisol. They not only help to block pain, but also regulate mood and boost the immune system.

Sunlight naturally enhances endorphins, which also play a central role during exercise. Long-distance runners refer to a 'runner's high' – that feeling of immense pleasure, even when they are experiencing significant physical discomfort after pounding the streets for kilometres. Recent research also suggests that when we cry, not only are stress hormones released, but endorphins are stimulated, making us feel better.

Serotonin

Serotonin syndrome is the body's response to a drug overdose. At normal levels, serotonin regulates body temperature, mood and concentration and contributes to a sense of wellbeing. Excessive levels of serotonin result in nausea and irritability. Conversely, a serotonin deficiency presents as a depressed mood, insomnia and a lack of confidence.

The gut contains more than 95% of the body's serotonin. This may explain why people say things like: "I feel sick to the pit of my stomach," or why we talk about "gut instinct". Serotonin probably also explains why so much anxiety expresses itself in recurring digestive problems.

The brain is far more complex and sophisticated than the 'CODES' outlined. Growing insight into the area of neuroleadership suggests that we are developing a richer understanding of the 'influence of influence' in so many areas of our daily lives.

If we think back to the idea of influence as different modes of payment, then as we move to a cashless economy, we are now being offered everything, from tap-and-go cards, to fully-fledged (open, semi-closed and closed) mobile wallets. Just as payment modes become more convenient and cashless, so, too, leaders have more opportunities to influence, along with increased sources of power and persuasion at their disposal.

How do you like to be influenced? If you can answer that question, it may give you some insight and clues into possible ways to engage with those in your network. Identifying the various approaches from other influencers that make you more open to requests, ideas, suggestions or new ways of thinking, could be really helpful. Knowing how I like others to approach me from an influencing perspective has definitely made me more aware of what I need to consider when looking to influence those around me. It is certainly not a case of 'one size fits all'.

Six Factors for Influence

During my interviews with several leaders in global companies about their most important considerations when people influence them, six broad themes, or influencing factors, emerged. Consider these in the same way you would if you were trying to get through a toll booth. The more of these factors you can combine (depending on your audience), the greater your likelihood of success.

1. **Analytical factors**
2. **Approach factors**
3. **Alignment factors**
4. **Authenticity factors**
5. **Attractiveness factors**
6. **Association factors**

1. **Analytical factors:** Is there fairness and logic in the request/presentation? Is there evidence to support the position? To what extent does this information line up with my current facts? What is the source of the data? How current is the data? What do I stand to gain here? What do I stand to lose here?
2. **Approach factors:** Is the request polite, concise and presented in the appropriate tone? Is the application, presentation or position supported by a particular purpose? Is the timing, right?

3. **Alignment factors:** Does the request/presentation line up with what I need to achieve in terms of my own needs and priorities? Is there an alignment of interests?
4. **Authenticity factors:** Does the request/presentation appear legitimate and credible? What is the influencer's track record?
5. **Attractiveness factors:** Does this request/presentation appeal to me? To what extent does it line up with my needs? Is there a sense of care for my priorities and point of view?
6. **Association factors:** What level of a relationship, if any, do I have with this person? Who else can endorse/sponsor the position or idea of the influencer? Who in my network can validate this person's situation, request or presentation? What are other people's opinions or perspectives on this request/presentation?

Understanding and answering these questions before you try to influence is no guarantee of success, but your chances of winning someone over will be improved. Selecting the most suitable combination of factors increases your leadership efficacy in both a one-to-one and one-to-many situations.

A richer appreciation of the power of unconscious bias impacts our understanding of influence. Social pressure, individual motivations, and the limits on our processing capabilities mean that we are prone to more bias than we realise. Decision-making and feedback are two of several instances in which bias and influence collide. We unconsciously sort people into preconceived groups.

Harvard's Project Implicit designed a series of association tests to highlight the extent and depth of these assumptions.[90] Researchers used the choices participants made on alternatives to investigate implicit social cognition (those thoughts and feelings that are mostly outside of our conscious awareness). The problem is that even with hundreds of people completing the association tests, one of the original designers now argues that there is still insufficient evidence to measure bias solely by one test.

2020 has been a watershed year on many fronts, not the least of which has been the groundswell of support for the Black Lives Matter movement. One can only hope that we will all become more aware of often deeply-held and systemic biases, and acknowledge where we need to change. Having lived in South Africa for more than 40 years, and having travelled internationally extensively, I have witnessed first-hand how deeply these divides run and the impact they have on society at large.

If, as author and speaker John Maxwell says: *"Leadership is influence,"* I believe that we need to make a concerted effort to understand influencing dynamics. What are the inputs to influence, and what are its effects? How will influence look in a post-Covid-19 world? With access to information and misinformation at an all-time high, every statement, action or inaction can be interpreted and misinterpreted.

Leaders will need to work hard to ensure that they adopt an authentic approach to influencing. Otherwise, we all run the risk of being discredited on the wastelands of unreliability.

5 / EXERCISE

INFLUENCE QUESTIONS

For you to consider:

- How would your stakeholders describe you, as a personal brand?
- What are your dominant influencing currencies?
- What are you doing to better understand the impact of your influence on others at a neurological level?
- Do you influence from the basis of stress or trust?
- When you influence, have you considered the six factors?
    1. **Analytical factors:** Is there fairness and logic in the request/presentation?
    2. **Approach factors:** Is the request polite, concise and in an appropriate tone?
    3. **Alignment factors:** Does the request/presentation line up with what I need to achieve in terms of my own needs and priorities? Is there an alignment of interests?
    4. **Authenticity factors:** Does the request/presentation appear legitimate and credible? What is the influencer's track record?
    5. **Attractiveness factors:** Does this request/presentation appeal to me?
    6. **Association factors:** What level of a relationship, if any, do I have with this person?
- What are you doing to foster a greater awareness of your areas of unconscious bias?

6 / COMMUNICATION

UNDERSTANDING, CERTAINTY AND CLARITY

"Information is giving out. Communication is getting through."

Sydney J. Harris

The Bee Waggle

Some years ago, I had the privilege of writing, producing and directing a television documentary on the Maale people, who live in the southern regions of the Rift Valley in Ethiopia. My team and I took two days to travel from Addis Ababa. We overnighted at Lake Awassa and then travelled into the remote Omo River Valley, and finally to Maaleland. Through a network of interpreters, the chief of one village invited us to his homestead, not far from the riverbank.

On arrival at the camp, I couldn't help but notice the difference in design and quality between two, adjacent rondavel dwellings. On the right was a circular structure: A house best described as a lean-to. It was cobbled together with sticks, mud and a dense covering of thatch. Although it was waterproof, it didn't appear to offer much more than basic protection from the elements. If anything, it lacked the finesse of its neighbour. Although they were about 30m apart, the only thing the two dwellings had in common was their size. Otherwise, the houses could not have been more different.

With the house on my left, I was struck by the attention to detail displayed in the tightly-packed mud floor, and by the deft touch evident in the carefully trimmed acacia branches interwoven into upright supports. Roof beams extended from the centre point in a radial pattern, visible as they protruded in a perfectly even cut; suspended over the edge of the carefully trimmed walls. A large, smoothly-combed thatch roof covered the trusses. The thatch, delicately sewn together, was tied to the ceiling with grass rope. Just below the roofline, carved acacia logs (about 50cm in diameter and two metres in length) hung symmetrically through the walls; lying parallel to the roof trusses and equally spaced at regular intervals around the building. A seal placed on the end of each log meant that a series of nine or ten disc shapes were all that was visible from the outside. Calabashes and woven baskets hung neatly on the outer walls. The care and creativity taken in constructing that building was apparent. Compared to its neighbour, the house looked almost palatial.

After showing us the rest of the camp, the headman offered us something to drink. We sat on small tree stumps and chatted about the ancient Maale traditions of hunting with bows and arrows, and of how a young man needed to prove his manhood by killing a lion. The conversation was cordial and relaxed, considering that I was only the fourth or fifth outsider the family had ever met.

The Maale people had desperately tried to maintain their independence and isolated lifestyle, but finally, they were looking to introduce visitors to the area. Eventually, the conversation circled back to a discussion about their hunter-gatherer existence. Our interpreters asked if we had any questions. There was something I had wanted to ask since we had arrived.

"Who lives in this house?" I asked, indicating the lean-to structure on the right.

"My wife and my children," explained the chief. "I live alone in the house on the left," he added. "My wife comes to visit me, but she always goes back to the children." He stood up and pointed to the round logs with the covered discs. "Yes," he grinned, "in this house, it's just me and my bees. I must look after them."

Suddenly, it all made sense. The house on the left was an apiary. In Western terms, the beehive was the equivalent of a bank. Honey was food, balm and medicine; it was liquid gold. In a society with no formal currency, ownership of the hives predated land ownership. The round log hives contained numerous bee colonies. At night, the headman would harvest both the honey and the beeswax, unsealing the hollowed-out acacia logs using a homemade smoker. For him, the comfort, safety and protection of the bees took precedence over the comfort of even his own family.

"If you are really quiet," smiled the chief, "at night, you can hear the queen bee singing when the royal cells hatch."

The chief could have been on to something. Scientists have known for more than 50 years that bees encode and decode messages to each other. It is only more recently that humans have gained some insight into the sophistication and complexity of these messages. Here's what we know:

A returning scout bee interacts with waiting bees in the colony by regurgitating newly-acquired nectar. If the nectar is of a high quality, the scout bee begins vibrating or 'dancing'. This dance, combined with the release of odour from scent glands, provides incredibly detailed information to other bees about the source of the nectar. Not only are there different dances, but the bee also moves with varying levels of intensity, depending on how far away the bees are from the food source.

The 'round dance' is straight forward. If the food is up to 100m away, then the scout bee moves in a circular motion, leaving it up to the rest of the bees to locate the source purely from scent and nectar fragrance. But this is where it gets interesting: When the food source is further away, the scout bee shifts to a 'waggle dance' that communicates both distance and direction. Through a series of longer or shorter dance circuits, the scout bee tells the others how much energy it will require to get to the nectar. The fewer the circuits, the further away the nectar is likely to be from the hive. This method communicates flight distances of up to 2 000m.

But what about direction? Believe it or not, during the 'straight' portion of the dance, the scout bee angles itself relative to the sun azimuth and the hive. The other bees are then able to work out the required direction of flight to get to the nectar.

In the darkness of the colony, the scout bee also uses sound (thrumming on the honeycomb) to indicate direction.

There are so many lessons to learn from these amazing creatures. They can certainly teach us about getting our message across succinctly.

Communication: A duplication of ideas; the meeting of the minds.

Attention, all Passengers

I was excited at the prospect of trying out a new internal airline. As we taxied from the gate, I buckled up and listened as the attendant ran through the safety briefing. Like the rest of the team, her body language revealed her inexperience. Neatly-pressed uniforms and eager greetings belied the fact that the team was new to the vagaries of in-flight communication.

Halting and uncertain, the attendant started to read. At the first mistake, she drew away from the PA system in a fit of nervous giggles. Passengers chuckled in sympathetic laughter. Too embarrassed to continue, she quickly handed both the script and the microphone to her assistant and hid her face behind the door panel as her colleague struggled to complete the briefing. It was clear that she, too, had not done this very often. Her eyes glued to her script, her head turned away from the passengers, she gave a staccato, monotone delivery, as she paused after every few words to look up at the first attendant for reassurance. The gain setting on the amplifier reverberated the distorted sound of her voice through the cabin. A high pitch rang out every time she pressed the 'Talk' button. After several excruciating minutes, the briefing ended.

The flight was not very full, and I spotted the open seats at the emergency exit doors. Always glad for some extra leg room, I asked an attendant if I could move before take-off. On cue, I swapped seats. A third attendant walked past me and, realising that she had not given me a run-down on the emergency exits, turned around, smiled, and outlined the evacuation procedures. Unlike the stammering of the first two attendants, her briefing was precisely the opposite: A double-action, rapid-fire delivery that was more like a horseracing commentary than emergency briefing.

Information transmission had happened in both briefings, but whether communication had occurred was debatable. If communication is about recipients ensuring understanding of content, intent and meaning, then passengers had been left, at best, mildly confused and, at worst, highly frustrated.

I was left mulling over the fact that, as far as communication was concerned, my in-flight experience was certainly not the exception to the rule. Research confirms that although followers generally have high communication expectations of leaders, those expectations often remain unfulfilled. Successful communication requires leaders to focus on the cognitive processes of how individuals acquire, store, retrieve, and apply that information.

In the technology-savvy world of social and electronic media, it's certainly worth considering the degree to which our communication is improving (or not) as a result of these advances. Even with the modern luxuries of email on our mobile phones, instant messaging, and video conferencing, the possibility for misunderstanding, ambiguity, and even confusion, still exists. So, how then do we move on to understanding, certainty and clarity?

Leaders spend 70-90% of their time in communication. When you consider speech, written text and behaviour (including non-verbal), it's clear that a large part of leadership is precisely that: Communicating. But conveying a message is not limited to what we say. It is multimodal and incorporates leaders' behaviours, decisions, and actions. Leadership communication takes place in the cauldron of interpersonal interactions. What's more, there is a positive relationship between the frequency and quality of leader communication and follower-performance.

As I write, the Dragon capsule (Endeavour), manned by astronauts Robert Behnken and Douglas Hurley, has just returned after docking at the International Space Station for more than 60 days. What makes this trip so historic is that it is the first commercial public-private partnership between Nasa and SpaceX.

I asked Prof David Block, Professor Emeritus, astronomer and author, to comment on what impressed him most about the recent completion of the Nasa Space X Dragon mission. He didn't hesitate:

"At any one point, the astronauts only listened to one voice, the voice of mission control and it made me realise that for any successful endeavour, the key to successful leadership is to listen to one singular voice, or if you've got a group of people around you, possibly as a CEO, to listen to a common voice. In other words, surround yourself with champions who have the same idea, who have the same goal and then listen to that common voice. That was the singularly most important facet of SpaceX, which riveted my attention throughout the mission."[91]

Understanding the Dynamics

Leaders appreciate and understand the dynamics and principles of communication. The first consideration is the **context and channel** of the message. The second and third considerations, respectively, are the **content** of the message and how one **conveys** the message. The leader's ability to speak with **candour**, and to **connect the dots** is also paramount. The extent to which global leaders successfully communicate **cross-culturally** is a further consideration.

Compelling communication occurs across a range of different contexts (**audience**). Communication context refers to both **intrapersonal** (talking to yourself – self-talk) and **interpersonal** (one-to-one, group), public, and even mass audiences. Identifying the 'who' of the audience precedes the 'why' and 'what' of the message.

You might find yourself talking to some followers who are deeply and passionately committed to what you say, but in the same room communicating with those who are not only disinterested, but possibly even passively resistant. They may even blatantly oppose your ideas. Considering your audience before deciding on what you want to say is a principle that applies whether you are drafting an email, sending out a press statement or facilitating a video conference.

Intrapersonal Audience

Eloquent communicators recognise how essential it is to understand what is going on inside themselves. That voice in your head wants to be acknowledged. When discussing the topic of this internal voice with my students, it is fascinating to see the various iterations that arise in response to the instruction: "Describe your inner voice as a person by completing the following sentence: 'I would describe my inner voice as …'" Some of their responses include:

- "My safe place."
- "A naysayer."
- "An inner critic."
- "A bully."
- "My creativity flow."
- "A nag."

- "A doubter."
- "A pessimist."
- "My problem-solver."

This 'inner speaking' might not be a voice at all. It may be reflected as images, memories, and even heightened sensory awareness.

"The intuitive mind is a sacred gift, and the rational mind is a faithful servant. We have created a society that honours the servant and has forgotten the gift."

Albert Einstein

Interpersonal Audience

In one-to-one conversation, articulate communicators focus all of their attention on the individual. They ensure that they are not distracted while communicating. They resist the temptation to try to do too much at once. Leaders are often so inclined to focus exclusively on the next pressing issue, or on the next project, that when they do engage with their followers, they struggle to offer their undivided attention.

From a communication perspective, what's also fascinating to note is the disconnect between the leader who is a great public speaker, able to ignite an audience of hundreds, or even thousands, yet struggles to hold a conversation on a one-to-one basis. As a professional speaker, I have been in several situations where a 'sage of the stage' (who commands the attention of an entire convention space filled with eager delegates) has confessed to me that they find personal, one-on-one conversations awkward, or even frightening.

In this technologically-connected world, we have to resist the temptation to allow the smartphone to suck our focus. Continuous partial attention seems to be an increasingly looming blight on our conversations. The idea that we can be 'always-on', hyperconnected to the digital universe, means that we run the risk of being in contact with everything and with no one at the same time. We seem to falsely believe that, as consultant and writer Linda Stone describes it, we can be everywhere except where we actually are physically.[92] Effective communicators are fully present.

The Artist is Present

A colleague of mine took his family to the Museum of Modern Art in New York to see a performance piece by Marina Abramovic called *The Artist is Present*. When they arrived at the museum, the queue snaked around the back of the building. People stood for hours to get into the room to see Marina's performance, held in an expansive, but empty, gallery, except for a table positioned in between two upright, wooden chairs.

Marina sat silently, dressed in a long, flowing, red gown; her back straight; her hands resting in her lap. One by one, audience members took their position in the other chair. Marina simply gazed deeply into their eyes without saying a word. She held that position for eight hours a day over a period of three months. Almost 1 000 people experienced that undistracted engagement. One enthralled audience member returned more than 20 times! People described being overcome by emotion at the deep sense of connection they felt in that moment. As brilliant as the performance art was, I wonder what it says about our society at large. What might we be missing in our daily one-on-one interaction with one another?

Active Listening

Almost without fail, thought leaders make a point of linking listening and leadership.

> Listening first; listening deeply; listening respectfully; being attentive to what is said; being accepting of ideas, criticisms and feedback; listening more than telling; and listening to learn and without judgment are just some of the ways that active listening has been described.

Active listening is not necessarily something that comes naturally, but it is something on which must leaders focus and develop. It's essential to be conscious of facing the person you're talking to, and to maintain eye contact. Be attentive to keeping an open mind as you listen to what is being said. Resist the temptation to formulate a response before you have all of the information. It's also vital that you resist the temptation to interrupt. Seek to gather more information and to fully understand what is being said before responding prematurely.

> How can we be fully present and avoid talking past one another?

Let's revisit some commonly accepted communication concepts in the leader-follower relationship. This model could represent any interpersonal communication between two parties, but a context might be helpful:

George is a 45-year-old manager of multinational IT firm XNet, based in Singapore. He is on a conference call to his subordinate in Bangalore, India – a woman named Sumitra. Sumitra is a systems engineer who has worked for XNet for the past three weeks. She is new to the XNet account and is still learning the ropes of the management of the shipments between Bangalore and Singapore.

One specific delivery is late, owing to a problem with XNet's raw materials supplier. Consequently, George's key account has lost revenue. George represents the sender; the source of the communication. He asks Sumitra for an update on the shipment and an explanation of why the problem occurred.

Notice that the model indicates an interesting phenomenon: The sender **encodes** his message (a subconscious act) through his personality style; the words he uses; his education; his background; and a host of other assumptions and biases. Just to complicate matters further, Sumitra **decodes** the message from George through her own set of assumptions and biases and receives this message via those filters. This provides the second opportunity for misunderstanding.

She then **encodes** her feedback to George, including a step-by-step analysis of the reasons behind the late shipment – once again, filtered through the feedback channel. All that George hears (all that he **decodes**, because of his frustration) is a list of excuses.

George is not someone who enjoys conflict, and he responds to Sumitra with stony silence. Sumitra, in turn, interprets the silence as consent on George's part. She incorrectly assumes that George is happy with her explanation.

All that has happened is that George has retreated into himself and refused to discuss the matter any further. Sumitra has incorrectly assumed resolution on the issue. Not only have these two individuals not understood one another, but they have talked *past* one another. The cross-cultural component only exacerbates the communication breakdown.

But does this model go far enough to explain what really happens in the communication process? The short answer is: To some extent.[93] We know that communication is not a linear process. We also now know that meaning moves beyond the mere words we use. Although the model illustrates a flow from sender to receiver and back again, in reality that process happens almost simultaneously. It is virtually impossible to freeze the communication and isolate one person as the sender and the other as the receiver.

The medium itself also plays a massive role in influencing just how effective you are in communicating. George and Sumitra's interaction on the phone (without the luxury of non-verbal feedback) limits the extent to which they achieve a 'duplication of ideas'. We shouldn't simply throw out the communication model, but rather, acknowledge that leaders need a deeper appreciation of the complexities of communication.

Group Audiences

Most of the men and women at the top levels of business and government share a common skill: Expertise in a particular industry or function, combined with the ability to present their ideas effectively. In a recent survey, 1 500 executives, promoted to the position of chairman of the board, president, or vice president of leading American corporations, were asked to identify which course they considered most important in preparing them for their management careers. Of the respondents, 72% said: "Communications."

In a broader survey, 3 000 people named their greatest fear. The most common answer was: "Speaking before a group."

A sound understanding of finance, law or marketing will make you effective on the job, but your ability to present your conclusions, insights and recommendations will set you apart.

Faced with the need to make an effective presentation, we often become our own worst enemies. Instead of directing our attention to where it could provide the greatest benefit, too often we focus on the uncertainties of the speaking situation:

- How will I come across?
- Will my message be accepted?
- Will I forget something important?
- Will I achieve my purpose?

The first critical step on the road to presentation excellence is placing the spotlight on the source of your anxiety: **The audience**.

An audience is not a faceless entity. Each person listening displays a variety of characteristics. Understanding particular needs, interests and attitudes relieves much of the anxiety you've come to expect when giving a presentation.

Your purpose is not only what you want to accomplish, but what you can reasonably expect the listener to think about, or do, after your presentation.

What does all of this mean for the future of our virtual meetings, and even good old face-to-face communication? How can leaders ensure that communication really happens – and that it happens effectively?

Understanding the dynamics of **asynchronous** and **synchronous communication** means that in order to increase the chances of being understood, 'raising the bandwidth' is really important and is a concept I explore in more detail in Chapter 9 in the context of collaboration. While successful virtual communication tends to default to asynchronous interactions, sometimes there is no replacement for 'eyeballing' the other party – even if it is through a camera. When it comes to effective communications, many companies are recognising the dynamic relationship between context, meaning and the need to optimise the correct point on the bandwidth spectrum. The issue is not just about tools or platforms, it's about suitability and matching the intended meaning in the communication with the most effective communication channel.

In explaining how Zapier built its distributed team, Julia Elman, then Director of the Design team commented:

> *"We have three primary tools for text-based communication overall at Zapier: Slack (virtual office), Async (internal blog) and Quip (internal documentation). One way to think of how we communicate and collaborate is along a 'bandwidth' spectrum, from asynchronous, text-based communication to spending time in person in the same location. When working through tricky issues together, it's sometimes helpful to 'raise' bandwidth – from text-based chat to a video call, for example."*[94]

Julia Elman
Senior User Experience Designer

Public and Mass Audiences

Although the lines between synchronous and asynchronous audience types remain somewhat blurred, public communication involves engaging with members of the public with whom you exchange ideas. One of the big drawcards of social media is how it creates a feedback loop and unlocks a more two-way communication process. In an attempt to manage their own narrative, leaders now use Twitter, Facebook and Instagram to shape their messages and create a sense of immediacy with their audiences.

Content and Delivery Congruence

It's essential to match your content to the audience. The most effective communicators pitch their message at an appropriate level. Timing, empathy, relevance and a call to action all support this goal. Effective leaders convey their ideas through verbal and non-verbal communication.

In our executive coaching programme, *Presentation Excellence*, we work with leaders who are subject matter experts with years of experience, but find themselves unable to speak with confidence in front of a group, or to sell their ideas. The issue is not that they don't know what to say, but rather that they lack confidence in how to say it. Much like flight attendants going through the motions, they focus on information rather than on effective communication.

A vital aspect of this communication competence is ensuring that our face-to-face communication demonstrates verbal/non-verbal congruence.[95] Whether we like it or not, our spoken communication is combined with non-verbal messages. Congruency occurs when the verbal and non-verbal messages agree. When this happens, your audience is not only more likely to agree with your message, but they will also show greater understanding of that message.

Conversely, when there is incongruence, your audience will doubt what you are saying without even knowing why. An expression that describes this effect of incongruence is: "Your actions speak so loudly; I can't hear what you are saying."

Research indicates that the non-verbal aspect may contribute up to 70% of the total message. The net result is that while your verbal message **might** be getting through, your non-verbal message definitely will. This means that the spoken word is either supported or countered by facial expressions, gestures, functional movements and posture.

A critical non-verbal cue is eye contact. Although in many parts of Africa, not making eye contact is a sign of respect, for the most part, direct eye contact indicates confidence and clarity in delivering the message.

Delivering with Candour

"In a time of universal deceit, telling the truth is a revolutionary act."

George Orwell

Assuming positive intent is an important first principle of effective communication – an idea that we will revisit when we explore constructive conflict in Chapter 8.

Candour: To play open cards with your stakeholders.

Twenty-one days into South Africa's lockdown, a recording of the CEO of a national retailer talking to suppliers went viral. Grant Pattison, leader of Edcon, broke down during a briefing as he explained that, as a result of the pandemic and the subsequent lockdown, suppliers should not expect payment. He shared how turnover was down 45% year on year, and that the company saw a $20 million-drop on forecasted sales and cash for that month. He went to explain that the company only had sufficient liquidity to pay salaries.

Effective leadership requires effective interpersonal communication. Practising this kind of communication means being willing to review and assess the extent to which you, as a leader, are communicating to achieve a duplication of ideas. There is sufficient evidence that there is a causal link between organisational candour and performance.[96] Put simply, this means that when leaders are open, honest and transparent in their communication styles, there is an increased chance of followers not only being clear about what has been said, but of them being able to act on the communication. This results in more effective followers.

One of the most powerful tools in verbal communication is honesty – particularly if you're lost in a conversation. If you don't understand something; if someone is speaking too rapidly; or if you are having trouble understanding someone's accent, be honest. They have lost you. While we continue to negotiate the challenges of the electronic age, let's make sure that our communication to our followers always facilitates an exchange of shared meaning.[97]

Leaders who can think strategically are also able to take in different pieces of information and 'connect the dots'. From a communication point of view, followers often only have several pieces of the puzzle. A strong leader can step back and bring all of those different pieces together before providing followers with a clear understanding of how their actions/ task fit into the overall objectives.

Unfamiliar Territory

A client booked me to spend two days in Lusaka, Zambia, with a group of senior leaders from one of the major finance houses. They wanted to work on time management and planning. Looking for a hook – a title for the programme – my marketing team came up with the idea of 'Time Navigation'. This built on the idea that rather than trying to manage time, one needs to approach it in the same manner that one would navigate a river: Sometimes the water is calm and tranquil, and at other times there are many rapids that need to be negotiated.

My client loved the concept and then confirmed all of the travel logistics, accommodation and conferencing facilities. Imagine my surprise when, on arrival at the hotel, I saw my company's name, my client's name and the directions to the conference venue beneath a large sign displayed in the hotel: 'Time Nagging'. This was yet another example of how things can get lost in translation (even when one speaks the same language).

As companies look to expand to the far-flung reaches of the globe, leaders face the challenge of communicating cross-culturally. The way we relate to each other, the way that we communicate ideas, and the way that we execute projects is not universal. I see this in facilitated interaction between leaders from different parts of a business, based in different parts of the world. We are separated by time zones, distance and culture. We need to know how to develop our cultural intelligence to effectively communicate with followers who possibly see things from a different perspective.

Some years ago, I was contracted by an international energy company in Malaysia to do a week-long leadership development programme. Their client office in Cape Town insisted that I spend time with them in South Africa before travelling. I needed to learn how to exchange business cards. What I had assumed was a universal and commonly-held practice turned out to be full of intricacies and protocols that I had never even stopped to consider. Cultural intelligence addresses a specific set of skills that allows an individual leader to become more effective in interacting with people from diverse backgrounds, languages and cultures.

> So, how can leaders ensure effective communication?

In the post-pandemic, obligatory shift to video calls, I was inundated with requests for advice on how to conduct effective virtual meetings. After weeks in lockdown, with no other way of meeting face to face, many leaders complained of 'Zoom fatigue'. It became clear that technology was only amplifying communication challenges. As we navigate the complexities of communication in the remote world of work, it's worth going back to some fundamental communication principles

Let us consider some helpful techniques for self-evaluation and conclude with some suggestions on how leaders can take practical steps to improve communication.

> How can we avoid talking past one another?

Let's revisit some commonly accepted communication concepts in the leader-follower relationship. Communication improvements need to be made consciously. Here are some ways to improve communication.

Verbal communication

- It's a good idea to reconsider the speed at which you speak, particularly when communicating with somebody whose first language is different from your own.

- Try giving people time to think about what you're saying, and then an opportunity to make valuable contributions.
- Ideally, some form of turn-taking protocol should be put in place, particularly if meetings are happening remotely.
- Try to avoid interrupting or completing other people's sentences.

Since the dawn of aviation, airline pilots have learned to understand the importance of contact with a controller, who could be 200 miles away on a line-of-sight communication, or 5 000 miles away, when they are crossing the ocean and making contact on a very high-frequency (VHF) channel.

To make that system work, airlines use standards or rules – what is referred to as a playbook. The first rule is that one person speaks at one time. In order to communicate, pilots use a standard phraseology, a format they have learned, so that if the communication is a little bit crackly, there's an accent they recognise. Standard communication is something that works well for remote operations.

Tips for global communication

- You may find that people from certain cultures need time to work through ideas and suggestions. Try to avoid putting people on the spot and then expecting them to give you an immediate answer on a particular proposal.
- Keep your language simple by eliminating difficult words. Remember that idioms and slang may work well in a local context, but they can get lost in a global context. It may, in fact, reinforce confusion.
- Try to avoid acronyms altogether.
- It's a good idea to reinforce what you've discussed on the telephone, or even face to face, with follow-up written communication.
- Ask the person to whom you are speaking to slow down. Then try to focus on the content rather than being distracted by a particular communication style. If you are unsure about something, ask questions.

In observations of thousands of interactions with people from different parts of the world, nine verbal categories have been identified that can be effectively integrated into conversation:[98]

Proposing

Proposing can be described as a verbal behaviour that puts forward a new suggestion or idea. This is a superb technique for stimulating conversation. It is something that every effective leader should add to their communications skills set.

Enhancing

Enhancing, or what has been referred to in the USA as 'building', is a behaviour that also takes the form of a proposal. Enhancing verbal behaviour extends, develops or builds on a proposal that has already been made by someone else. This is a really helpful technique for those leaders looking to create common ground in their conversations with followers. It does two things: Effective building requires effective listening; and it really makes your followers feel that their contributions to the conversation are adding value.

Supporting

Supporting is a verbal behaviour that could be considered simply 'agreeing'. In a verbal context, one uses supporting to make a conscious expression of that agreement in the form of a verbal statement that expresses support for a particular point of view.

Disagreeing

Leaders should not avoid disagreeing with followers. In fact, research indicates that the high level of disagreement in a conversation – provided those disagreements have been validated with supporting evidence – before reaching consensus – the tighter the agreement. The trick is how you disagree. Disagreeing as a verbal behaviour states direct disagreement on an issue. People do not hear what comes after the word: "No." For the disagreement to be effective, make sure that you give well thought-through reasons as to why you disagree, before disagreeing.

Avoid Defending or Attacking

Effective leaders understand that it is important to separate out communication that focuses on issues from defensiveness or attacks on individuals.

Defensive postures usually involve some kind of value judgment and emotional overtone ("Don't blame me, it's not my fault. It's his responsbility."). Defending/attacking is to be avoided in leader-follower communication because it's usually about people and not issues.

Testing (Checking understanding and summarising)

Leaders need to work on effective ways to minimise misunderstandings and ambiguities in communication. One of the most powerful techniques that can be employed is simply recapping and summarising what has already been communicated. It is also highly effective to check your understanding of what has been agreed upon and communicated. Words such as: "Am I right in saying?" or "Can I just check my understanding?" go a long way to reconfirming what has already been communicated and what the receiver of that communication has understood you to have said. Clarifying is probably one of the most important leadership-communications skills a leader needs to learn. Recapping, summarising, checking understanding, and reconfirming are all superb ways to eliminate misunderstanding, ambiguity and confusion.

Seeking and Giving Information

When communicating, leaders need to ensure that they do not rely purely on the giving of information. This kind of communication approach is not inclusive, and there is no guarantee that your audience (**followers**) will absorb, internalise, or even understand what you have told them. Although giving information during communication cannot be avoided, it is important to balance this with a focus on asking questions.

Bringing in or shutting out (Involving and interrupting)

All nine behaviour categories that have been mentioned can be used to either bring people into a conversation or to shut them out. Bringing in (**involving**) is a technique that can be effectively used to include people who are not participating fully in the conversation. Shutting out (**interrupting**) is a communication technique that should be used sparingly. However, it may be necessary to limit the participation or contribution of a particular individual who is taking a conversation in a direction that you, as a leader, don't want to go. In order to either bring in or shut out, one can use any of the verbal categories described in this section.

Storytelling: The Power of Metaphor

People love stories. They evoke emotions, making it easier for people to feel engaged. Even if leaders do not feel that they are storytellers, the power of metaphor should not be discounted. On 11 February 1990, after being freed from Victor Verster Prison (now Groot Drakenstein Correctional Facility) after 27 years of incarceration as a political prisoner, Nelson Mandela delivered his first public address. He employed metaphor as he referred to the dark days of history:

"I pay tribute to the endless heroism of youth, you, the young lions. You, the young lions, have energised our entire struggle. I pay tribute to the mothers and wives and sisters of our nation. You are the rock-hard foundation of our struggle. Apartheid has inflicted more pain on you than on anyone else."[99]

Nelson Mandela

At the deepest level, the metaphors leaders choose to convey their message are incredibly significant. On announcing South Africa's lockdown, President Cyril Ramaphosa, as Commander in Chief, could be seen in military fatigues as he commissioned the National Defence Force.

In other parts of the world, leaders talked about 'being at war with an invisible enemy,' and being a 'war time president'. Others referred to the virus as 'the enemy'. This was notably different from the approach taken by German Chancellor Angela Merkel. Along with other German commentators, she very carefully avoided any such rhetoric. Instead, she chose to refer to the response to Covid-19 as 'a long-distance run'.[100]

Myth, archetypes, visual imagery and metaphor all play a significant role in the storytelling process. Author Simon Lancaster does a superb job of exploring this idea in his book, *Winning Minds*.[101]

"The greatest thing by far is to have command of a metaphor.
This alone cannot be imparted by another; it is the mark
of genius, for to make good metaphors implies an eye for
resemblance."

Aristotle

Effective communication remains an essential component of leadership. Indeed, the exponential effect is possible with a deeper understanding of what is required to ensure understanding, clarity and certainty.

6 / EXERCISE

COMMUNICATION QUESTIONS

> **Four Key Techniques to Evaluate Communication**
>
> Use these techniques to evaluate your interpersonal leader communication style:
>
> - Openness
> - Supportiveness
> - Motivation
> - Empowerment.

For you to consider:

Openness

- Are you being open enough in your communication to make use of appropriate self disclosure? To do this, examine the level of trust that exists in your leader-follower relationships.

Supportiveness

- Do your followers clearly indicate that they feel supported by you in both the frequency and quality of your communication?
- Are you supportive when you provide feedback to your followers?

Motivation

- Is your communication motivating? Are you able to get people to do things willingly as a result of your communication?
- Do you communicate your vision clearly and with a compelling appeal to both logic and emotion?

Empowerment

- Is your communication empowering?
- Are followers able to execute and carry out tasks based on a clear mandate? Do they have the authority to act?
- Do your followers feel that you have communicated everything that they need to know in order to do their jobs? Do they have a clear understanding of what is required?

If the answer to any of these questions is: "No," it might be time to consider reviewing a few guidelines on how to improve your interpersonal communication.

Having considered some of the critical elements of leading others, it is worth stopping to reflect on our journey thus far.

In this part of the book we have examined 'Leading Them': Developing those around you as followers. In the next section, we will shift our focus to the context of the high-performing team and explore the importance of team alignment; principles of constructive conflict management; and the key ingredients for team collaboration.

PART | **THREE**

LEADING US
(DEVELOPING TEAMS)

7 / ALIGNMENT

INTEGRATING INDIVIDUALS INTO A COHESIVE WHOLE

> Integrate individual choices, strengths and ambitions into a cohesive whole with a singular, collective purpose.

"There is no such thing as a dysfunctional organisation, because every organisation is perfectly aligned to achieve the results it currently gets."

Jeff Lawrence

The Royal Air Force Aerobatic Team, more commonly known as the Red Arrows, was formed in 1965. Since then, they have performed almost 5 000 displays. I remember seeing the team for the first time as a young boy in the early 70s at Yeovil Air Base in the United Kingdom.

I have always been fascinated by the team's speed, agility and tight formations. At any moment in time, nine individuals manoeuvre their aircraft with high precision at speeds of over 900km/ph. Some of the manoeuvres result in the pilots 'pulling up to 8Gs' (eight times the force of gravity). I've often thought about what it must be like to perform these highly synchronised formation aerobatics. Recently, I was afforded a bird's eye view without being in the cockpit. Using modern camera technology, the team recorded a number of their sequences from the pilot's perspective.

The intricate manoeuvres have names such as The Corkscrew, The Heart and the Spear and, my own personal favourite, The Champagne Split. The team works through its paces with pinpoint accuracy, often flying with wingtips less than two-and-a-half metres apart. In the Gypo Pass, four planes fly in such a way that two planes fly in one direction and the other two planes fly in the opposite direction. They then turn towards those first two planes before they bear down on each other. At the very last moment, they pull away to avoid what looks like an inevitable mid-air collision. The net result is an astounding display of planning and execution.

Recently, an amateur photographer posted an image of the exact moment when two of the aircraft passed one another. The timing of the fly-past, combined with the precision of the photographer, was so accurate that rather than celebrating the pilots' proficiency, the photo looked as if the planes had narrowly avoided a mid-air disaster. Ironically, the manoeuvre was so convincing that on publication of the picture, a spokesperson for the Red Arrows issued an official statement reassuring the public that everything had gone entirely according to plan.

During my work with global organisations over the years, several recurring questions have emerged, including: What are the elements of a high-performing team?

My spontaneous answer is that for a team to be high-performing, all of the individuals in the team must correctly aligned and strategically using all of their resources. Let me explain further.

Alignment: Integrating individual choices around a collective purpose.

In a high-performing team, individuals, with unique strengths and personal ambitions, choose whether or not they are going to co-operate. This choice is more than merely a tacit acceptance of a 'big idea'. There is an initial buy-in that evolves into an unwavering commitment.

A team choice precedes a willingness to work towards a specific aim in which individual capabilities and expertise are harnessed in a logical, coherent unit. The team aligns around the commitment to the success of the activities of the whole.

On an alignment continuum, the reverse also holds. Author and consultant, Miles Kierson, demonstrates how a lack of alignment gradually becomes only 'buy-in', which then slips to a 'compliance mentality' and eventually degrades to 'surrender'. Where things become complicated at this end of the continuum (symptomatic of misalignment), is where team members start demonstrating signs of 'resistance', 'apathy' and, in the very worst cases, even 'sabotage'.[102]

To illustrate the concept of alignment, it's helpful to look at another team discipline: Formula One motorsport.

At the 2019 Brazilian Grand Prix, Max Verstappen's pit crew achieved something quite remarkable. On lap 21 of a 71-lap race, he entered the pits and the team jacked up the car, removed and replaced all four wheels and then lowered the car again – all in an astonishing 1.82 seconds! While Formula One fans may be somewhat blasé about what happens in the pit lane, let's pause for a moment and consider these magical less-than-two-second interludes.

Much of the detail is lost when you see the team operate in real time. However, watching the slow-motion footage reveals the sheer elegance of the timing; the almost surgical precision and attention to detail; and the brilliant interplay between the 16 crew members and the driver.

The car slows down in the pit lane and comes to a stop. In the nano-seconds before the car hits its mark, tyre swappers use pneumatic wheel guns (spinning at 10 000 rpm) to unscrew the wheel nuts. The front and rear jackmen raise the car while two team members act as stabilisers, ensuring that the vehicle remains in place. Four tyre carriers (one per wheel) take responsibility for removing a wheel, while another four members stand by with the replacement.

What is often not apparent from the top-view cameras in the pit lane is the perfect harmony of the tyre carriers and swappers. Side-on, close-up cameras highlight the precise height of the wheel gun preceding and then trailing the actions of the carriers. The team works with exact angles to synchronise the wheel removal and replacement. The speed and timing of the entire operation is expertly co-ordinated. This sequence is another powerful illustration of how planning, the assignment of roles and responsibilities and communication all come into play in this high-pressure environment.

When things go wrong, they go horribly wrong. Numerous clips record collisions in the pit lane: Fuel hoses still connected as a car drives off, bursting into flames; and even an instance of a car leaving the pits with only three wheels. Pit crew have been driven over and even inadvertently set alight. When even one part of the team is misaligned (even performing the correct action, but at the wrong time), the results can be fatal. When a team is aligned, it's magical; but when a team is misaligned, it can be fatal.

Salvaging the Ship

In Chapter One, I referenced the events that lead to the Costa Concordia tragedy. Twenty months after the ship collided with the rocks, Master Mariner, Captain Nick Sloane, led the salvage operation of the wreck, co-ordinating a total of 500 engineers into a high-performing team that practically illustrates may of the principals we have discussed.

Seven key elements emerge around the issue of alignment. Every organisation needs to negotiate and clarify these elements, to ensure that everyone on the team has a common understanding of these fundamentals. They then need to work hard to articulate them in some form of a team charter. Although teams might not use exactly this language to refer to what they are doing, a recurring pattern reveals something of the 'black box' of team dynamics.

Seven Building Blocks

These seven 'A's' are the basic building blocks around which every high-performing team need to establish themselves.

- The **AIM** of the team (The purpose of our team is …)
- The **ATTRIBUTES** of the team (The values of our team are …)
- The **AGENTS** in the team (The roles in our team are …)
- The **ACCOUNTABILITY** in the team (The decision-makers in our team are …)
- The **ASSETS** (the resources in our team are …)
- The **ACTIONS** (The plans for this team are …)
- The **ACHIEVEMENTS** (The results we are working towards in this team are …)

Aims of the Team

Many times, on my *High Performing Teams* programme, I ask intact team members (members of an ongoing organizational unit that is usually stable and functions together on an ongoing basis) to articulate the aim of their team. Three things usually occur:

Some people initially respond that they have not taken the time to define their team purpose. Alternately, they write down something so complicated that they begin to confuse themselves. Most impressive, though, is when members of the same team give me as many different answers as there are members. They have purpose, but it is not singular, and it is undoubtedly not unifying. I have even read examples in which team members produce an 'aim statement' that is not only not aligned; but contradictory. Thrashing out a singular unifying aim (SUA) is a critical element of any good team charter.

I asked Captain Nick Sloane how he went about designing a plan and creating alignment for everyone on the team to successfully execute this 800 million-dollar salvage operation.

Nick recalled how, in the early stages of the project, getting people to believe in the project was not easy. One of the significant components of the approach to raising the vessel was a technique called 'parbuckling' – rotating the ship into an upright position. Nick explained the complexities and risks involved in parbuckling – if the vessel was not in one piece.

"Firstly, we looked at the project globally. What was our aim? What did we have to achieve? We divided up all of the different components that required our focus on a one-by-one basis.

"The ship was one massive crime scene, three rugby fields long, with accommodation for 4 500 people. Bedding; detergents; food; curtains; mattresses; pillows and carpets were all floating in suspension, along with all the passenger and crew luggage. All of that material would have just drifted into the aquatic environment if we did not remove (the ship) in one piece.

"In trying to cut it up, you would actually open up the ship, and things would just drift out from inside those long passageways. A vital part of the plan was attaching huge steel blister tanks, creating 66 000 cubic metres of external buoyancy wrapped the around the ship."

The idea of creating buoyancy on the bow came from a situation where, to use a metaphor; a patient needed stabilising – requiring a neck brace before being transferred to the helicopter. The question was how to stabilise a vessel of that size. Nick remembers:

> *"We were waiting in a coffee shop and looking at the 'stretcher' and 'the patient', and it came to me what we needed for the ship: We needed a neck brace around the bow. It was the same shape. Literally, within a couple of hours, we came up with some brilliant solutions, written on the back of a serviette, then transferred on to a piece of paper. Then we called in the engineering companies and said: 'Right, what do you think of this?'*
>
> *"And they said: 'Yes, that's perfect!' and then engineered it a bit more. We said: 'If you stabilise the patient, the whole spine is improved.' We could rotate the patient if we supported the neck."*

Nick and the team ran a simulation with a German company called Overdick GMBH. They told him that the brace would require 5 000–6 000 cubic metres of buoyancy. They reduced the weight of the bow by that weight, reran their models and came back and said:

> *"Not only does this support the bow, but it also improves the mid-ship section – the spine – as well."*
>
> *"At that point, we knew we had a solution. It was a much bigger tank than we expected. It doesn't sound big, 6 500 cubic metres, but when you see the three-dimensional shape, it's massive. As you sink the air bubble, the shape changes as the water depth changes. To try to control an air bubble of three dimensions is almost impossible. We then divided those compartments into smaller compartments, and we said its either 100% full or 100% empty. You can't have an air bubble that's changing shape as you go through the water column."*

With the parbuckle, they ran the risk of the bow falling into deeper water, creating a domino effect: The shock loads of the bow breaking would transfer through the hull. There was a possibility that the stern would also fail and they would end up with three separate pieces, or maybe even more of the ship in deeper water.

> *"It was a bizarre concept. Even when I first saw it, I thought it was crazy. No one was going to pay us to remove the ship in one piece. Out of the eight international companies that tendered, we were the only company that said*

we could do it. Two others said that they could rotate the vessel upright and then cut it in situ. But the Italian authorities insisted that we move the ship in one piece.

"We had an email from the client to say that we were strictly forbidden to proceed. It is impossible to design, fabricate, deliver and install before the parbuckle date. I just said: 'If we don't try, there is no parbuckle,' so we went ahead and ordered the steel the same day.

"When we ordered the steel, a message arrived that we would only receive payment after installation. It took a while for the shareholders (and my boss) to realise that we were undertaking this component at our own risk. It made them all a lot more nervous, but we knew that without the neck brace, the bow would most probably fall off during the parbuckle. With that insight, we decided to go ahead and install it. We only worked out a week before it arrived how we were going to install it because, with every other model (simulation) that we ran, it failed and capsized underwater. It was literally at the last minute.

"We assigned a crisis team one weekend to sort out the installation sequence. Late on the Sunday, they came back to us and said: 'That's it, we have found the solution!' And we decided that's the way we would do it."

The team used the blister tanks almost like water wings on a baby in a swimming pool to keep it afloat and deliver it to Genoa. Imagine a vast reservoir 22m x 20m, and then the entire beam of the ship connected as a three-dimensional shape to take the flare of the bow.

The blister tank system needed to be installed at a 65-degree angle underwater, with a clearance of 400mm off the reef. Two hinges on the blister tank joined port and starboard on a long hinge beneath the ship. The top hinge allowed for complete free rotation of the two sides, and then the second hinge would only allow 10 degrees of rotation. That was to try to lock it in a certain angle so that they could try to install it. However, they found that the 10-degree rotation was too much. By reducing the rotation of the lower hinge to five degrees, they could then control the degree of rotation of the vessel.

"But the blister tanks had already been fabricated, and the hinges had already been installed. The team cut out little half-moons and put those into the lower hinge, just to restrict the movement.

"Even the day it arrived, the owners and underwriters said: 'This is impossible. It will be embarrassing.' We said: 'Just relax, let's watch.' We knew we had no choice."

Attributes and Non-negotiables

Very few teams with whom I interact have considered the importance of their distinctive attributes. In this instance, I'm referring specifically to what makes the team distinct. How does the team function? What are the team's fundamental non-negotiables? It's all too easy to simply go to the company mission statement, vision and values and to copy and paste those into a team charter. However, what is needed is an in-depth, inclusive discussion on those components of the team that enable it to work in the way that it does.

Some might refer to this as an 'operating agreement', or 'ground rules'. Whatever you call it, these are the fundamental beliefs and behaviours that begin to give richness to your team culture.

Take the time to clarify how your team interacts with one another and with external stakeholders. How often will you meet? What are the consequences of non-performance? What are the principles on which you are not willing to compromise along the path to task execution?

I asked Nick about the rules and principles that guided his operations. He explained how there were intense periods of work along with long periods of waiting – specifically when the weather was involved.

"Team members wanted to go ashore and have some r 'n r. As soon as we had bad weather, then we could do that. But the challenge was that team management get distracted by managing people who are focused on going out and having a good time. When they are despondent or depressed, or possibly concerned that the project itself is not going in the right direction, that can have an impact. They can bring each other down.

"At the time, we had to maintain daily meetings and keep on striving and emphasising that we were there as guests on the island. Firstly, there were a couple of cardinal rules. If you broke those rules, you would be on the next ferry. As a result, we sent about five divers home after that first winter storm. Sacrificing those five people sent a powerful message and helped us to manage the rest of the team."

> **Ubuntu:** An African philosophy that emphasises 'being self through others'. At its core is the idea: "I am because you are," or "A person is a person through other persons."

I asked Nick about the idea of non-negotiables, team attributes and principles. Nick explained how he introduced the concept of ubuntu into his team.

"I had two posters on ubuntu: What it meant from Nelson Mandela's perspective, and (one) from Archbishop Desmond Tutu's perspective. Our teams comprised many different nationalities. The way you talk to a German can be far more direct than when you speak to someone from an Asian culture. Some cultures don't want to 'lose face', even if they are wrong. It's essential that they understand the significance of what they are doing, but I always wanted to let them walk away without the feeling that they had been beaten over the head. With a Dutch or South African guy, you can just tell them: 'You are wrong, get a life and pull your act together!'

"You also can't just shout at everyone. I noticed how some of the Dutch and Italians tended to raise their voices when they argued. Some of the other team members would say: 'Don't raise your voice to me!' We had to manage that type of thing."

Agents, Assets and Accountability

Whichever context you consider, one of the commonalities of a well-aligned, high-performing team is role assignment and responsibility clarification. Over and above the specific roles that a team may require, some companies we work with use the **RASIC** model:

- **R:** Who is responsible?
- **A:** Who is accountable?
- **S:** Who will provide support?
- **I:** Who needs to be informed?
- **C:** Who needs to be consulted?

Whatever approach you use, one thing is clear: Without clarity on roles, teams run the risk of either duplication of effort, or they experience significant gaps in the execution process.

Nick told me: *"You have to identify the people and put them in the right positions. It's no use placing someone who prefers to be detail-oriented on the operational conceptual side. When you identify your project leaders, they have to be the right people for those positions, rather than just who is available.*

"Even if you have to delay appointing someone, it's far better to find that right person for that specific function, so that they are capable and can take ownership. They might all be competent, but you are looking for people who are capable of a particular part of the project. I think if you can get capable project leaders or team leaders to take ownership, then a lot of the challenge of running a big team is taken away.

"You have to divide people into smaller teams, but you need the team leaders to be the right people. We then looked at the people available to us and asked: 'What are their individual work preferences in terms of their specific skill sets?' There are many different types of divers: Boilermaker divers; fireman divers; even qualified civil engineers, all who want to become commercial divers. Once we had a sense of the available resources, we then asked who could head up those individual teams.

"So, that is how we got the seven individual teams right: From logistics; to ship fabrication; to commercial; financial and then the four operational teams. We set up the management structure, and then from there, each one could control, take ownership and responsibility and authority to drive those teams."

A high-performing team is the sum total of the individual skills, experience, insights, talents and strengths that make up that team. Increasingly, I recommend team leaders do a formal skills audit to identify these unique strengths. All too often, people are assigned roles that do not necessarily allow them to play to their strengths. One of the important decisions Nick had to make was assigning people to work according to their strengths. A massive part of the operation was building the platform that would support the ship's hull.

Nick explains: *"One of the biggest components of the salvage operation was the grout project, which involved 24 000 tons of grout cement. We knew that was the number-one dive project, so we needed someone who had many years in the dive industry, who had been on many salvage jobs, but who was also a saturation-qualified diver with the highest training from the oil and gas side. He could then be in charge of all of the other dive teams.*

"We had 13 individual dive teams running 24 hours a day, with 130 divers in the water every day. We needed someone competent and capable, who could take ownership of the project and the teams. Historically, teams would work eight weeks on, four weeks off. We were asking the dive crews to work a bit longer: Four months on, one month off, so we could maintain the focus and the same project plan without being distracted by a change of leadership. They had to be competent; they had to be capable; and then they had to take ownership.

"During the first couple of months, everyone was quite keen to take ownership, but when we had the first winter, things got quite bad (the ship collapsed two metres in one night during just one storm). The doomsayers on the outside were starting to influence the people's perspective of the project and saying: 'Maybe it is a project too far,' or 'The concept is perhaps a bit too extreme to be successful.'

"So, by the time we had gone through the winter, we had lost a couple of people who said: 'You know what'? This isn't for me.' So, we had to find a new team at the end of the first six months. We realised that was the start of the rollercoaster ride. We knew that it was going to get rough, but that it was going to succeed. We knew what the challenges were, and we had solutions we thought would work – we hoped they would work. Then the rest of the team committed to stay until the end.

"We realised that we needed to take those timelines into the global project schedule and then ask: 'What resources do we need in order to achieve this?' 'Which of these resources are on the critical path?' Once we had the critical path, all of the other 'mini-projects' that were part of the larger project had to stay off that critical path. We could then confirm that we had the right resources to maintain that schedule.

"Each night we would say: 'Do you need any extra resources? You're starting to drift on to the critical path, so keep off the critical path. This project's costing us thousands of dollars an hour; 24 hours a day; 365 days a year.

"Whatever you do, you want to be off the critical path, because then the whole project is going to be focused on you, and it's going to be far more uncomfortable. We said that before you get on the critical path, let's identify where you are going to have a problem; try to see what resources you need; and then let's mobilise those resources, because we can't afford to stop.

"We didn't want excuses; we wanted solutions. That was the motto."

Action Plans and Achievements

"Every evening we would have a 'wash-up' meeting. All of the different team leaders would be there. I would give them a few minutes to report back on what they had performed during the day. Were they going to achieve their objectives? We had a daily plan, a weekly plan and then we had a monthly plan. We had the global plan, but the weather, logistics, difficulties encountered during the operation dictated the daily plans.

"We would have back-up dive strengths, back up ROVs (remotely operated vehicles) and a couple of spare divers as well. You can get a lot of ear, nose and throat infections on a dive team, and the moment that happens, you have to isolate the people with the flu and get them out of the main accommodation block where the divers are so that you did not infect the rest. You have to look at how you manage your team; at their progress on a daily and weekly basis; and then how that impacts the global schedule."

Using the RAPID (Recommend; Agree; Perform; Input; Decide) decision-based approach is one way to increase accountability and execution. This key idea will be explored in Part 4 of the book.

During our interview, I asked Nick how he found a balance between leading from the front and ensuring that his followers bought into his vision and leadership:

"We had a specific challenge with the large diameter drilling for the platforms that would support the vessel. We needed to drill into granite rock, at an angle of 25–30 degrees. It was a big challenge with two-metre diameter holes, and the vertical tolerance for those holes was less than half a degree from the vertical. Their footprint had to be perfect to match the platforms. That was one of our biggest challenges.

"The press quoted me at a particular meeting in the January, in Italy, where we had six different engineering companies working for us. We

brought all of the engineering companies together, and said: 'We are battling, things are not going the way we wanted. Let's come up with some solutions.'

"On about day three or four, we held another crisis meeting with about 30 or 40 engineers (including some academics). We had two or three possible solutions: One we could try to implement in about five or six days, and the other one was going to take two months of research and development, and another month of delivery and mobilisation.

"We said we could not afford three months. We could look at it as a back-up solution, but we were not going to go in that direction.

"One of the Italian professors said: 'We think you are wrong. We would like to take a vote in the room.'

"That was when I said: 'This is not a democracy. There is only one vote, and that is mine.'

"Of course, they said I was acting like Mussolini and not a democratic leader. I said: 'We have two solutions, with a possible third one – one we can implement within a week. The other one is months away, and that is not an option. We cannot sit around doing research and development, and it's very unlikely that we can make that work anyway. The fact that is your preferred option – your solution – doesn't mean that we have to accept it.'

"But every day, we would have these evening meetings so that everyone could update us on their progress and specific challenges. If they had a solution, or if they needed more resources, I would listen to them and focus on how that impacted the global schedule. Some team members were not interested in the other finer details of the other operations because they were under pressure themselves. As a result, they didn't necessarily follow the whole global schedule. And at that stage, you have to say: 'We can't drift from the plan; we can't allow what you are doing to negatively impact the other options or projects, or the global project as a whole.' At that point, you have to say: 'That's my decision. Let's go with it.' It seemed to work.

I asked Nick if he had taken away any specific leadership lessons from the Concordia salvage job.

"Never give up! I think as Gary Player said: 'The more you practice, the more you plan, the luckier you get.' That is exceptionally true. I worked with pipelines projects in South Africa, and also the Caspian Pipeline Project in Russia. When it seems that doom and gloom are around you, that is the

time to go back to the basics and ask: 'What did we think of when we first started it? Did we know that we would have these challenges? Yes, we did.'

"So, when you face these challenges, don't let the obstacles beat you because you knew they were going to be there. Sometimes, the solution does not jump out at you straight away. Don't give up. What you think is impossible can be done, and you won't know until you push yourself. You have got to push yourself, too.

"I learned an incredible amount on this project about different facets. I didn't know much about extensive diameter drilling, deep-water grout installation and some of the engineering that we did. There was a long journey to learn what I needed to learn. You will never know everything before you start, so you may as well start anyway."

Asked about some of the other complexities of the operation, Nick responded:

"It took us 10 months from the time we finished the parbuckle to the time we delivered the ship in Genoa. We had one winter in between, and we lost three to four months of actual onsite productivity, when we did all the engineering on the mainland.

"The first winter was horrible! It was the worst winter in 45 years. It started with the 'Halloween Storm' (which carried on) into the first week of November. They told us that we would not get lousy weather until January or February. The ship collapsed a further two metres on itself and on everything that we had put in place."

"A lot of equipment was damaged and destroyed. That was a shock, because we thought that if that was the start of winter, if we have two or three more storms like this, then that's it. The job's over. Then a lot of people said: 'It's crazy. We are spending all this effort, time, and money to work on being able to install everything, and the ship is going to break up before the end of the winter.'

"And we said: 'That's right; it might. All we can do is just carry on.' You can't beat the weather. The weather will always win. It is your worst enemy on a salvage job. You can manage your time, but you can't beat the weather. You have to ask: 'What other things can we do?' When you have 100 divers sitting and waiting for a week, their frustration levels are increased.

"And then we had to say: 'Listen, don't worry! The ship went through that storm, and it is still reasonably strong. It did collapse two metres, but

that was on the lower side – most probably the ship's balconies that were resting on the reef. But the project hasn't changed. The plan stays the same, so let's get on with it!'

"I think by the time we got to spring, there was a bit more belief. When we installed the platforms and managed to get the drilling tolerances so that we could get them to slide into the predrilled holes, that was also quite a technical feat. As we achieved those milestones, that seemed to lift the morale."

Alignment remains a critical component of 'the exponential effect' and of high-performing teams. In the new world of work, and as remote teams become the norm, it is really worth taking the time to consider developing a team charter and formulating these alignment pillars. The exponential effect of this synergistic process is something I will revisit in Chapter 9. First though, let's consider the impact of conflict and conflict resolution.

7 / EXERCISE

ALIGNMENT QUESTIONS

For you to consider:

- The **Aim** of the team:
  Can you answer the purpose question? (The purpose of our team is …)
- The **Attributes** of the team :
  Have you identified and agreed on the core values of your team?
- The **Agents** in the team:
  Have you clarified the roles and responsibilities in the team?
- The **Accountability** in the team:
  Who are the decision-makers in the team? Who will be answerable and accountable for the final outcomes?
- The **Assets**:
  Have you done a thorough audit of all of the resources in your team?
- The **Actions**
  Are your specific plans clearly stated and laid out, with specific milestones?
- The **Achievements**
  Is there agreement and shared understanding of the common and agreed results to which everyone on the team is working?

8 / CONFLICT

RESOLVE AND RESOLUTION

"Almost all conflict is a result of violated expectations."

Blaine Lee
Vice President of Franklin Covey

When Things Fall Apart

> A leadership team that will not confront issues will always have turbulence in the team.

In a team context, conflict is expressed at many different intersection points. The underlying causes of these tension are varied and driven by multiple factors. These include, but are not limited to, personal egos and differences in perspectives. The history of the relationship between the parties, misunderstandings and even unfulfilled expectations, can also play a role in fueling underlying tension.

What one party says might be correct, but their tone, timing or approach could be enough to start a running battle. A lack of follow-though or broken promises could also contribute to heated arguments and confrontations. The more diverse a team, the greater the chances of conflict.

Handled badly, conflict can be a death knell to trust, team dynamics and solid solutions. Constructive team conflict stimulates lively debate and fosters innovation and high-quality solutions. In the context of a high-performing team, a commitment to addressing conflict positively is a critical element of success.

Nick Sloane offered me some insights into the way he managed conflict in his team. He also explained how, in his early years as a salvage master, it was often easier to work with a more homogenous group of people because it was easier to get things done.

"When I worked with Penta Marine it was quite easy: We had 100% South African teams. In the late 90s, we were bought by Smit International (Smit Salvage), the market leader. We then became a Dutch-South African company. But we would find that the South African team got the African locations; the Middle East, Papua New Guinea and China; and the Dutch guys would get the Mediterranean, Caribbean, Brazil and Australia. They would handpick their locations. It got to the point where I was running a large salvage operation in Pakistan, with four Singapore teams, two Dutch teams and three South African teams.

In the Concordia salvage, Nick realised that this approach would not be sustainable. For the project to be completed, he needed a different solution.

"With the Costa Concordia, we had 15 nationalities in the dive team (26 nationalities in total). Initially, there was ongoing conflict, specifically between how the Italians and Dutch teams approached their day-to-day operations. After about six months, we said: 'Listen, at this stage, with the in-fighting, we won't do something a specific just because it's the 'Italian way.'

"To alleviate this, we divided them into multinational teams. We didn't have a 'Dutch team' or an 'Italian team'. We mixed them up. We made a conscious decision to integrate the International Oil and Gas Standards, (IMCA) as the standards for the project.(We said:) 'It doesn't matter what your background is; you will be part of a team. If you don't want to be part of a team, then we are quite happy for you to take the next ferry and leave the project.'

"At first, there was some resistance. We had two senior guys who resisted, and we said: 'We are serious. If you can't accept it, and if you are not happy, take the ferry and go'.

"They said: 'You can't fire us!'

"I said: 'I'm not firing you; I'm saying that you are not part of this project. You can go back to your company, but you are not going to be part of the Concordia project.'

"Then people realised that we were serious about integrating the teams."

During one of my recent leadership development programmes, leaders shared instances in which they had become really angry about something, or even 'completely lost it'.

One sales manager described working with his team towards a shared quarterly financial target. Everyone had given their commitment to reach the goal. It was a complex structure that involved each person selling a certain number of units, but also maintaining a minimum profit margin. The sales team was individually incentivised, and the sales manager was incentivised on the team's performance. If the team hit the target, not only would he enjoy a personal discretionary bonus, but he had a mandate to pay out a performance-based team reward over and above individual commissions.

Where it became complex was that each salesperson had a fair degree of latitude in how they could offer their clients discounts. The challenge was that in order to achieve the quarterly team target, both unit sales and profit needed to be in line.

One team member boasted that her next sale would get them over the line. Naturally, the rest of the team was ecstatic. What she had omitted to tell her manager was that, in order to secure the business, she had committed to such a big discount that almost all of the shared gross profit would be eroded. Targets were set up as an all or nothing, which meant that if either one was not reached, no quarterly incentives were paid.

Realising the implications of the deal, the sales manager described how he began to boil inside. Almost instantaneously, he had jumped out of his chair and hurled a huge arch-lever file against the partition between his office and the rest of the room. As the reinforced glass reverberated, people on the other side looked on in disbelief. The manager realised that, if nothing else, he had made his point. One member's actions meant everybody would suffer. The team was about to turn on one of their own.

I remember facilitating a session for a large multinational that had undertaken a dramatic restructure. Three different teams were to be merged into a central operating unit. This was a major upheaval for two-thirds of the organisation. Staff members who had been assured of a role in the new structure, but who were not currently based at the centre, would have to move across the country. Those who had not been reassigned at all had seen their positions closed. The memory of how things had been in the good old days loomed large in the room and the atmosphere was thick with tension.

I had been asked to provide input into the drafting of a new team charter, and to help the new team navigate the way forward. In trying to understand the dynamics of the new operations team, I shared how constructive conflict was a key component to team success. I wanted the people around the table to face the underlying issues, to 'surface' them, and then to come up with a plan as to how to address the root causes of these tensions.

After about 15 minutes, a senior member, a specialist in his field who relied on others to provide critical technical support, made the point: "The relationships in this team are so bad that I would happily sit on the sidelines and watch this team go down in flames!"

Over many years of facilitating conflict-handling sessions, I find it fascinating how we approach disagreement, depending on the context, the nature of the conflict, what's at stake, and the parties involved.

As complex human beings, consciously or unconsciously, we are able to adapt to different approaches for different parts of our lives. I have seen leaders who are highly competitive and only focus on their own needs in a work-based situation, then shift to total avoidance when handling conflict in their personal lives.

I like to get leaders to think about difficult conversations and the most common underlying drivers that lead to challenging interactions. Some examples might include:

- Convincing other team members of the validity of a specific proposal.
- Disagreements over targets.
- Having to acknowledge poor performance.
- Questions around approval and decision-making rights.
- Last-minute changes to scope, timelines and budgets.
- A perceived lack of communication or ambiguity as to what is required.
- The timing, location or in/frequency of communication.
- Competing priorities.
- Differences in opinion.
- Bullying and harassment.

- Competing goals or priorities.
- Lack of planning.
- Lack of responsibility.

The list is endless.

Embracing the Dragon

It is impossible to be part of a high-performing team without some degree of conflict. In many instances, conflict has had a bad rap. When I ask leadership teams to throw out words they associate with 'conflict', unsurprisingly, their associations are negative. If we are really honest, for most of us, conflict is not something to which we look forward and definitely do not enjoy.

However, there does seem to be a high correlation between teams that manage friction well and the opportunities that come from 'thinking in the alternative'. In these teams, conflict is embraced as a necessary component of interpersonal dynamics. Polarities and differences of opinion, rather than being shut down and switched off, are celebrated. These teams look for reasons why things cannot be done. There is a commitment to stimulating constructive conflict.

Jerry Hirshberg, an American former auto designer at Nissan, called this "*creative abrasion*", or "*embracing the dragon*".[103] This productive conflict was best realised when team members with differing, and even contradictory, perspectives enjoyed equal airtime.

A key part of Hirshberg's process involves people in a team with opposing views sharing their perspectives. Having heard each other, both parties are then required to 'embrace the dragon', to switch roles, and then repeat back and defend the opposing position or idea. Not only does this approach give the opponent a better understanding of a position, but it also allows for what I call 'reasoning with empathy'.

This approach to conflict may appear to be contradictory to what was outlined in the previous chapter on alignment, but I don't believe this has to be the case.

Alignment doesn't have to mean agreeing on everything. Alignment certainly does not have to mean an absence of conflict. In fact, quite the opposite.

There is a growing understanding that when people have been allowed to share opposing ideas, and those ideas have been understood, even if not necessarily embraced, on consensus, the team is far more committed to the way ahead.

A portfolio manager of an investment firm told me: "*Once we had done our research and taken a decision on where we saw the market going, we would always be willing to pay good money to an analyst who was prepared to provide us with the counterview. We want to be shown that we are wrong.*"

Differences in experience or perspective can provide creative tension that, when harnessed correctly, makes for far more elegant solutions. For that to become a possibility, it's worth reflecting on how you see conflict.

> What is your personal view of conflict?
>
> - Neutral?
> - Negative?
> - Positive/ Constructive?

Language is important. How can leaders move conflict management from 'resolution' to 'transformation'?

Prof John Lederach of the University of Notre Dame in the US, proposes that conflict transformation is a "*way of looking, as well as a way of seeing*".[104] Understanding the immediate situation, as well the underlying patterns and contexts that shape a specific conflict, provides the first steps in the transformation process.

> Are you a peacekeeper or a peacemaker?

Peacekeepers will do whatever it takes to keep things from boiling over – even if that means avoiding underlying issues. In the short term, this may be a worthwhile approach, but typically, relatively minor issues left unresolved can escalate into far more serious, often intractable, situations.

Peacemakers, on the other hand, are committed to having difficult conversations in order to 'surface' and address underlying issues that threaten the success of the team.

Here, the nuances of culture and worldview should not be overlooked. I am very conscious of my largely Western, English mindset. I can't apologise for my upbringing, but I also must acknowledge that my approach to resolution is largely shaped by my worldview. Dr Cathy Bollaert has done some very insightful work into the role that worldview plays in shaping interpersonal conflict.[105]

While I might prize the explicit calling-out of concerns, frustrations and non-delivery, a chat to one of my Japanese associates about his typical responses to conflict revealed a different perspective. During a phone call, without the benefit of eye contact, I asked Akihiko how he typically dealt with disagreements. The line went silent as he paused for a moment. He then responded: *"You'll know when I disagree or when I am angry because I will give you my quiet face!"*

Cultural sensitivities aside, the overwhelming consensus in high-performance team thinking is that the proactive surfacing of conflict issues is far more beneficial to the team in the long run.

Online Disinhibitions

One of the many challenges presented by social media is the fact that people tend to lose their inhibitions. Suddenly, they feel emboldened to make responses or comments in an online chat forum or email response that they would never dream of making in a face-to-face setting.[106]

The tendency towards online disinhibition may have a mitigating effect on empathy. At the same time, the largely asynchronous nature of remote work means that responses can be more considered and measured than in the immediacy of a collocated environment. This doesn't necessarily mean that conflict is more likely to arise in a remote setting, but the way that disagreement is expressed may look different.

As much as some team members may appear more direct – even brash – in a remote setting, one of the more common indicators of a pending situation is 'radio silence'. Team members who are not collocated may be tempted to simply withdraw, rather than address and air differences.

One of the biggest challenges facing remote teams is the early identification of signs of potential conflict. Raising those issues and finding meaningful ways to address differences, all while separated by time zones, geography and culture, is challenging. Remote conflict mediation is par for the course in the post-Covid world.

Integrative vs. Distributive Approaches

Conflict is rooted in a high or low desire to address specific concerns. An **integrative approach** to conflict focuses on finding solutions that are mutually acceptable.

A **distributive approach** assumes that for one party to be more satisfied in a conflict, the other party will have to be less satisfied. This balancing act of 'concern for self' versus 'concerns for others' is what leads to outcomes that may or may not be sustainable.

In a team setting, it makes no sense to continually opt for a distributive agreement, as this will weaken team dynamics. The net effect could be that people start to feel their contributions or ideas are not valued or appreciated and that they would be better off not being part of the team.

Understanding the Triggers

Psychologists have proposed three different sources of conflict:[107]

- **Economic conflict:** Competing for scarce resources.
- **Value conflict:** An apparent incompatibility of principles and practices.
- **Power conflict:** These occur where there is a battle to maximise influence at the expense of the other party.

Underlying forms of team conflict are typically explored in terms of four broad categories: Task; relationship; process and status conflict.[108]

Task Conflict

- Letting the side down through lack of follow-though or completion.
- Disagreement on the work to be done, or the task content.
- Differences in ideas or opinions.

Task conflict is not necessarily negative. If task conflict can be used as an opportunity to relook at how a problem is addressed, it can be positive.

The challenge arises when disagreements around task, process or status detrimentally impact on relationships.

Relationship Conflict

- Clique mentality.
- Friction among team members.
- Personality differences.
- Tension among team members.
- Emotional conflict among team members.

A recurring theme in literature surrounding the high-performing team is the importance of not allowing task conflict to spiral into relationship conflict.

Process Conflict

This third category needs some consideration. A team may disagree about how they will work together; the logistics of task completion; and even on protocols concerning roles and responsibilities.

Before the pandemic, only 5% of the European work force, and 7% of the US population worked remotely. Now that an ever-increasing number of people are having to navigate the complexities of this new work world, it is inevitable that there will be tensions about not just what needs to be accomplished, but how it will be achieved. In a team context, conflict around 'how' something should be done may also produce high levels of fresh thinking and creativity.

Status Conflict

In a team context, a conflict around status is as much about power as it is about perceived hierarchy. As organisations become flatter and teams more matrixed, the 'networked' effect of teams mean that perceived hierarchy and 'dominance competition' will need to be mitigated. This type of conflict is often about individuals feeling that they are not being respected. In an attempt to redress any perceived imbalances in the power dynamics at play, these individuals may then be tempted to look for insidious ways to score points.

When exploring the nature of conflict and the triggers that may lead to conflict, it's also worth considering possible strategies to de-escalate a negative conflict situation into a more constructive approach.

Strategies for De-escalation

1. **Create a climate of open expression.**
   Decide early on to have a conversation with all of your members on your team philosophy around conflict. Let team members know that while you encourage lively debate and welcome differences of opinion, these need to be based on fact and not presumption. If two team members have a disagreement, they try to get other team members involved and lobby for support. Don't be afraid to step in and encourage the original two parties to address the issue one-on-one before the disagreement escalates to a toxic level in the team.

2. **Check your temperature: Leave fevers at the door.**
   As the economy opened up after the lockdown, health and safety representatives, armed with temperature monitoring devices, appeared at the entrances to many buildings. The procedure is simple: Allow the sensor to be pointed at your forehead. If your reading is within acceptable limits, you will be asked to sign the register and then be allowed to proceed into building. If your temperature is too high, not only will you be barred from entering, but you will need to seek medical attention. If you refuse to have your temperature, access will be denied, too.

   This metaphor of 'leaving fevers at the door' is really helpful as a first principle of conflict management. If we are unable to keep our emotions in check and 'run hot', there is every chance that we will say things that we will later regret. When we allow passion to supersede persuasiveness, we run the risk of inserting 'more heat than light' into our responses. This is not to suggest that we should bring emotion into conflict, but rather, that conflict is best managed from the basis of issues and interests than how we feel in the moment.

3. Status is all-important and unimportant.

Cultural dynamics; age; gender; hierarchy; and length of service can all play a critical role in the conflict resolution process. In an African context, where a lot of my work has focused, we have often failed to recognise the role that seniority and patriarchy play in conflict situations. Although we may not personally agree that these factors should play any role in team dynamics, disregarding cultural mores could mean that any attempt to resolve conflict is disregarded as illegitimate.

Addressing cultural patterns while working hard to negate adversarial power dynamics in a team is a delicate balancing act. It will be really interesting to see how more traditional views towards hierarchy and position will stack up in this super-networked, hyper-connected world. I do think it is too simplistic to argue that status is simply an insidious issue in a high-performing team. For this reason, I propose that status is both all-important (it must be acknowledged in specific cultural contexts) and unimportant (only focusing on power and hegemony in a team context often serves to hinder performance). Of course, team members should always be treated with courtesy and respect, but rather than getting hung up on status, it might be more helpful to think about the importance of acknowledging team members' autonomy.

4. Take time to really hear the other, and use looping techniques.

In our need to put our point across and then stick to our position, there is always the very real danger that we will fail to hear what the other party is saying. Experienced mediators use a technique called looping.

> **Looping:** Repeating or paraphrasing the statements that aggrieved parties make in order to show that you really understand and are able to approach the conflict from the basis of empathy.[109]

It's important to remember that looping does not equal agreement. The fact that I am able to demonstrate an understanding, or even an acknowledgement, of a colleague or team member's perspective does not necessarily mean agreement with their position. In fact, one of the most powerful tools in any conflict resolution strategy is being able to articulate someone else's point of view while still remaining convinced of your own point of view. Thinking in the alternative is both a logical and empathetic process.

Traditional debating uses a standard motion; proposer; seconder/opposer; seconder/open to the floor/vote format. The Long Now Foundation adopts a vastly different approach to its format. Once a debater states a position or proposes a motion, the opposer is not allowed to put forward a contradictory point of view without first summarising the proposer's position. Only when the proposer is satisfied that the opposer has correctly summarised his or her point of view, is the counter argument allowed to be introduced. Rather than looking for the 'straw man' – the weakest point in the opposing argument – one looks for the 'steel man' – the most robust and well-formulated elements of the contrary view, and then highlights those points.

5. Identify interests and perspectives

Conflict in teams often gets stuck at the level of issues. Disagreements flair up when people fail to clarify the interests and perspectives that drive those issues. By moving beyond the issue and then understanding the idea or the motivation behind a position, team members can find common ground for the sake of the team's goals.

6. Address the idea, decision or action – not the person.

Agree on a set of rules of engagement and work out how to express disagreement in a non-confrontational way. Of course, bullying and harassment should be called out, but even then, the action should be addressed, rather than attacking the individual concerned.

I have worked with a number of high-performing teams who have introduced a 'card system'. A friend of mine, who worked in a high-pressure financial services department on multimillion-dollar currency trade deals, came to an agreement with the colleague who sat opposite them about how to implement this conflict management process. He would often become frustrated at someone not following through on information he needed, right there and then. In that kind of environment, time (literally, minutes and seconds) has a massive impact on deals.

Both of them carried a set of cards in their desk drawers. They agreed on the behaviours that they felt were most constructive for them to work together. They also agreed that any behaviours that did not support those outcomes would, depending on the severity, be either yellow-carded, or even red carded. They also had someone to act as an early-warning system when the heat was on. That person's job was to provide immediate feedback on whether the way they were acting was conducive and in line with the kind of behaviours and outcomes that had been agreed upon. It was immediate, in real-time, based on strong levels of trust and confidentiality, and it certainly didn't take 12 months before any feedback was given on their behaviour.

> *"In those moments of madness, and at the risk of losing my cool, my colleague at the desk opposite would take a yellow card out of his drawer and hold it up. That wasn't so bad and was usually just a warning that I was on dangerous ground. Red cards were for particularly severe offences and involved fines that were paid into a central kitty for our end-of-year party. I was usually on the receiving end, but it was great fun to dish them out, too. The cards certainly helped to change the culture from indiscriminate attacking or blaming to one of dealing with issues."*

7. Choosing to respond, rather than react.
A response is well thought-out, measured, deliberate and considered. A response is based on facts; it is well-informed, seeks to understand the opposing view and welcomes new information. A reaction is quick and spontaneous, often rooted in emotion and can add fuel to fire. A reaction tends to be closed to new information and escalates quickly from focusing on the idea, decision or action, to the individual or people concerned.

Creative Abrasion Climate

In summarising the strategies for effective conflict transformation and creative abrasion, consider the COPPE-R Approach:

- Co-operative
- OPen
- Positive
- Emotional
- Responsibility.

This is an extremely useful diagnostic tool to help assess the degree to which conflict is framed as positive, or as negative and destructive. Many of these dynamics are incorporated into the principles of psychological safety covered in Chapter 9. Leaders of high-performance teams take full responsibility for ensuring that the climate is conducive to constructive conflict.

Co-operative vs. Competitive

Any idea or suggestion is always meant to contribute towards a better outcome and improved solution. Rather than going for zero-sum (win-lose/lose-win) approaches, team members are committed to co-operative conflict resolution approaches. In a competitive climate to conflict, the most dominant voice prevails. In a co-operative conflict approach, individual team members are willing to work through differences for the sake of the team. They reason from the whole to the part, rather than from only their individual needs and concerns.

Open vs. Closed

In a high-performing team, the focus on incremental gains requires a climate in which people are free to speak their minds and offer their opinions. The converse is a closed, opaque environment in which team members feel unable to freely express their opinions. In this kind of closed environment, conflict is discouraged, and alternate views are rarely considered.

Positive Emotional vs. Non-Emotional

The creative abrasion process means that at the moment of suggestion or proposal, negative emotions are set aside and that there are no 'stupid' ideas. As much as some might argue that we need to be non-emotional, practically, this is almost impossible. Rather than arguing for a non-emotional approach, the integration of positive emotions and expression of appreciation and affiliation, while respecting autonomy, play a critical part in the conflict resolution process.[110]

Responsibility/Task Decision vs. Personality Attack

The debate should never be about an individual. The discussion must always be about the idea, task or decision, and on who will do what and by when. The moment a conflict moves from the assignment of responsibility and actioning of the next task to attacking individuals, leaders need to intervene and steer the team back on track.

"I strive to work on harmonious teams in highly collaborative environments. I do not enjoy conflict, but will address it head-on in the attempt to drive a better outcome for all involved. I enjoy working in open and honest environments rather than environments that are highly political or where there are ulterior motives."

Erik Brinkman
Product Director at Gitlab

It is impossible to cover all of the various underlying triggers, types and variations of conflict. However, what I have tried to highlight is that conflict-handling needs to be an intentional part of any leadership role. Our approach to conflict has an exponential effect on both the individual and on team performance.

8 / EXERCISE

CONFLICT QUESTIONS

For you to consider:

- Are you able to identify the typical signs of conflict in your team?
- What is your personal view of conflict? Positive? Neutral? Negative?
- Do you tend to be a peacemaker or a peacekeeper?
- Can you identify opportunities to explore constructive conflict and creative abrasion?
- How do think you can move from conflict resolution to conflict transformation?
- From where do most of your conflicts arise? Task? Relationship? Status? Process?
- What steps can you take to encourage 'embracing the dragon' in your team?
- Are you able to separate issues from interests?
- To what extent are you able to apply the COPPE-R approach to conflict-handling?

9 / COLLABORATION

THE SCIENCE AND ART OF SYNERGY

Collaboration: An interactive process involving two or more participants working together to achieve outcomes they could not accomplish independently.[111]

Expressing the 'One'

I've performed with Steve Barnett on a number of occasions. His 'orchestra' does not rehearse together before a performance. Many of them have never met ahead of time. Most have never even played an instrument nor had any musical training. Steve is best known on the international professional speaking circuit as the Non-Speaker and the Silent Conductor. Using a range of tuned percussion instruments, he takes groups of people and, without saying a word, enables them to make music in incredible harmony. Just as comfortable performing in the Royal Albert Hall as he is in front of a crowd of thousands of sports fans, Steve has a magical ability to encourage strangers to collaborate.

When Steve conducts, audience members receive colour-coded percussion tubes that Steve has hand-cut to different lengths and tuned to a note on the pentatonic scale. Struck in unison with a small percussion stick, the sound produces a 'pulse'. Combined, they produce an indescribable, rhythmical melody. Standing at the front, Steve holds up one of five coloured tubes and only audience members with that specific colour 'note', work with him. That group continues playing, rhythmically following Steve's baton. He then moves to a different instrument and 'musicians' carrying that colour tube step into the performance.

This layering process repeats until an ensemble of five different sets of tubes play in harmony. Through mime and physical comedy, Steve creates a combination of corporate drumming, choreography and orchestration in an incredibly visceral demonstration of the power of people moving from synergy into collaboration.

But how does he do it? For fear of invading his space as a performer, I was somewhat reluctant to ask Steve to 'break the fourth wall' and talk to me about what led him to create these memorable moments. Part of me felt that the performance is best experienced rather than described. On the other hand, I wanted to try to understand the intersection points between both the science and art of what I and thousands of others around the world had experienced. I was sensitive about not 'asking the magician to explain his tricks'.

Surprisingly, Steve was as generous about his craft in conversation as he is on stage. His hesitation was not in sharing his insights, but rather in how to actually put them into words:

"It's not often, as a non-speaking performer, that I have to articulate what is happening on stage. I was doing what came naturally. When I left university, I joined the South African Volunteer Service and ended up teaching English and Maths in a village school in Lesotho. English was not their first language, but they loved Shakespeare. My students would sit in this mud hut, six to a bench, some in school uniform and most in traditional blankets.

"Even though I had a very basic understanding of Sesotho and they could hardly speak English, we met at the intersection of dialogue, rhythm and poetry. We learned to understand each other. I would often arrive on my horse and interact with the children through movement and sound, through call and answer."

Steve shared how, having worked with a number of ethnomusicologists, he learned that much African music is based around the idea of a polyrhythm, emphasising secondary beats rather than the primary beats that are the focus of traditional Western rhythms.

"From what I learned about cross rhythms, I started doing corporate drumming. We would play, and I would debrief and explain what people had just experienced.

"I kept getting feedback that my sessions were more powerful with no explanation, that the magic happened in demonstrating without speaking. You can play a 3/4 over a 4/4 at the same time. The pulse comes around every 12 beats. But the accent is not on the first beat, on the 'one'. Music goes in circles. It's knowing where the 'one' is that is critical to expressing the rhythm and projecting the pulse.

"I start with simple beats and then move to the more complex. I have a picture in my mind where I try to 'create a space' between the audience and myself – an imaginary space where the energy meets at the place of total and complete engagement.

"Groups work together as a body. They get support from each other. People are concentrating on what they are doing, but they don't always get the big picture. When you start to listen to what others are doing; when you hear 'the whole', you stop thinking about what you are doing. You give yourself to the moment."

At the end of Steve's sessions, people will often comment about how the experience has given them a practical, tangible demonstration of what is possible at an individual, team, and even an organisational level.

Collaborative Synergy

Now widely regarded as a buzzword, 'synergy' has been overused and, consequently, diluted in terms of its original meaning. However, that shouldn't mean we simply discount the idea. If collaboration is an 'interactive process', then the outcome, (one that individuals could not accomplish independently), is synergy.

High-performing teams co-operate and work jointly towards a common goal. They move to a 'higher order alignment'. They demonstrate a commitment to helping one another and to producing results in which the net effect is greater than the sum total of the parts.

> **Synergie (syn- co or together)** n.1650s; "co-operation", from modern Latin
> *synergia*; from Greek *synergia* "joint work assistance; help", from *synergos*
> "working together"; related to *synergein* "work together, help another in
> work"; from syn- "together" (see syn-) + *ergon* "work" (see urge (v.). Meaning
> "combined activities of a group", from 1847.[112]

It's a real pity that just because a word is incorrectly used, or overused,
in boardrooms around the world, it should be discredited. Effective team
leaders work towards creating an environment in which these powerful
team principles find expression. The question every high-performing team
has to ask is:

> How do we move from individual contribution to effective
> collaboration?

You can't 'create' synergy; it emerges at the intersection where vision,
capacity and chemistry collide. However, some very real challenges to
creating a culture of collaboration do exist. This approach often takes far
more time; multiplying the 'transaction costs' that come with more role
players, more decision makers, and the need for increased communication,
protracted meetings and even redesign.

The question of speed is an important one. Whatever you might be
working on as an urgent priority might not even be in my immediate field
of vision. The fact that you might need my input at a specific moment in
time is no guarantee that I will be able to offer support there and then.
Multiply that challenge by the number of stakeholders, and the challenge
can seem overwhelming.

Although collaboration should not have to mean a strict adherence
to rigid, inflexible processes, 'learning to dance' together requires careful
choreography and timing. High-performing teams seem to collaborate
more effectively when they really need to. The level of dependency and
interdependency in any given team will be a necessary precursor to
collaboration. When these are well defined, collaboration produces not just
faster results, but higher quality solutions.

> "**Collaborative synergy**: *An interactive process that engages two or more participants who work together to achieve outcomes they could not accomplish independently, in an open, integrated process (operational, procedural and cultural) that fosters knowledge collaboration, influenced by a transformational leadership that encourages participants to expand connections beyond typical boundaries and achieve required project outcomes."*[113]
>
> **Janet Salmons and Lynn Wilson**

The exponential effect of co-operation at this level of intensity is remarkable. But while you can't always orchestrate collaboration in the same way that Steve does with his 'orchestra', there are definitely some keys that will unlock any team's efforts to achieve this level of co-operation.

Collaboration requires a common understanding of the purpose of the team, relative to the problem to be addressed; an appreciation of individual creativity, psychological safety; alignment; shared processes; and agreement on the right tools. When all of these elements combine, an exponential cross-functional effect occurs. Leaders need to consider the roles they play in facilitating the collaboration effort, taking all of these dynamics into account.

Wicked Problems

Not everything requires a team approach. However, the increasingly complex and wicked problems that leaders are facing mean that an ability to network and collaborate to find elegant solutions will be paramount.[114] Wicked problems have specific characteristics:[115]

- They are highly unpredictable.
- They have an undefined time scale.
- They cannot be fixed with previously tried solutions.
- They cannot be solved by part-time committees.
- They involve multiple stakeholders and are socially complex.
- The issues are interconnected, and any single solutions may cause new problems.
- Solutions tend to be better or worse, rather than right or wrong.
- Their complexity means they can't be solved by individuals working alone.

Covid-19 fits perfectly into the description of a wicked problem. Added to this, the sheer scale of the problem means that nations, never mind companies or individual teams, have been forced to collaborate. At the time of writing, at least five or six different vaccine solutions are being explored internationally. Of course, teams do not only need to look at solving wicked problems as a reason to collaborate. Not everything is a wicked problem and we should not consider them as the only reason to co-create.

The clearer the alignment, the greater the opportunity and likelihood of collaboration. The more committed team members are to a single purpose, the higher the chance of a creative process that generates and expresses well through ideas.

Individual Creativity: Achieving Flow

Collaborative effort starts with individual creativity. Given the space to experiment on their own, and when people are then asked to share their best work, the results are often even more astounding.

"This whole idea of collaboration has become such a sacred word and concept, that we think creativity all has to emerge from this very collaborative place. But the same is also true of solitude. You can't really know what you and you alone think, unless you are willing to be by yourself for a while."[116]

Julia Elman
Senior User Experience Designer

Effective remote teams have a culture of 'respecting the creative process'. Research seems to indicate that one of the massive advantages of the virtual environment is that creators can work independently and then view the results of their efforts woven together.

During the lockdown period, I was impressed by a number of musicians around the world who recorded individual contributions that were then edited into overall productions. Although the artists could not be in the same studio at the same time, the results were extraordinary.

South African, Tim Greene, even managed to write and produce an entire movie, *Cabin Fever*, during lockdown. He cast actors and then directed them remotely. Group rehearsals took place on Zoom, and actors filmed their scenes on their own phones. Greene then edited the individual pieces of footage into the final production.

This dance between artistic solitude and combined expression, all supported by enabling technology, is fascinating. The freedom to shut off, pause, wonder, reflect and then work in an independent sanctuary is life-giving for creators. But in a remote team, the real wonder of that work – the magic – is when results, or 'creations' are brought back into the centre and shared. In an effective, high-performance team, that moment of sheer vulnerability is always trumped by the assurance that, in looking at your work, other team members only ever want to take an individual contribution and refine, enhance, shape and improve it.

There appear to be a number of preconditions to achieving 'flow':[117]

Clear goals

Knowing what the end goal is, and what is required as an individual contributor, can shape the creative process. Ironically, from a creative point of view, working with absolutely no constraints at all can sometimes be quite restrictive. From my own experience as an author and instructional designer, I find that the tighter the brief, the more creative I can be. It's almost as if I work best creatively on really well-defined rails. If the rails are not there, I need to first put those limits in place. The more aligned we are, the more collaborative we can be. While some may disagree, I see collaboration as both a process and an outcome.

A balance between opportunity and capacity

I might be given the opportunity, but do I have the skills to carry out that action? This links very closely to knowing your strengths. I am far more likely to give myself to a process when I know the opportunity presented is one that will enable me to perform to my full potential. The more freedom of choice individual contributors are given for their specific contribution, the higher the quality of that contribution.

Deep concentration and engagement

Personally, I lead and work best in that space of intense, focused and uninterrupted engagement. There is a discipline that comes with switching off to external distractions and giving yourself completely to the creative process. My own experience is that the more you intentionally step into that place of engagement, the easier it becomes to discover those internal wells of deep creativity. Flow almost seems self-fulfilling. Greater frequency and regularity produces greater success. The more productive and successful you are, the more often you want to find that nexus point.

In the new world of work, leaders will need to think carefully about how to support individual contributors to design optimal creative spaces. In the knowledge economy, the debate has moved from: "Should we be doing remote work?" to "Where is the place where I can be my most creative, productive and effective while still remaining connected to the whole?"

Unconstrained creativity

When I am in a state of flow, not only do ideas develop more freely, but time itself seems to speed up. This temporal illusion is usually an immensely powerful indicator of my depth of concentration and engagement. Finding that balance between creativity and implementation is a constant juggling act. There is plenty of evidence that intentional, dedicated time for unconstrained creativity early on in a project or strategy paves the way for higher quality outputs. This temporal interplay underpins the innovation process.[118]

Psychological safety

Do your team members feel that they can take risks with those they work alongside? When challenged to change as a result of ongoing organisational shifts, do you and your team members feel the need to focus primarily on self-protection? How readily do team members embrace collective problem-solving and goal attainment?[119] Are team members encouraged to speak up and offer individual perspectives?

Many of the principles explored in '*Conflict-handling*' and '*Alignment*' in this book create the foundation for innovation, critique and a sense of safety to bring individual work into the whole, and to submit it to the collective wisdom, expertise and experience of the larger team.

"Psychological safety is not immunity from consequences, nor is it a state of high self-regard. People know they might fail; they might receive performance feedback that says they're not meeting expectations... But in a psychologically safe workplace, people are not hindered by interpersonal fear."[120]

Amy C. Edmondson
Novartis Professor of Leadership
Harvard Business School

Learning to Dance

Collaboration is difficult to describe, and it's just as difficult to break down into its individual parts.

- How can we instil this philosophy of collaboration into our teams?
- What specific steps can we take to role model the drivers of psychological safety?
- How does understanding both the 'music' and the 'rhythm' of collaboration help us 'learn to dance'?
- How can leaders create an environment in which these powerful principles of co-operation are applied?
- What can leaders do to unlock this exponential effect?

Create a high culture of respect

Respect is not tied to hierarchy: It is linked to the intrinsic worth of the individual contributor rather than to the contribution itself. Collaboration works best when everyone knows and experiences that their time, energy and effort is highly prized. Each team member is seen as valuable and deemed to be important. It is not enough to say this to each other; this principle needs to be role-modelled and recognised when it is demonstrated. There is nothing more powerful that being invited to be part of something bigger than yourself, knowing that your team members are doing all they can to make you shine. When you shine, the team can shine, and the end result shines!

Be comfortable admitting your own limitations

Successful specialists are often poor judges of their own limitations, and even poorer delegators. This can result in at least two unintended consequences: Firstly, there is the risk that people who can contribute to end results are not consulted and, consequently, the solution is not optimal. Secondly, there is the risk that in not collaborating, in an attempt to 'fly solo', timing or execution is affected.

In the collaboration process, delegation should not mean assigning a task and then disengaging. Perhaps it means being vulnerable enough to invite people in early on in the process because you see that they can add value. Be as intentional in expressing your limitations as you are about showcasing your strengths. Even though collaboration is the twin of co-creation, that doesn't mean it is instinctual. We are often more comfortable working autonomously. Asking for help doesn't come naturally.

Leveraging the benefit of peer contribution and review only happens when you are specific about why, where, and how you need input. If necessary, be candid about where you have gone wrong. Do that early and often. Leaders can be wrong – we are fallible. In the knowledge economy, however, those failings are often going to be more glaring and obvious. When you do reach out to collaborate, it's important to bring in people in a way that gives people clear guidelines as to both the level and extent of involvement and responsibility that you require. Communal learning is a critical component of the collaboration process.

Timing matters

The more complex the problem, the earlier you should consider collaboration. This ability to do the right thing at the right time and to demonstrate dependability, is a vital component of the collaborative process. I have seen too many instances in teams where, by not reaching out early enough, opportunities for collaboration were lost.

As much as we may rely on machine learning to improve dependability, this intersection of people, tools and context is critical to the collaboration process. Just as Steve Barnett needs to bring in different musicians at specific intervals to play the beat, off-beat, rhythm and cross rhythm, so it is in a high performing team. Bringing in people can set the tone for the rest of the process. It can determine not just what they are able to do, but also how well they do it.

Cross-functional solutions need cross-functional input

As organisations become more matrixed, the need and opportunity to collaborate increases. Silos are broken down by incorporating groups of people with varied levels of expertise and experience. Boundary spanning and working across departmental or business unit divisions sounds logical, but it is often not easy to get right. Remote teams may find that they are placed at the intersection of process and function, or between design and strategy. Clarifying both individual and team priorities will help to ensure that cross-functional interaction is optimised.

An atmosphere of trust

Trust was covered at length in Chapter 4, but now let's look at the need to trust your own creativity and to trust others – as well as the importance of trusting the process and then the outcome. Collaboration does not necessarily mean consensus.

"This creative collaboration produces innovation, but to many, this kind of engagement is hard and can be emotionally draining. The sparks that fly can sting or, at minimum, create tension and stress." [121]

Linda Hill, Greg Brandeau, Emily Truelove and Kent Lineback
Authors of *The Collective Genius*

Steve Barnett shared with me that even though he has silently conducted thousands of sessions, he is never entirely sure what will happen when he steps on stage. He knows that even though he puts all of the ingredients together, the outcome is never guaranteed. But the chances of achieving the outcome are increased when he is clear about what he is seeking.

Shared Processes

1. **Agree on an optimal outcome.**
   In a post-Covid world, leaders have had to become more comfortable in a 'results-only' environment. Sometimes a desire for clarity will need to be moderated by flexibility. Mapping out the preferred solution, what 'could be', needs to be separated from the discussions on how to get there.

2. **Create the collaboration space and communication platform.**
   The need for a central workspace and agreed communication platform is critical to collaboration. This is true in both collocated and remote teams, and needs to be considered early on. The notion of the 'obeya', or large collaboration room, comes from lean manufacturing. The idea is simply an open space in which shared charts, graphs and drawings are displayed, providing a visual dashboard of a project's progress. Some project teams equate this with a 'war room'. More recently, we have seen leaders setting up virtual obeyas to achieve the same results without team members being collocated with virtual, remote teams.

3. **Map and connect the network.**
   Identify all of the potential contributors early on – both from a creative and implementation perspective. It is so easy to get so obsessed with organisational structure that nothing actually gets done. One of my colleagues always asks: *"Why go to someone with a title if you can go to someone with an answer?"*

   Add in people as required.

   - Do you need more horizontal integration from project or process contributors?
   - Do you need more vertical integration from your supply chain or product engineers? Where do customers fit into this process?
   - Is this an opportunity for open collaboration?

In the IT world, there is a growing commitment to 'designing for ultimate user experience (UX)' and to acknowledging the benefits of collaborating with customers early on in the design process.

A leader's role as both 'mapper' and 'connector' in the collaboration process helps to identify potential contributors. They must then intentionally bring those stakeholders (both internal and external) into the creative space. High-performing teams make effective use of both communities of practice and communities of interest.

4. Help develop inner creativity and collaboration protocols.
The conversation around collaboration needs to start earlier than the moment of shared co-operation. Leaders can play a significant role in coaching team members to reframe deeply-held beliefs and emotional dispositions about both their individual worth and the value of their ideas. By understanding what leads to inner collaboration and creativity, leaders can help to unlock even higher quality contributions.

Steps to accessing internal potential through self-discovery and self-knowledge may be worth considering. Team leaders can play a role in tapping into individual team members' 'present capability ceiling'. This simply means finding ways to see how the world shows up for that team member; their perspective on the optimal outcome; as well as what they view to be their contribution in achieving that outcome. Each individual needs to find flexible and novel ways to come to the creative process.

It is beyond the scope of this book to explore all of the dynamics of 'the leader as coach', but the following would certainly be important components of that relationship:

- **Personalising:** Encouraging team members to approach a problem or challenge by tapping into their unique life experiences.
- **Co-inquiry:** A process of working with individuals through a set of questions to set up a number of possible options to approach a problem.
- **Discovery learning:** Giving individuals the space to work on their own, or with others, at a pace that works for them.
- **Feedback:** Specific, timely feedback loops on initial contributions.

5. Agree on shared collaboration protocols.
At some point in the collaboration process, the focus needs to intentionally change from the individual to the team. Self-directed work

teams need to agree on the frequency of meetings, feedback loops and monitoring. These shared collaboration protocols can be both informal and formal.

During my interactions with remote teams, I have even seen those that, on certain days, choose to leave their web cams on while working together, but keep their microphones on mute. That helps them to create a sense of proximity, even though they are geographically separated. They then just ping each other in the moment, rather than having to set up formal meetings each time they want to brainstorm something. Finding that balance between regularity, predictability, and flexibility is something that each team will need to work out, based on the nature of the task and the needs and maturity of the team. This practice is not the same as managers insisting on people being on camera throughout the working day as a form of 'remote control' or surveillance.

Collaboration Tools

In remote teams, the notion of 'bandwidth' in collaboration is really important. As a metaphor, bandwidth refers to how much attention is required at that moment in time. High bandwidth engagements require more planning and, therefore, more bandwidth. Low bandwidth engagements are more straightforward and are not as context-rich. In discussions with tech companies, like GitLab, it is clear that coders and programmers have a clear understanding of this in a way from which the rest of us can learn. In chapter 6, I referred to the idea of synchronous and asynchronous communication. If we extend this to the principle of collaboration then the relationship between communication, collaboration, and bandwidth becomes apparent. For teams that have transitioned to remote work, there are more tools than ever available to support three speeds of collaboration: Real-time, async and storage.[122]

Real-time Synchronous Tools

Here I am interacting with a team member in real time, and at the same time. I can see them, and they can see me. This requires more 'bandwidth', more 'data', and more of my focus and attention.

Characteristics of these tools include:

- **High bandwidth:** Immediate, but fleeting interaction (you need to be notified of the meeting and you need to be present). Once the meeting is over, the moment is gone.
- **Important when a balance of context and content is required.** Some issues require more intense engagement and discussion and cannot be resolved through email or instant messaging.
- **Excellent for really getting to know people,** for visual thinking and for complex discussions. In the early stages of collaboration, leaders should not underestimate the power of building in elements of social cohesion. In situations that require abstract thinking and discussion, creating opportunities to connect at the same time is paramount.
- **Synchronous.** For one-on-one and coffee chats. We are in the same space, physically or virtually and engaging with each other at that moment.
- **Face to face:** Meet locally or when travelling.
- **Video and voice.** Many companies are mandating that calls are now video- and voice-enabled to ensure non-verbal communication supports the collaboration process.

Asynchronous Tools

Here I am not interacting with a team member in real time. We do not have to be in the same space at the same time. Characteristics of these tools include:

- **Low bandwidth.** Slower, delayed and linear (you do need to be notified, but you don't need to be present or to respond immediately).
- **Persistent.** There is a record of what was discussed. I can go back and check an instant message, or the recording of a meeting I could not attend.
- **Useful for the generation of ideas,** day-to-day work and most decisions and conversations.
- **Discussions with straightforward outcomes.** When the issue at hand is straightforward, it is not necessary to get everyone on the same call at the same time.
- **Flexi-synchronous.** Record meetings using collaborative whiteboards.

- Examples of this sort of collaboration would also include asynchronous email, wireframes (a schematic or blueprint) or mock-ups (models or prototypes where different team member provide input).

Storage: Documenting the Process

One of the cardinal principles of collaboration is documentation. Sometimes referred to as storage, documentation enables high-performing teams to record content in a format that can be saved and retrieved by anyone in the team. We typically think of this as a written form, but should now include technological documents, such as video or audio recordings of meetings. These open up a whole new realm of possibilities for filing. Storage is typically both asynchronous and timeless, and works well when it is well organised and easily accessed

When I interviewed, Jean du Plessis, Engineering Manager at GitLab, he explained how their handbook is their 'Single Source of Truth'.

> *"We are very serious about documentation. Anything that a team member needs to know about how to do something at Gitlab that should be in there. We constantly work on the ability to contribute content and on improving the usability and discoverability of content as well as the experience of searching and consume that information."*

Collaboration then, is both art and science, principle and practice. It requires the right tools and application of tried and tested principles but also a willingness on the part of all concerned to give themselves to the process.

Stepping In

I asked Steve Barnett about some of the key lessons, from the perspective of collaboration, that are incorporated into his silent performance.

> *"What I do certainly falls into the realm of theatre. It's a process of developing audience reaction into participation and then interaction. Some people may initially feel vulnerable, but it's a very safe space. I understand the reluctance of the 'non-joiners' who initially hold back. It's wonderful to see the surprised*

look on their faces when they overcome that initial resistance and step into the performance.

"Actions speak louder than words. It's important to make work serious fun. We like to play. I try to work with the power of the one-to-one. Making eye contact with individual people is really important. I make sure I'm having a good time because that encourages the audience to step in.

"It's important to encourage the good stuff and to demonstrate a sense of belief. I want the whole audience to feel the 'pulse of the one' and to be able to express that together."

There is a new pulse, a rhythm, that is inviting deep commitment to taking on some of the biggest challenges through co-operation. What we need are leaders who will be brave enough to take up the baton, to create safe spaces and to allow for teams to discover the wonder of the collaborative process. **Collaboration** is a dance between **creativity, capability and convergence.** The extent to which we get that right largely determines the solutions that we find and the results we achieve.

9 / COLLABORATION

EXERCISE QUESTIONS

For you to consider:

1. What holds you back from collaboration in your team?
2. What are some of the challenges or problems your team is facing that could be best solved through collaboration?
3. What can you do to foster individual creativity in your team?
4. How would you rate the current level of psychological safety in your team?
5. What immediate steps can you take to improve the level of psychological safety in your team?
6. Do you have agreement in your team on shared processes? Is everyone clear on what those shared processes are?
7. Do you have agreement in your team on shared tools? Is everyone clear on what those are and how they will be used?

The purpose of Part 3 was to start some conversations around what it takes to create and develop and lead a high-performing team. By building the story from self-leadership, to leading others, to leading teams, we are now in a better position to explore what it takes to lead for results and to deliver solutions.

LEADING FOR RESULTS
(DELIVERING SOLUTIONS)

10 / EXECUTION

DELIVERING ON THE PLAN

Execution: Ensuring that a strategy is carried out; steps to implement an agreed course of action.

Incremental Gains and Losses

Wilhelm Steinitz was a world-champion chess player. Widely credited for a systematic approach to the game, he moved from a style of play characterised by strong, frontal development leads and fierce attacks, to focusing on the accumulation of small, positional advantages. Where novice players are often happy to sacrifice lower-value pieces in an attempt to monopolise the queen, Steinitz proposed that small changes in the positioning and structure of pawns could lead to significant gains over the period of a match. His 'accumulation theory' premised the idea that over time, a chess player could build up small temporary advantages and convert them into permanent positions.

Pilot Alex MacPhail uses this same principle at an individual level when he flies:

"Find those small incremental gains for tomorrow so you're going in prepared. You give it your best but then you look at yourself within the context of the team and you find just that small improvement, so that tomorrow is a better day than today. You are looking for something small and you're not worried

about what other people are doing. Your focus at that moment is not your competition on the field or in the boardroom. You are just worried about your performance today and what you are going to do make tomorrow just a little bit better."

In a leadership book like this, application of every chapter is a step closer to achieving something concrete. This final part of the book is about leading for results and delivering solutions, and effective execution and delivering on the plan. This requires a combination of self-leadership; leading others; team leadership and leading for results. At a high level, this entire book is about execution, so why are we addressing this topic specifically? There are a number of reasons:

- Leadership is about leading followers to achieve an outcome.
- It is necessary to see the links between leadership principles and leadership practice.
- A strategic mindset needs expression in strategic execution and follow-through.

For many years, the institute I founded has been involved in facilitating strategic planning workshops. We've run these session for multinationals, non-profits and even for local municipalities. Over time, it has become increasingly apparent that implementing a strategy is far more difficult than writing one. It is now well documented that a large percentage of strategic plans fail.

Having worked with many international MBA holders and hundreds of participants in executive education programmes, I have seen that when it comes to getting things done, many clients struggle to make the links between the leadership theory and practice.

In recent years we have shifted the focus from strategic planning to strategic execution. Although my background is in leadership and marketing, it is my conversations with experts in the field of project management that have helped to shape and refine much of my thinking around execution. What follows may seem quite elementary if your expertise is in the project management realm, but the ideas are no less important when it comes to leadership. There are extraordinarily strong correlations between strategy execution and the principles of effective project implementation.

Even the notion of project management has changed. We can no longer simply talk about a straightforward, linear process in which we plan everything ahead of time and then implement a project. In this increasingly dynamic world, there is a need for more adaptive and iterative methods to getting things done.

With the application of Agile principles, a multidisciplinary, cross-over effect between leadership, teams and project management is emerging. We are seeing a shift in Agile methodology, from a narrow focus in software development (where the principles were first conceived) to broader, more generalised applications – not just in the field of project management but also in organisational leadership and development. We've reached an intersection between Agile project management expertise and adaptive leadership principles. The conversation around execution is evolving to focus on how to develop adaptive, Agile leaders who effectively deliver value to stakeholders.

Insights from the World of Project Management

While I fully appreciate the differences between implementation and execution, from a strategic point of view, I believe that we need to consider both elements. We need those elements that are put in place to start a course of action (**implementation**), as well those required to see it through to completion (**execution**). In this chapter I want to answer these questions:

* How do leaders effectively get things done?
* How do leaders execute and make things happen?

I interviewed a number of project managers on what they identified to be principles of effective implementation. First, I asked Llewellyn Thorne, a seasoned project manager in the IT sector, based in Raleigh in the US, for his insights on the parallels and differences between the concepts of implementation and execution. With more than 30 years' experience, including 14 years as Global Program Manager at Cisco, I was keen to hear his thoughts:

"The differentiator in my mind (comes with) the 'stove-piped' project manager who is less mature in their thinking. The less expansive the experience of the project manager, the more inclined they will be to think about pure project

implementation, rather than the execution of the strategy. The more mature, experienced and expansive the mindset of the individual, (it doesn't really matter how long they have been in the game), the more they will see that project management isn't just about 'building houses'. It is not just about implementing a plan and putting something in place. There is a reason the plan is there, and that plan can iterate.

"Execution is about delivering on your strategy, and it is a top-down thing. Implementation is just delivering on the tactical plan. The difference is primarily in the minds of the people who have a less expansive view and a less expansive experience."

Small changes (positive or negative) in one part of the system can have significant, even dramatic, effects in others. Nowhere is this principle better illustrated than in an understanding of the role of leadership in execution. This notion of leading from the basis of incremental or marginal gains; of looking for minor adjustments that have major impact; is widely applied across a range of leadership contexts.

Russel Delmar also has more than 30 years' international experience in the project, construction and engineering management of tunnels; light-rail transit; railway; energy pipeline and heavy civil projects. He has led and managed large, multidisciplinary teams in the procurement and implementation of complex projects. I asked Russel for his insights on the concept of incremental gains and losses.

"A leader's ability to influence the cost, or cost outcome, of a project at the beginning, by making relatively small changes, has huge implications on the out-turn cost. Enabling a team to function well, to operate efficiently, is where you can definitely spend your best money.

"In instances where distractions and politicking take precedence in a team, a project can take far longer, if it even happens at all. In situations where costs are escalating, there is the very real danger that everybody retreats into their contractual positions. In the early stages of a contract, the consequence of that kind of dysfunctional environment are clear in the graphs. If you have a dysfunctional team right up front, rather than optimising the project, you may find the exponential costs (due to ignored scope, lack of attention, or missing or perpetuating gaps), take on higher orders of magnitude. But your ability to make these changes reduces over time and starts costing more and more. The extent to which a team is

dysfunctional, misaligned and pulling in different directions will inevitably result in huge, increased costs down the road.

"In project management, both leadership and management are important. Management is concerned more with processes, and leadership focuses more on direction, culture, and trust. You need both in implementation."

Russel then reflected on two of his top projects and what, in his mind, made them successful. The first was the $1.8 billion Niagara tunnel, which was an impressive upgrade to the Sir Adam Beck Hydroelectric Generation Complex:

"It was a 10km tunnel from above Niagara Falls to the hydroelectric power-generating station below the Falls. We worked really well with Ontario Power Generation because the scope of the project was so clearly detailed. The remarkable thing about it was that the tunnel was close on 14m in diameter. At its deepest, we went down to 140m below the city. We used the biggest rock-tunnel boring machine ever built.

"It was just one of those projects where everything clicked. Everybody knew what they needed to do. Nobody was trying to out-compete anyone else. Everybody just stuck to what they did, and they trusted and respected the input of everybody else. It was just one of those unique teams! There was incredible synergy. I think this was probably a function of the right people in the right positions: Not only technically qualified, but also the right personalities and the right technical fit. We worked well together because everybody set out to create a high-performing team with high trust and high respect. I spent four years in that team. The tunnel increased generating capacity by 150MW."

Llewellyn Thorne reflected on projects of which he was a part, and the leadership lessons that could be drawn from an execution perspective:

The biggest one, the most impactful one, was the introduction of Wi-Fi into the enterprise environment of Cisco Systems. It was so effective because we had the authority and liberty to execute according to our current understanding, without having to go up and down the command chain to get funding. Because there was an abundance mindset and sufficient budget, we performed better. We had the right level of authority (when) controlling the implementation, and we had the right level of liberty when executing it, in order to be able to buy equipment, roll out infrastructure and appoint resources to manage – all inside of a global team.

"The implementation of what became Wi-fi – wireless overlay in the corporate enterprise – had such a powerful net result: The empowerment of mobility in the workspace. You could now wander around with your computer, and that was a game-changer. People could walk to each other's desks with their computers and start doing the work that we do today.

"Prior to that, there was a VOIP (voice over internet protocol) transition. That was a massive disruption to the marketplace as it knocked out other regular telco companies and completely sidelined them while the VOIP infrastructure came into place. We went hard at it in Cisco, and that was a very powerful change in two places. One that was particularly significant to me was the Internet Protocol (IP) Contact Centre. I was responsible for that development.

"Three integrated projects, all running on converged architecture for voice, video and integrated data systems: Converged network systems, all streaming on a single IP network. These three projects, combined, had a massive impact on the company and a huge impact globally. The company remains a very strong market competitor, even today.

"From a leadership perspective, the key factor was the correct balance of authority and autonomy within the teams, and the ability of the team to respond without inhibition, prohibition or control that slowed them down from actually doing things. They could make decisions and execute them because funding was never withheld."

The second project Russel shared, he described as *"the highlight of his career"*:

"The $ 1.4 billion light rail transit (LRT) project in the City of Calgary comprised 8.5km, with six stations connecting to an existing operational environment, all within a very busy urban context.

"We were constructing in a busy downtown environment with all of the associated traffic and stakeholder and public issues. The significance of that project was that the client was both very proactive and progressive. They structured themselves and their service providers with exactly the right levels of authorisation and organisation. The champion of the project was a city director who had direct access to the city general manager. As a result, the project enjoyed both support and facilitation authority at the highest level.

"The way was cleared by the city to make things happen, rather than what often happens on those big projects, where everybody has competing interests and tries to raise roadblocks to things happening. We had a progressive client in a progressive organisation, with progressive authorisation

and a high appreciation of the expertise that we, as service providers, were actually bringing. That led to a motivated contractor, a motivated service team and ultimately, a project that was completed in record time. I don't know if another transit project has been completed with as big a monthly construction 'spend'.

"I think the project's success was owing to a combination of these very progressive external factors and some strong internal leadership in the project team.

Through these conversations, several patterns emerged. Independently, two experts with more than 60 years' project management expertise shared unique, yet similar, leadership lessons. Understanding of context; a clear charter; clarity on scope; the right team; the right mindset; the right levels of authority; adequate resourcing; timely feedback and strong leadership all seem to be critical to effective execution. I have attempted to distill the key lessons from these conversations into critical execution best practices.

Leadership Lessons from the Field

1. **Preparation: Understand the context and think adaptively.**
   Leadership is about context. There is a very real danger that by focusing only on the personal attributes of a leader, we fail to appreciate how execution requires a deep understanding of the situation at hand. A leader's 'adaptive capacity' determines the extent to which he/she understand and adjusts to the unique context for a contracted service or implementation. Adaptive leadership mobilises adaptive work; supporting followers through *"sustained periods of disequilibrium so that the organisation can thrive"*.[123]

   The technical outworking of adaptive methods is that we become more agile in the way that we work. Adaptive thinking means having iterative concepts built into the way we execute. Adaptive leaders need to be comfortable working with repeated cycles of improvement. They should also be comfortable taking on the responsibility of being catalysts for change.

2. Define the project charter.

Leadership execution starts with proving the reason behind a strategy; setting out the scope and the objectives; and then resourcing the project with the right people. An effective charter maps out the objectives and constraints of the project. It also carefully defines what is in or out of scope. Included in all of this groundwork is the need to identify key stakeholders and clarify the risks, benefits and costs of the project.

3. Balance authority and autonomy.

Execution begins with two important components: A clearly defined project charter and clear authorisation. You need to understand exactly what the charter is; exactly who has authorised it; and how it has been authorised. Often projects fail because of a lack of understanding that the correct authorisation and authority, and the correct champions have been given to the project. One sure way to fail in a project is having to deal with those who aren't authorised to make the decisions.

Llewellyn then highlighted the importance of self-determination in execution: A delicate balance between authorisation, autonomy, competence and relatedness.

"The leadership element is the self determination on the part of the leader. They are going to be more successful if they understand the principle of self-determination and apply it appropriately to adaptive methods. I need this adaptive, iterative thinking across the board and top to bottom across my stack, my org and my effort.

"I need to lead understanding. I need to be self-determined and understand and adopt adaptive methods in my own practice on a daily basis, in everything I do and in all my relationships. I can't just be handing out what I see as the strategy and the plan for execution. I need to ensure that I drive that down the stack. As a leader, I need to route development paths in my organisation for this thinking. I create the routes and I build the opportunity into my strategy and execution to nurture this thinking and behaviour."

4. Set out the scope.

All too often projects are derailed because of a misunderstanding of the scope of a project. It seems that you can't over-define the scope: The more definition the better. You've literally got to build your project on paper to the nth degree, to the appropriate level of detail, so that you're able to correctly define and encapsulate exactly what is required. Scope definition is critical. It's a huge exercise and you could spend years including all of the design, engineering, procurement and contractual elements involved in how a project is going to be implemented. Only when you have verified the scope with all of the key stakeholders and clarified the limitations can you move on.

5. Be comfortable with change.

In an increasingly ambiguous online environment, it becomes even more critical for leaders to identify emerging threats as early as possible and to adapt accordingly. We need leaders who will not only anticipate change, but who are comfortable dealing with the extent and speed of it.

> The most important component of execution in the modern adaptive environment: On an ongoing basis, we have to become more focused on an iterative development of our strategy. Iterative conversations are an essential component of the execution mix.

6. Understand the rules of engagement in a results-only work environment (ROWE).

In strategy execution, the emphasis for the project lead is shifting more from command-and-control, and even a push-down-the-stack approach to servant leadership and a facilitator role. The leader needs to clear the hurdles to allow the team to get where they need to go.

In a remote context, leaders now have to trust that team members will deliver, despite not being collocated. Rather than dictating from central headquarters, the team leader or product owner is there to ensure that the team doesn't go too far down a road and completely 'miss it', from a product perspective. How the team gets there is completely their own doing. This empowers all of the individuals and maximises team efficiency and ownership.

"We suggest common things we value to create
consistency across projects but give product teams the
power to organise and execute however they want. To do
a great design, your team doesn't have to be in the same
room."

Julia Elman
Senior User Experience Designer

An idea put forward by some IT companies over the past couple of years is the notion of being 'execution agnostic'. The focus is on interoperability in terms of technology, tools and methodology and even business processes.

The word 'agnostic' is used very specifically in the IT context and refers to a heightened sense of flexibility when it comes to methodology. This is about aligning all of the resources; tools and technologies to the specific needs of the organisation, rather than the other way around. In discussion with companies that embrace this philosophy, I have found that they are actually usually passionate about execution and about getting things done. They prioritise shipping, going to market, and impact. But what they don't seem to get lost in is becoming too attached to any one set of tools or being totally prescriptive. The focus is much more on leading the 'why' and focusing on delivering results. In a world where there is an abundance of tools to support execution, they opt for a less-is-more approach.

7. Work inside and out with stakeholders.

Stakeholder interests are playing an increasingly important role, and effective execution requires a great detail of stakeholder involvement, understanding and appreciation of stakeholder interests. It's worth knowing not just how your project is internally organised, but also being able to identify how it fits into the broader external organisation and into society at large.

All of the experts I interviewed noted that you can't underestimate the power of external stakeholders and the influence of social media. All of this means that execution requires a high degree of transparency and upfront openness. Leaders need to prioritise taking those stakeholders along with them through the process.

8. Don't forget your own people.

"As important, if not more important is the people part, the soft skills side of it. The cultural element is as important as the mechanics. You can have all of the mechanics in place, and you can totally fail because you don't have real buy-in and real engagement from your team."

Lewellyn Thorne

As students of leadership, we know the importance of people and engagement, but there is always the risk that in driving towards an outcome, we treat people as cogs in a system and not with the care and respect they deserve. A culture of execution should be underpinned by a culture of care.

Feedback Loops

9. Understand the Dynamics of Tight Feedback Loops.

One of the main differences between a traditional waterfall approach to project management and an Agile approach is the difference between a top-down, sequential, linear view and one that allows for an iterative approach to execution. Feedback loops play a critical role in enabling that process. The longer the period of time between the implementation and the feedback, the higher the risk that opportunities for improvement are lost.

Leaders who still view execution from a command-and-control perspective negate that approach and potentially miss out on critical stakeholder feedback or customer experiences. In systems thinking, we consider a feedback loop in terms of the cause and effect relationships involved.

> A feedback loop has four essential components:
>
> - An **input** (data) stage
> - A **relay** to an individual
> - A **consequence** stage
> - An **action** stage.

Lewellyn Thorne described this point excellently:

> *"This whole 'feedback and iteration' principle is not down in the trench and not up in the executive suite. It has to flow and integrate from top to bottom in order for the enterprise, organisation or the project to be maximally effective."*

Once again, the principle of incremental gains means that you can try something, then get feedback and then make the necessary adaptations. This is not just about fixing mistakes, it's also about making marginal improvements.

Wearable technology has dramatically impacted our day-to-day lives. More than ever, we are tracking blood pressure, sleep patterns, daily steps and flights of stairs climbed – all from the convenience of our smart phones and watches. The ability to get accurate, personalised, real-time feedback is often enough incentive for us to keep entering the data, making changes and then seeing the results in real time. These tight feedback loops introduce a level of personal control in which we have a real sense of being able to manage small, but significant, changes in our lives.

A number of my friends are sound engineers and musicians. Andrew Greeff has been involved in sound mixing in recording and broadcast for more than 40 years. He has travelled the world supporting international artists as a front-of-house engineer and was also the sound engineer for host broadcast services for the 2014 FIFA World Cup in Brazil.

I asked him how the shift from traditional floor or 'wedge' monitors on stage to working with in-ear monitors has changed feedback for musicians and vocalists. With an in-ear system, the sound is transmitted to a wireless receiver connected to the earphones.

"With a wedge monitor, there is always the danger of a negative feedback loop. When someone points a microphone at a speaker, the original signal goes back on itself. Sound from the speakers ends up back in the microphone and is reamplified, causing a howling noise. Having no negative feedback is a big plus with an in-ear system.

"The secret of in-ear monitors is that sound is set, so each person hears specific instruments or vocals. In a big production, we will have a front-of-house engineer who controls what the audience hears, and a monitor engineer, who is responsible for setting what the artists (musicians or vocalists) hear. Each individual can tailor the volume of their input relative to everyone else. The mix is cleaner, you hear yourself and others clearer. You are also not limited to having to stand in one spot to get feedback, as you would with a wedge. You can also get the feedback in stereo.

"Some of the basic systems allow for a three-drive setting of base, mid-range and treble, but the newer set-ups go for eight- or even 12-drive settings. The monitor engineer can select the pre-fade and hear the exact feedback the musician is getting, and then adjust that, if necessary. The drums might be lagging because the click track is too soft, and this can be corrected immediately."

Andrew's metaphor started to take on a life of its own.

If execution requires tight feedback loops, how do you put those in place? What lessons can we learn from the field of sound engineering?

- Leaders should do all they can to try to eliminate negative feedback.
- Ensure that everyone hears what they need to hear as soon as they need to hear it.
- Ensure that team members receive feedback in real time.
- Make feedback personal.
- Early user feedback is helpful.
- Ensure that individual feedback is given relative to the performance of the whole.

> - Leaders need to intentionally place themselves between the feedback and the team member to hear what others are hearing. Leaders may need to change perspective to increase understanding of how feedback is being received.
> - Appoint specific people as guardians of feedback channels.
> - The higher the quality of the feedback for the team (the musicians), the better the output for the customer (the audience).
> - Allow for iterative, adaptive changes to be made as a result of the feedback.

I asked Andrew if there were any negatives to the in-ear system. He laughed and made the point that because sound is processed in our heads, there was always the danger that what individual musicians hear is not necessarily at the level or quality of feedback the music director want them to hear. Andrew reflected on how feedback loops had to be managed.

"I've been in many sessions where the lead musician is playing the right notes but is 'off'. She is not feeling the nuance or the subtlety. One of the first things that we do is go and listen to what that musician is hearing. Often, they have set their individual instrument to a level where they can't hear anyone else. This can render the musician completely useless, as they are locked in their own world, playing on their own time, even if all the notes are right.

"You can put too much feedback in someone's ear! When that happens, the musician can end up isolated and miss the ensemble. In other instances, we've seen trained musicians singing flat because they cannot hear the harmony in their ear. It's as if they are singing on their own. The noise-cancelling effects of in-ear can also mean that the artist becomes disconnected from the audience."

> So, does this mean that there are any pitfalls in tight feedback loops?

Tight feedback loops can create a false sense of reality in complex systems.

- Tight feedback loops mean that we may start focusing on expedient, quick wins at the expense of long-term, sustainable goals.
- Tight feedback loops can be seductive as they provide speed, but not necessarily accuracy.
- Sometimes, having more noise in the system can be helpful in order to get a more comprehensive overview of what is really going on.
- When we give feedback, we need to shift the focus from individual shortcomings to identifying what followers are doing well, and then reinforce more of the same.

Iterative and Incremental

From an execution perspective, leaders need to combine the iterative and incremental. In order to make that possible, it is important to understand the difference between micromanagement and micro monitoring.

Micromanagement

The classic signs of micromanagement are when tasks are delegated with responsibility but not authority. There is a retention of power, characterised by a strong desire by the delegator to hold on to control. Micromanagement is often linked to a lack of trust, or an underlying misgiving about the real competence of those to whom tasks or responsibility have been assigned.

Micromonitoring

Micromonitoring involves providing your team members with an agreed set of milestones that will help to ensure they are on the right track and heading towards the target or end goal. If people are not hitting the agreed milestones in the agreed time periods, that is an early-warning indicator that the overall target is unlikely to be achieved. Language is important.

Because this term sounds so similar to micromanagement, people often display an initial resistance to this idea. Micromonitoring is simply about frequent, consistent interim measurement. In working with a set of predefined metrics (inputs and throughputs), there is a higher chance of achieving the outputs. Monthly financial statements; performance areas related to sales; cost management or other key performance areas; the corporate culture itself; and even management review processes, are all seen as enablers to achieve overarching success. Some industries call this practice 'flash reporting'. These dashboard reports are an excellent way to track and tack, and reinforce the feedback loop process.

We can't talk about execution without discussing measurement and review. You cannot execute unless you work from a culture of 'accountability first'.

10 / EXERCISE

EXECUTION QUESTIONS

For you to consider:

- How well do you understand the context in which you are working?
- Can you identify some practical instances in which you can look for incremental gains in your execution?
- Have you carefully crafted your project charter, and clarified the risks, benefits and costs of the project?
- Is everyone you are leading clear on the scope, identified solutions and intended results?
- What steps can you take to balance authority and autonomy?
- How comfortable are you with an iterative approach to strategy execution?
- How would working in a ROWE environment change your execution plan?
- Have you mapped out the key stakeholders?
- What you can do to create tighter, more dynamic, immediate feedback loops?
- How is the prevailing team culture hindering or helping execution?

11 / ACCOUNTABILITY

DECISION-MAKING RIGHTS AND ABILITIES

Accountability: The ability to give account; accounting for your abilities and actions.

"When things go wrong in your command, start searching for the reason in increasingly large circles around your own desk."

General Bruce Clarke
US Army General

The Final Frontier

The space shuttle Challenger exploded 73 seconds after lift-off from the Kennedy Space Centre on 28 January 1986. Seven astronauts lost their lives. Prior to this tragic event, the shuttle programme saw 24 successfully completed missions. Now, with more than 30 years' hindsight, we can look back on this tragedy not just from a technical point of view, but also from a leadership perspective.

The technical flaws on the spacecraft, particularly linked to the failed O-ring seals on the rocket motor, have been well documented in numerous publications. What is less clear is why the flight was initiated in the first place, given that a number of engineers had pointed out the potential dangers of launching the spacecraft in low temperatures.

In trying to manage the expectations of multiple role players (both inside and outside the organisation), Nasa faced the very real pressure of an ambitious launch schedule. This, combined with the fact that key contractors felt obliged to defer to customer demands (even in the face of growing evidence of a problem with the O-ring seals) meant that important recommendations were not acknowledged.

The chain of command was complex, hierarchical and bureaucratic – so much so that any reservations there might have been about ice on the launch pad were never escalated and, eventually ignored.

From a leadership perspective, the investigative reports into the Challenger disaster do show that Nasa was hampered by *"inappropriate accountability mechanisms"*.[124]

But what do we mean by 'accountability'? How would things have been different if the decision-making rights and the decision-making process had differed? In an attempt to answer these questions, it is important to explore the differences between responsibility and accountability. Both are critical leadership concepts.

I mentioned previously that the Dragon mission was the first commercial public-private partnership between Nasa and SpaceX. One could almost imagine Elon Musk's awareness of how the expectation of history weighed heavily on him. Accountability was paramount.

> "I'm the Chief Engineer of this thing, so I'd just like to say that if it goes right, its credit to the SpaceX-Nasa team. If it goes wrong it's my fault."

Elon Musk
Founder and CEO of SpaceX

Before we explore accountability, it is worth understanding responsibility – an idea introduced in Part 1, which has become a recurring theme throughout this book.

What is Responsibility? What is Responsible Leadership?

Responsibility: The ability to give a response to completing a task or action.

Taking responsibility: Taking ownership for completing a task or action.

Responsible leadership: Value based; built on ethical, principal-driven relationships between leaders and stakeholders who are connected through a shared sense of purpose and meaning.[125]

Responsible leadership occurs at the intersection of the person; the roles the leader fulfils; the ethics of the leader-follower relationships; and the responsibilities and ethics of what a leader does.[126]

Responsibility begins with an internal decision. In a world that emphasises personal liberties and personal freedom, it's worth considering the important counterbalance of responsibility.

An Idea Whose Time has Come

I had only ever seen pictures of the *Statue of Liberty Enlightening the World* (to give her full and correct name). Finally, there I was, with my family in New York, travelling on the Hudson River and making our way around Manhattan, past Chelsea and Tribeca; past Jersey City and then into the open water towards Liberty Island.

It was a windy, cloudy day and the entrance to the statue itself was still closed, owing to the after-effects of Hurricane Sandy. This did nothing to dampen our enthusiasm. As we sailed past, we were able to see Liberty for ourselves: Her right hand raised, bearing the gold leaf-covered torch; her left-hand clutching the tablet, recording the date of the American Declaration of Independence.

As we looked closer, her now-famous green tinge from years of copper oxidisation appeared in sharp focus. As my two children stood in the front of the boat, we moved quickly to photograph them with the statue in the background. I was not impressed by the scale of the statue, or even by the seven spikes on the crown. Rather, I was impressed by what I could not see.

Liberty seemed smaller than I had imagined (maybe that was the result of seeing *Planet of the Apes* and *Independence Day*). Just before I had arrived in New York, I'd been rereading Victor Frankl's timeless classic, *Man's search for Meaning*. What really impressed me was what Frankl had written:

"Freedom, however, is not the last word. Freedom is only part of the story and half of the truth. Freedom is but the negative aspect of the whole phenomenon whose positive aspect is responsibleness. In fact, freedom is in danger of degenerating into mere arbitrariness unless it is lived in terms of responsibleness. That is why I recommend that the Statue of Liberty on the East Coast be supplemented by a Statue of Responsibility on the West Coast."[127]

On my return to South Africa, I learned that in fact there is a 15ft prototype for this Statue of Responsibility at the Utah Valley University. It was sculpted by Gary Lee Price, a fellow of the US National Sculpture Society, whose works are displayed around the world in galleries, libraries, museums and educational institutions and private collections. He describes his work as *"lifting the human spirit through sculpture"*. It is a journey on which he has been for more than 40 years.

Gary, and his wife, Leesa, are based in Arizona, USA. I approached them both to discuss the background to the planned full-scale Statue of Responsibility, which will stand 300ft high.

"In the mid-2000s, Dr Stephen R. Covey reached out to me and told me about one of his mentors, Dr Viktor E. Frankl, a holocaust survivor who had this incredible idea that he'd been talking about since the 1960s. Dr Covey said that he had collected some of my work, and he asked if I would be interested in designing Dr Frankl's idea of a statue of responsibility. At the time, I was not aware of such a concept, but I very quickly warmed up to the idea of a Statue of Liberty on one end of the country, on the east side, and then bookending our nation with another statue. I thought: 'Wow! What a great vision! What a big-picture idea to have!'

"As a holocaust survivor, and having seen what happened to his motherland of Austria and the entire European continent, Frankl came away with some incredibly enlightening and powerful ideas, realising just how crucial and important responsibility was. I then reviewed my other works and tried to figure out how to design something that represents responsibility.

"I'm part native American. My grandmother was part Cherokee, and so I was very drawn to the native American genre. I had done a piece depicting

two native Americans – indigenous people, as we now call them – helping each other up a cliff. In that depiction, one is reaching down. He's holding on to the cliff, but he's reaching down, interlocked with the figure below him, assisting that person up. The piece was called 'The Ascent' and I subtitled it: 'They rise highest who lift as they go'.

"It just so happened that the minute I put that out in the marketplace in the early 80s, it became extremely popular. Galleries would tell me all the time how people would stand in front of the piece and actually get emotional. It is about helping each other out and being there for each other. What I think is fascinating, too, is it ended up being a right and a left hand, and we can all make that (symbolic association) ourselves. It just so happens that responsibility starts with us, and then we reach out to other people and help them."

Gary went on to relay the story of how he had travelled to Vienna to meet Dr Frankl's wife, Eleonore 'Elly' Katharina Schwindt. He showed me some photographs of him standing in front of Dr Frankl's desk where he had penned *Man's Search for Meaning*. Elly had shown him a statue that Frankl had bought after he was released from the prison camps. It was called *The Suffering Man* – a figure reaching up to the heavens, which he had used as a metaphor for responsibility. Elly explained to Gary how Viktor had always commented: "Where is the hand reaching down?"

Gary reflected: *"Elly pulled me aside before our little entourage left Vienna and she said: 'Gary, I know where this needs to be! Hopefully, it will end up in San Diego. That was like our second home in the USA.'*

"Up until that point, I had no idea whether I was even on the right track with my concept or not. One of my foundational beliefs is a quote by Victor Hugo, who wrote 'Les Misérables' and 'The Hunchback of Notre Dame'. He said: 'Nothing is more powerful than an idea whose time has come.'

"I'm a very impatient person. I guess that's why I've been so prolific in my career. A lot of my pieces are not so detailed that you see every line; it's more of an impressionistic feeling that represents that kind of impatience of wanting to get the idea out there.

"We believe this project is in Higher Hands. We're talking about a three- to five hundred-million-dollar project that could probably take a good couple of years to create. It will have elevators, and there will be occupied levels and a look-out tower at the top. I would think it would take probably a year to get all of the permits from coastal authorities, and it could take

two to three years to construct. But, in spite of my impatience, wanting to have this 300-footer done already, it hasn't been the right time. With what we're going through here in America specifically... but of course it's reached globally... it is like we have been handed the perfect timing for responsibility on a silver and golden platter, and all that comes with this gal here holding up that torch of freedom!

"We are optimistically hoping that within three years, people will be going there and teleconferencing people in in New York Harbour, communicating back and forth, going: 'Okay we're here! What's it like over there? Look at what we have created! Look how we're all connected!'

"We have monuments all over, and a lot of them are (shrouded) in controversy right now. It's more than a monument, it's a movement. We need to call out to something much, much bigger, that transforms humanity and gives us purpose and reason and guidelines on how to interact with each other. We are accountable, and the bottom-line boils down to us."

The Bill of Responsibilities

In South Africa, progress has been made in drafting a Bill of Responsibilities to support the existing Bill of Rights. The twelve responsibilities are:

1. The right to **equality** places on me the **responsibility to treat every person equally and fairly**, and not to discriminate unfairly against anyone on the basis of race, gender, sex, pregnancy, marital status, ethnic or social origin, colour, sexual orientation, age, disability, religion, conscience, belief, culture, language or birth.

2. The right to **human dignity** places on me the **responsibility to treat people with reverence, respect and dignity**, to be kind, compassionate and sensitive to every human being, including greeting them warmly and speaking to them courteously.

3. The right to **life** places on me the **responsibility to protect and defend the lives of others**, not to endanger the lives of others by carrying dangerous weapons or by acting recklessly or disobeying our rules and laws. Live a healthy life by exercising, eating correctly, by not smoking, abusing alcohol, or taking drugs, or indulging in irresponsible behaviour that may result in my being infected, or infecting others, with communicable diseases, such as HIV and AIDS.

4. My responsibility in ensuring the right to **family** or parental care expects me to: honour and respect my parents, and to help them, be kind and loyal to my family, to my brothers and sisters, my grandparents and all my relatives. To recognise that love means long-term commitment, and the responsibility to establish strong and loving families.

5. The right to **education** places on me the **responsibility to attend school regularly, to learn, and to work hard, cooperate respectfully with teachers and fellow learners and adhere to the rules and the Code of Conduct of the school**. It concurrently places on my parents and caregivers the responsibility to: Ensure that I attend school and receive their support; and places on my teachers the responsibility to promote and reflect the culture of learning and teaching in giving effect to this right.

6. My responsibility in ensuring the right to **work** carries with it the **responsibility for all learners, parents, caregivers and teachers** to: work hard and do our best in everything we do, recognise that living a good and successful life involves hard work, and that anything worthwhile only comes with effort. This right must never be used to expose children to child labour.

7. My responsibility in ensuring the right **to freedom and security** of the person is upheld by my taking r**esponsibility for: not hurting, bullying, or intimidating others, or allowing others to do so, and solving any conflict in a peaceful manner**.

8. The right to own **property** places on me the **responsibility to: respect the property of others**, take pride in and protect both private and public property, and not to take what belongs to others, and to give generously to charity and good causes, where I am able to do so.

9. The right to **freedom of conscience** requires me to: **Allow others to choose and practice the religion of their choice, and to hold their own beliefs and opinions, without fear or prejudice**. To respect the beliefs and opinions of others, and their right to express these, even when we may strongly disagree with these beliefs and opinions. That is what it means to be a free democracy.

10. The right to live in a **safe environment** assumes the **responsibility to: promote sustainable development, and the conservation and preservation of the natural environment, protect animal and plant-life**, as well as the responsibility to prevent pollution, to not litter, and to ensure that our homes, schools, streets and other public places are kept neat and tidy. In the context of climate change, we are also obliged to ensure we do not waste scarce resources like water and electricity.

11. The right to citizenship expects that each of us will be good and loyal South African citizens. This means that we are **responsible for: Obeying the laws of our country, ensuring that others do so as well, and contributing in every possible way to making South Africa a great country.**

12. The right to free expression is not unlimited, and does not allow us to: Express views which advocate hatred, or are based on prejudices with regard to race, ethnicity, gender or religion. We must therefore **take responsibility to ensure this right is not abused by ourselves or others, to not tell or spread lies, and to ensure others are not insulted or have their feelings hurt.**

13. I accept the call of this Bill of Responsibilities, and commit to taking my rightful place as an active, responsible citizen of South Africa. By assuming these responsibilities I will contribute to building the kind of society which will make me proud to be a South African.[128]

This notion of a Bill of Responsibilities is not unique to South Africa and has been proposed by leaders in other countries, too. Although the list comes in various guises, the message with these responsibilities is clear. Only focusing on individual liberties or rights distorts the picture. By balancing rights with responsibilities, leaders operate from a mindset that acknowledges that:

- Responsibility is mutual.
- Responsibility is co-dependent.
- Responsibility is best exercised out of relationship.
- Responsibility demonstrates a duty of care.

"We are made wise not by the recollection of our past, but by the responsibility for our future."

George Bernard Shaw

The concept of the responsible leader is central to the exponential effect. The responsible leader acknowledges the need to align actions with purpose; actions with principles; and actions with outcomes. With this understanding of responsibility established, leaders can then consider their accountability. The ultimate goal is to create an environment in which people move from responsibility to self, to responsibility to others, and then look to take accountability. In order to unlock the exponential effect, leaders need to acknowledge the importance of counterbalancing the principles of liberty with the equally important principles of responsibility and accountability.

"Sooner or later everyone sits down to a banquet of consequences."

Robert Louis Stevenson

* What is accountability?
* How is accountability different from responsibility?

Justifying Actions or Decisions

ac|count|able

Pronunciation: /əˈkaʊntəb(ə)l/ Required or expected to justify actions or decisions[129]

I asked 'Dr Meaning', Alex Pattakos, the founder of the Global Meaning Institute, for his thoughts:

"Responsibility can be shared and delegated. Accountability cannot be shared or delegated. I view them along a motivation continuum – from intrinsic (responsibility) to extrinsic (accountability) – with MEANING as the 'bridge', if you will, between and connecting them."

Accountability, in its original form, was an accounting or bookkeeping term. It meant to "give an account". Rooted in the history of the 11th century, the *Domesday Book* held records of all of the assets possessed by landowners. Combined, these assets made up the sum total of the king's realm. Landowners were required to demonstrate accountability to the Crown.

Over time, 'accountability' has taken on a broader meaning. Rather than simply referring to financial records, we use the word in a leadership context to refer to principles of decision-making, governance and consequence. It's also worth noting how the word has seen a complete reversal of fortune. Where 'accountability' was originally used to refer to followers' obligations to leaders, the word is now more widely used to suggest how general citizens expect their elected officials to explain and justify their conduct in office.

It has been said that accountability sits at the intersection of responsibility and relationship. To show responsibility means that you care; to show accountability means that you want your words and actions to count.

"Leaders not accountable to their people will eventually be held accountable by their people."[130]

Mike Myatt
Author and CEO coach

Accountability is defined as:
- The leader's willing **acceptance** of the responsibilities inherent in the leadership position to serve the wellbeing of the organisation.
- The implicit or explicit **expectation** that he/ she will be publicly linked to his/ her actions, words, or reactions.
- The expectation that the leader may be called on to **explain** his/ her beliefs, decisions, commitments, or actions to constituents.[131]

The idea of a leader willingly accepting responsibility is an important one. Leaders also need to acknowledge that in the new world of work, it is not just their followers who have implicit or explicit expectations. This now extends to a much broader range of stakeholders. Today's leaders understand that under the glare of social media, anyone with even only a slight interest in a leader's actions, believes they are at liberty to ask for an explanation for the leader's comments or conduct. It's a hard lesson to learn when we give little or no thought to comments we make on online platforms.

Effective leaders acknowledge their postings as a permanent record for all to see and scrutinise. Accountability is certainly one of those critical, but much-neglected components of leadership.

In a recent interview I conducted with political analyst Daniel Silke, he made the following point:

"One of the critical issues really remains the fundamental that we all need to be accountable. Whether you're in a family, a corporate environment, and certainly if you're in an elected position paid by the taxpayers, you need to be accountable."

The Essential Components

For leaders to embrace effective accountability (rather than viewing it as some kind of modern witch hunt), they must understand the components that need to be in place:

1. **Agent**. Accountability requires a party to give account.
2. **Domain**. Accountability requires a set of responsibilities; an area that will be subject to the accountability process.
3. **Principal**. Accountability requires a person to whom the initial party will give account.
4. **Feedback**. Accountability involves the rights of the principal to require the agent to inform, explain and justify decisions and actions with regard to the domain.
5. **Sanction**. Accountability involves the explicit acknowledgement by the agent that the principal has the right to choose to sanction the agent if it is felt that decisions or actions can't be justified.[132]

I would like to add one more component to this list:

6. **Reward**. Accountability involves the explicit acknowledgment by the agent that the principal has the right to choose to reward the agent, based on previous decisions or actions.

> **Accountability:** The ability and willingness to give account. It is the lifeblood of effective execution.

With these components in place, let's apply this to a specific case study.

> Basic Education Minister Angie Motshekga denied accountability in the Limpopo textbook saga where schools were without books for the first seven months of the school year: *"I'm not responsible for delivering textbooks in Limpopo; I can't be blamed."*[133]

It is clear from this report who the agent is (the minister) as well as the extent of the domain (the timeous and complete delivery of textbooks). The problem begins with a tacit conflating of responsibility and accountability.

The minister is right when she says that she is not responsible for the physical delivery of the textbooks. That job was probably outsourced or subcontracted to a logistics company. However, that does not change the fact that, as the Minister of Education, she is still ultimately accountable for the outcome.

Not only is the domain not acknowledged, but it is also not clear (at least, from the article) who the minister sees as the principal (the president, the schools and the general public). Because the domain and the principal are not acknowledged, the correct feedback channels break down and the sanction/reward process cannot be executed. The net result is a failure of decision-making and a failure of accountability.

Consequence Management

The tension in the room was palpable. I had been tasked by a new client with taking hundreds of line managers through their new annual performance appraisal process. The organisational goals were clear and the process for creating individual performance expectations was established. The methodology for creating line-of-sight between individual behaviours and the business objectives was in place, and the scorecard, bell curve and moderation system were all accurately mapped out. There was only one problem: No one believed a word I was saying…

The last couple of years have seen a number of extraordinarily successful, global companies relooking the traditional annual performance review. Accenture, Adobe, General Electric, IBM and Microsoft have all been very public about the fact that they are moving away from very traditional, cumbersome, administration-heavy review processes.

"Performance appraisals are very expensive, complex systems for making people unhappy."

Kevin Murphy
Colorado State University

These companies have identified that for accountability to really work, they need to be able to give and receive feedback in a frequent, fast and technology-enabled way. Proponents of this approach argue that it is far more important to evaluate an individual on the tasks and role that he or she were initially assigned, rather than benchmarking and ranking that person on a normal distribution curve and then comparing them to everyone else over a 12-month period. Only time will tell how all of this will impact on pay grades, but what is clear is that businesses have identified the direct correlation between a culture of accountability and improved performance.

Although accountability is at the core of leadership, it is often a tough reality for leaders to accept. It is a natural human temptation to try to duck and dive when things go wrong. When faced with a complex issue, the natural human inclination is to try to get other people to accept co-responsibility, or to at least dilute the accountability on ourselves.

The effects of a lack of accountability are evident all around us. Many are seemingly inconsequential, but because they are so ingrained in the way we interact, it is as if we have become immune to their effects. A late arrival (or no-show) at a meeting, or a non-returned voicemail soon escalates into more dramatic non-performance. Every leader is an accountant. Responsibility is for the task; accountability is for the result.

"When we prepare for the pandemics and crises of the future, which will come, we need to be accountable, and we need to make sure that we build up a resource base that's not squandered through patronage or the whims of elected officials."

Daniel Silke

> How do leaders develop accountability?

Accountability is one of those times when you need to be using 'I' statements. Accountability is about seeing it, owning it, solving it and doing it. Accountability needs to be both positive and principled: Making, keeping and answering personal commitments.

"We seem to have normalised doing and saying nothing …
and that's not okay."

Michele Wucker
Commentator and policy analyst

Accountability is not simply expecting people to do what they are told to do, when they are told to do it. It is about holding yourself and others to the actions of your commitments:

- State the commitment.
- Check that everyone understands the specifics of the commitments.
- Clarify the commitments.

Accountability is easier when there is strong relationship and clear motives, and if your followers see that you take both big and small things seriously. The small things are often much more powerful, such as phoning back when you promised to do so, and responding to a seemingly insignificant email. Holding people to the principles of accountability may mean having to make some difficult decisions.

"UNLESS someone like you cares a whole awful lot, nothing
is going to get better. It's not."

Dr Seuss
The Lorax

There is a long-standing joke in the scuba diving community: Always dive with a knife. When confronted by a shark, stab your buddy and swim away. You might not be able to outswim the shark, but you can outswim your buddy. This is a tremendous lesson in how *not* to be responsible or accountable.

Businesses are full of people who, when faced with any sort of challenge, look around for someone on to whom they think they can shift the responsibility, problem or the blame. They then look for the nearest escape route.

It is also worth pointing out the value of peer accountability. This involves a willingness to be vulnerable. Let's return to scuba diving, which is a great metaphor to illustrate this: Scuba involves working in pairs;

checking each other's equipment; sticking together; looking out for each other; communicating clearly; completing the dive together; ascending together and then logging the dive. Break anyone of those cardinal rules and you endanger both you and your buddy. It requires allowing others to see your weaknesses and to help you.

Peer accountability involves giving each other the right to speak into the areas of responsibility, decision-making and actions. You also agree to the other person calling for an explanation of your actions at any time.

Peer accountability involves a mutual submission, in which there is a spontaneous willingness to allow a colleague to be a sounding board and a confidante. Being able to ask trusted colleagues for their input and perspective on important issues provides incredible opportunities.

One of the key differences between peer accountability and the essential components of accountability mentioned earlier is that the agent and the principal become interchangeable roles.

"If you want to inculcate a sense of responsibility and accountability, then demonstrate that you take both the small things and the big things seriously and behave accordingly."

Brand Pretorius

Accountability Avoidance

Accountability and buck-passing are inversely related. There are typical signs of accountability avoidance for which we should be looking out. Although there are many different examples and warning signs, here are several that we are likely to encounter:

- **The standard delay. ("We'll get back to you.")**
  Delay tactics are common when avoiding accountability. Stonewalling, and/or buying for time are often nothing more than a blatant refusal to be put one's actions or decisions under the microscope. If you, as a leader, are confronted with this approach, it's really important to make sure that you agree on milestones and timeframes with the individual concerned.

- **The outright denial. ("Not on my watch.")**
  Denial is often used when people know they have no wiggle room. Rather than acknowledging liability or responsibility, people often feel it's easier to simply deny any involvement. When individuals feel compelled to take this approach, it's really important that you collect or provide clear evidence in order to help them understand where the buck stops.

- **The direct shift-blaming finger point. ("It was so-and-so's fault.")**
  This tactic is apparent when people confuse responsibility and accountability. The fact that you have delegated responsibility for a task does not mean that you are not ultimately responsible. It's never enough for leaders to say that they are not responsible.

"Part of the reason for our limited response (in South Africa) was the fact that we have squandered resources, perhaps for the last decade or so, through graft, corruption and poor policy decisions, where there wasn't enough accountability from our national leaders."

Daniel Silke

- **The deft side-step of ignorance'** ("I don't understand."; "I didn't know.")
  Used as a tactic when people have few, if any, alternatives at their disposal. That's why, in the accountability process, it's important to keep records of any discussions, and to confirm ahead of time that everyone understands the nature and specifics of the commitment.

Matching Performance with Promises

Unless you start with personal responsibility, it will be almost impossible to expect accountability. Although a formulaic approach is never able to cover all situations, these six principles may go some way to increasing your chances of matching performance with promises:

D6 Approach

D1: Define your expectations clearly and concisely.

Watching leaders communicating, it is interesting to see how often they are totally convinced that they have described exactly what they want and that they have made their expectations clear. This assumption can be dangerous – they are the enemy of accountability. At the same time, the person receiving those expectations isn't always on the same page. If expectations are not clearly and concisely defined, then the accountability process is set up for failure before it even starts. If expectations are vague, or too broad and generalised, then that is exactly the quality of work that will be delivered. The first step in the accountability process is making sure that people are clear that they will need to give account.

> Accounting precedes accountability.
> Ensure accountability by confirming accountability.
> Accountability is the mirror of answerability.

D2: Determine the individual's ability and willingness.

Any leader looking to delegate a task, project or set of responsibilities would do well to confirm that the person to whom they are delegating has both the ability and desire (willingness) to complete the task. The question of ability is concerned with the issues of capacity, resources, skills and time. Before assigning a specific project, it is probably as important to have a discussion around these elements as it is around the project itself.

The question of willingness is a little bit more difficult. There will obviously be times in any leader-follower relationship when people will be asked to do things that they don't necessarily want to do.

D3: Decide on mutually agreed outcomes and consequences for non-performance.

Accountability works best when both parties agree on what success looks like, right from the outset. Leaders ensuring accountability will take the time to clearly articulate what outcomes he or she has in mind. You might be tempted to micromanage the process, but the best leaders are more interested in the outcomes. There is an especially important relationship between decision-making and accountability. Keep these outcomes visible and let people understand the implications of non-performance.

D4: Dialogue regularly.

The word 'dialogue' used here is intentional. Effective conversation makes for effective accountability. Create opportunities for regular feedback, updates and insights into the progress individuals are making with respect to particular tasks. Everything discussed in the previous chapter on micro-monitoring applies here.

D5: Debrief and disclose the results.

Measure, track, take stock and reward appropriately. Leaders need to find ways to create an environment that encourages trust. Build a culture in which accountability allows for the public disclosure of the leader's behaviour, along with the organisational expectation of consequences as a result of that behaviour.[134]

Biometric tracking and time and attendance software, programme evaluations and customer surveys can go some way to raising the level of accountability through objective measurement. However, none of those external measures will achieve anything if leaders are unwilling to take responsibility and accountability.

D6: Be consistent.

The more consistent you are in adopting and applying this approach to yourself and to those with whom you interact, the quicker followers will see that you are serious about leading by example.

Black Swans and Grey Rhinos

An emerging debate has seen leaders classify world events as 'black swans' or 'grey rhinos'. A black swan is a metaphor for an unpredictable event that is beyond what is normally expected of a situation and that has potentially severe consequences. Black swan events are characterised by their extreme rarity, severe impact, and the widespread insistence that they were obvious in hindsight.[135]

Grey Rhinos, on the other hand, are highly probable, high-impact yet neglected threats.[136] In an interview with author, commentator and policy analyst Michele Wucker, she made the point that the black swan has been misused to normalise complacency. In contrast, the grey rhino provides an alternative that challenges decision makers to be held accountable for failing to prepare for, and head off, clear and present dangers.

"If (you find) yourself saying 'black swan', that's a red flag already. People don't think enough about the possibility of some big thing 'whooping them upside the head with the two-by-four', as they would say in Texas, where I grew up. Build in some resiliency, build in some reserves. Think about how you're going to deal with some of those things. If something happens, don't just wash your hands of it by saying: 'Oh black swan, nobody could have seen it coming!' In a lot of cases, people did see it coming. As a leader, you want to listen to hear people who are saying: 'This is coming.'

"Listening is such a big part of it that if you find yourself talking about black swans in hindsight, then you need to do a real rethink of how you're looking at the world. Don't just be looking through the rearview mirror and using a cop-out and making excuses for not having gotten in the way.

"In some cases, you can learn: 'Here's what I could have done better and here's how I'll do it next time.' You really want to keep your eyes in front of you, to be forward-looking, and when you're taking actions, continue to ask yourself: 'Is what I'm doing working? Do I need to adjust?'

"So many people will see a problem and then say: 'Okay, here's what I'm going do about it and then I'm going wash my hands of it, even if it doesn't solve the problem.' You need to really hold yourself accountable, not just for paying attention to what's in front of you; for listening to the people who are warning you of things, but also for being accountable for your actions and adjusting when things aren't working the way that you think that they should."

Leadership accountability should be regarded as the scoreboard of responsibility. True leaders are always willing to answer both for their decisions as well as the consequences of those decisions. When that happens, there is often more reason to celebrate.

11 / EXERCISE

ACCOUNTABILITY QUESTIONS

For you to consider:

1. What areas in your life require greater self-responsibility?
2. What tasks or duties have you been assigned, but failed to carry out?
3. What specific outcomes are you both accountable and responsible for?
4. Who can you approach, as a trusted friend or mentor, to begin a peer accountability process?
5. In terms of commitment, what stated actions do you need to follow through on?
6. What can you do to develop personal accountability? What will you do to develop personal accountability?

12 / CELEBRATION

IN FOR THE WIN

"Colleagues should take care of each other, have fun,
celebrate success, learn by failure, look for reasons to praise
not to criticise, communicate freely and respect each other."

Richard Branson

From the angle of the aerial photographs, the wording was clear: "Tien's dream is Nice in the Cote d'Azur." A sea of blue lettering stretched out across the Promenade des Anglais in the southern resort town of Nice. On closer inspection, it became apparent that a human chain of 6 400 people formed the letters, making up, what Guinness World Records described as: "*the longest human-made phrase*" visible from the sky, ever recorded.

Li Jinyuan was the man behind the event. As Tiens Group Founder, Li organised a vacation (a free, four-day trip to France and Monaco) for almost half of his employees, in celebration of the 20th anniversary of the company. The sheer scale of the celebration was staggering. As part of the largest tour group France had ever hosted, Tiens Group required 5 000 hotel rooms in Cannes and Monaco, as well as an additional 140 hotels in Paris. Moving the group around required 7 600 train tickets. It took 147 buses to get the tour group from their hotels to the promenade in Nice. It is estimated that the four-day event saw about $36 million flow into the French economy.[137]

The world record was performed in 2015. Now, writing this chapter at the 100-day mark of lockdown in South Africa, it feels a little bit tone deaf to be talking about celebration. Infection rates continue to climb, along with an increasing number of business closures and job losses. But this is probably the best time to contemplate the power of celebration – provided we are celebrating the right things.

It was Bill Hughson, President of DeVry's Healthcare Group, who said: *"An organisation produces most what it honours most."*

If we honour complacency, that's what we produce. If we honour accountability, that's what we will produce instead. Celebration becomes an indicator of personal, relational, team and organisational priorities.

While very few leaders could be expected to go to the extreme of the Tiens Group, there is more than enough evidence to suggest that celebration is a critical part of the leader-follower dynamic. Yet, this is often one of the most neglected elements of the team success.

- Effective teams track progress.
- Effective team track results.
- Effective teams celebrate.

What do we celebrate?

When discussing with leaders this important principle of leading for results and delivering solutions, the conversations usually focus on outputs; victories; successes; achievements; attainment and progress. Although there is certainly nothing wrong with that, two themes emerge: Firstly, we tend to celebrate after the fact. Secondly, of those interviewed, less than half took the time to recognise their team, or even to reward individual contributions.

There is now plenty of evidence from psychologists, such as Dr B.J. Fogg, Director of the Design Lab at Stanford University, that tiny habits can have an exponential effect. Celebrating those habits is an essential component of habit formation.[138] Teresa Amabile and Steven Kramer have also shown the power of small wins and how celebration is critical to acknowledging meaningful progress in meaningful work.[139]

Acknowledgement and Appreciation

It seems almost ironic that we need to be reminded about the importance of celebration. In the midst of a year of social distancing and austerity, it is worth reminding ourselves of what's really important. Years ago, one of my mentors in the USA was staying at my home at a time when I was juggling multiple projects and priorities. On the way to the airport, he leaned over and said: "Andy, it's been a great time seeing you and the family, but can I ask you one question? What do you do for fun?" My silence spoke volumes.

Learn to Acknowledge and Celebrate the Individual

I have always been a firm believer in acknowledging the individual before their contribution. It's often easy to forget that behind every person you lead, there is a human being with their own responsibilities, challenges and unique circumstances. This reality was brought to the fore again this week in a conversation with a masters students I am supervising. She was bringing me up to date on her progress with her thesis.

"How are you?" I asked, knowing that she was working in a department where a number of people had contracted Covid-19.

"Not too well!" she said. "My tests have come back: I'm Covid-19-positive and I'm in isolation at home! I'm not coping with this research methodology section and I'm feeling dreadful."

The conversation shifted very quickly to her wellbeing and that of her family. "Right now, your children need you more than they need you to have this MBA," I said. "Your health is far more important."

Let's learn to see the person before we see their work. Some of my most rewarding work with high-performing teams has been when leaders have taken the time to make appointments with me for no other reason than to say: "Andy, I appreciate you!"

Correct Privately but Celebrate Publicly

I have seen too many instances in which these two practices are reversed. Public correction runs close to humiliation. I have seen all too often how teachers who cannot control a group of rowdy teenagers resort to what I call "the flip" – calling out young people in front of their peers in a disparaging and humiliating way. They then only ever acknowledge good work privately.

I recognise that there are some people who don't like it when a fuss is made of them, but those people tend to be the exception. Appropriate celebration understands how individuals want to be acknowledged. As a rule, public celebration is a great way to honour excellence.

Celebrate Character, Purpose and Resilience

The high school I attended seemed to hold many awards ceremonies. I can still see the table on the stage covered with the school flag and laden with trophies and plaques of various sizes. There were always the big ones – including the Victor and Victrix Ludorum – overall awards for the top boy and girl who excelled in sport in that year. Then there was the coveted Headmasters Award.

No one, not even the staff, knew ahead of time who the recipient would be. That award was made purely at the principal's discretion. He might have consulted with his executive team, or asked for input from individual staff members, but the headmaster made the choice to honour one individual learner.

What I will always remember about that award is that it was very rarely given to the most popular child, or to the one with the best grades, or even the one who was the most successful on the sports field. No, that award was always based on character, service, contribution and respect. Wouldn't it be magnificent if we could find ways to make a similar award part of our organisational culture? Leaders set the tone. Remember, an organisation produces most what it honours most.

Celebrate Trust, Positive Influence and Effective Communication

During my career, I have been part of a number of collocated and distributed teams. As a member of remote teams, I have seen the power of choosing to trust people I have never met, and the power of positive influence and effective communication.

We should not take that trust for granted. We should be celebrating the fact that even though working conditions have changed forever, for those of us who can, we still have the privilege of interacting with people who demonstrate authenticity; who have no hidden agenda; a high degree of self, social, and situational awareness (insight); and who show care, empathy and competence.

When positive influence brings about meaningful change, we need to celebrate. When leaders and teams see a clear and effective duplication of ideas and demonstrate understanding of the context and dynamics of communication, we need to celebrate.

For more than 20 years, my friends, Craig and Gina Rowe, have run a Holiday Club for primary school children in their local community in Muldersdrift, South Africa. Most of the children who attend are from disadvantaged backgrounds. I asked Craig to reflect on some of the memorable moments in the programme:

"Holiday Club runs every year during the mid-year school holidays, sometime around June-July, in the middle of the South African winter. Hundreds of children (between 400 and 1 500) arrive each day for planned activities, spiritual input and games. We identify high school children as leaders, supervised by young adults and a few volunteer moms and dads.

"Young leaders are given ownership and responsibility from day one. We take them through a three- to six-month process before the time, planning themes, educational activities, fun and games. We have three primary purposes: To raise up the next generation of leaders; to give children an entire week of the most fun they have ever had; and to introduce them to Jesus. Although we do provide transport for a lot of the children, we've had some instances of children leaving home in the dark, walking in just T-shirts and shorts in the middle of winter, just to get there in time.

"We started with one site, but over the years, the programme has grown to include anything between six and 12 satellite sites, spread over a 20–30km radius. Multiple sites make it more accessible for more children, which means we can also create multiple leadership teams.

"The highlights for me are the young leaders who develop their own ideas and run the programme. Over the years it has been so encouraging to see a number of those same young leaders, who now, many years later, are involved in nation-changing activities of their own. A number of them relate back to Holiday Club as their first tangible experience of goodness and love.

"One young person said to me the other day: 'At Holiday Club, I was trusted to be a leader when no one else trusted me.'

"For the children, the Friday celebration is a well-established tradition and highlight. The local community contribute all of the ingredients and then the children construct the biggest banana split you can imagine! It runs

for metres. We've even lined steel drums and placed them end to end! They get to eat as much ice cream, banana and pudding as they want.

"The Holiday club has been so successful that it has now been rolled out in multiple provinces. It has been replicated using the same model as far afield as Brisbane, Australia, and even reaching the island of Vanuatu in the South Pacific.

One of the most powerful celebrations has been to see adults, who attended Holiday Club 10–15 years ago, now successful in their own right; running their own careers and with their own young families, mobilising their colleagues and friends to fund the initiative. It's as if we've come full circle!"

Celebrate the Team, Team Alignment, Positive Conflict and Collaboration

More than ever, the power of team, of being on the same page, and of being aligned around a common set of values, is critical. Being able to embrace creative abrasion and principles of collaboration is essential to the high-performing team.

We need to celebrate these components when we see them in practice. We need to call it out, point to it, and keep showing team members how their behaviour reinforces collaboration. Give the team time to share in the benefits. Reward the enablers of hard work and not just the results of hard work. Celebration motivates the team.

More than ever, we need to learn to appreciate the team member support systems that make success possible. Take time to celebrate spouses and children who are behind the scenes and sacrifice time away from loved ones, who are far more than providers or breadwinners.

Celebrate Execution

Of course we should celebrate getting things done; of course we should celebrate results; and of course we should celebrate solutions; but in a world where it is so easy to move on to the next project – if nothing else – the pandemic has taught us to reprioritise what, when and how we celebrate. Quick wins, alternative options and coming in under budget are all brilliant reasons to pause, acknowledge, reflect and learn from what we have done well. Celebrate institutional memory (the combined knowledge and learned experiences in the team) and celebrate innovation.

I have consulted with far too many organisations that regret not nurturing positive enablers when they were present.

Celebrate Accountability

If we celebrate accountability, it will become more deeply entrenched in organisational culture.

A friend of mine, Mike Davies, a previous mayor of West Devon in the United Kingdom, quit the Conservative party as a councillor over the actions of a senior leader in the party during the lockdown. He was widely praised for taking such a drastic step to highlight inconsistencies in his own party.

In June every year, Transparency International (TI) celebrate whistle-blowers – people who are prepared to put their jobs and livelihoods on the line to uncover environmental crimes, fraud and corruption with respect to public funds, and even mismanagement or theft within private companies. TI doesn't just celebrate the whistle-blowers, it also celebrates the implementation of policies and practices that guarantee individual safety and protection from retaliation.

More and more companies are implementing governance practices which add a duty of care to the triple-bottom-line of people, profit and planet. Professor Mervyn E. King, Chairman of the International Integrated Reporting Council and the King Committee on Corporate Governance, has done excellent work in the area of corporate governance and accountability.

The history of corporate governance shows that companies began to challenge the notion of the primacy of the shareholder in order to consider the growing *"legitimate and reasonable interests and expectations of stakeholders"*.[140]

From the mid-90s, intangible assets (company strategy; supply chain; human rights; stakeholder relationships and particularly how the company actually makes money) began to make up an even larger percentage of the overall market value of companies. These intangible assets needed to be both accounted for and reported on, so that boards could effectively discharge their duty of accountability. But what is also clear is how governance needed to move from being seen as a set of compliance processes and procedures to actually underpinning the way companies do business.

Corporate governance works best when 'value' is seen as *"a sustainable lens in a resource-deprived world"*.[141] Prof King has highlighted how corporate governance requires leadership at board level that is both ethical and effective.

> Prof King coined the acronym 'ICRAFT', to describe ethical leadership that is exemplified by:
>
> - **Integrity**
> - **Competence**
> - **Responsibility**
> - **Accountability**
> - **Fairness**
> - **Transparency.**

The *King Report* describes ethical leadership as the: *"anticipation and prevention, or otherwise amelioration, of the negative consequences of the organisation's activities and outputs on the economy, society and the environment and the capitals that it uses and affects."*

Effective leadership is results-driven. It is about achieving strategic objectives and positive outcomes. Effective leadership includes, but goes beyond, an internal focus on effective and efficient execution.

Corporate strategy should focus not just on outputs, but also on outcomes in society. Where corporate governance is underpinned by both ethical and effective leadership, the expected outcomes include:

1. Ethical culture.
2. Good performance.
3. Effective control.
4. Legitimacy.

Governance principles and best practice need to interface with enterprise judgment calls (strategy). These four outcomes ensure that, not only will the organisation have the licence to operate, but also that organisational reputation is enhanced. These outcomes need to be celebrated.

One of the most profound organisational components of the *King Report* is that the principles of the Code have been broadened to include not just corporate companies, but also non-profit organisations; state-owned entities; municipalities; institutional investors and small, medium and micro-enterprises. Organisations need to apply the 17 principles of corporate governance and also explain their application.

We are living in a world of global financial volatility shaped by the Fourth Industrial Revolution, with a broad range of stakeholders calling for a radical transparency. Prof King makes the point that nowadays, there really is nowhere for leaders to hide. This radical transparency also needs to be celebrated.

Celebrate Diversity and Inclusion

People like James Mpele remind us of the importance of celebrating diversity and inclusion. As a transformation specialist, James notes that most companies are still stuck on compliance and making sure all of the documentation is completed.

"Only a few companies have taken this a step further to say: 'How can we be creative?' This drive to transformation is still coming from the head, as opposed to the heart.

"The South Africa Board for People Practices has an annual awards ceremony that celebrates excellence in employment equity, diversity and transformation. We look at the quality of the approach, the strategic policies the company has developed, and their best practices. Is it just play, or is it real desire? What are the results of the planning? Then we look at application. Who is the communication to? Who is driving that communication?

"Thirdly, we look at the results achieved. How have individuals benefited from the policy? Have people really moved their diversity and inclusion policy beyond compliance?

"One of my recent celebrations is a company that has employed a number of people who are hard of hearing, and even deaf. The company found that without many of the typical audio distractions faced by people without hearing disabilities, their work performance was excellent. The company has also made money available for people within the organisation to attend sign language school. You can't just be bringing people who are deaf into an organisation and then not be able to communicate with them. This company has made a point of making money available for people who are deaf to feel included, and to feel that they are part of the organisation. For me, that's really thinking beyond the box!

"Language is important. If you see someone in wheelchair, what do you see first: The person, or the wheelchair? People in wheelchairs want you to see them as people, as individuals, before you see the wheelchair. We are often unaware of the damage that we can cause to another person.

"We have a rule that we often try to reinforce: It's the person first and other things second. For example, say: 'Person with disability', rather than 'disabled person'. In a roadshow, we will talk about our journeys, and about where we've come from as South Africans."

Women are still significantly underrepresented in leadership positions, particularly in listed companies. Seipati Mokhuoa is the Chief Strategy and Investment Officer at HD Afrika. She was recently appointed as a Senator for the World Business Angel Investment Forum. She is also the founder and CEO of SAWIL (Southern African Women in Leadership), a company that supports empowerment and transformation through leadership and management training, coaching, mentorship, dialogue and support. Seipati explains her role in developing African innovation and entrepreneurship through the HD Afrika Innovation Hub and her personal initiatives:

"The role of HD innovation hub is to mainly link start-ups to investors, funders, sponsors, incubators and accelerators globally.

"On a personal level, I like celebrating some of my milestones. I'm running an initiative called 35 for 35. From an innovation point of view, for my 35th birthday, I'm looking for 35 start-ups that I will mentor and help incubate, accelerate and connect to angel investors. Since I have a signature role and I have access to these things, I thought: 'Let me find 35 people that I can put in a better position to access funding and grow their businesses."

I asked Seipati to explain more about SAWIL, and also the plans for the Vision 2030 Pioneers Awards, which celebrate women in leadership:

"If you look at the South African Top 40 listed companies on the JSE (Johannesburg Stock Exchange), there is only one female CEO there. We've come up with a 10-year strategy to close that gap. We want to identify and celebrate trailblazers in the Southern African Development Community (SADC) region.

These women must be passionate about transforming leadership in the countries in which they operate and on the continent. They need to be 'extending the table', in terms of diversity and inclusion, with a particular focus on gender equality. We are looking for women who are extremely zealous and completely unapologetic about climbing the corporate ladder and changing the status quo. These women know who they are and what value they add. They are not easily swayed to leave when challenges arise."

Seipati explained that for many of the women with whom she's worked, it was really difficult to break through the glass ceiling in the corporate environment.

"It's easier for women to give up because they do not get enough support. You get tired of what goes on in the politics of corporates and then give up and start your own business. That's why we have more successful entrepreneurs than corporate leaders in terms of women in the SADC region."

I asked Seipati to share something of her journey and her leadership lessons for aspiring women who might want to follow in her footsteps.

"Self-leadership is at the foundation of excellence. You need to take time to invest in yourself. Growth and change are constants on this journey, so practice patience. Be compassionate with yourself at all times because nobody's going to do it for you. Once you are (in a position of influence), be the person you wish you had by your side as a woman rising in the ranks of the corporate.

"We can never place enough emphasis on lifting as you rise. The only way we are going to disrupt the status quo is to mentor and lift others. We need to look after one another and be truly passionate about opening doors for the women behind us. We need to be excited about having more of us at the table."

Celebrate Celebration... For No Reason at All

As much as we need to find reasons to celebrate, being unpredictable, spontaneous, using the element of surprise and having no reason to celebrate, but doing it anyway, is worth the effort. Effective leaders understand the power of acknowledgment and appreciation, and the impetus and excitement that comes with celebration.

I have learned to be grateful for so much that we took for granted before the pandemic: The liberty to walk around with no curfew; the luxury of relaxing in a coffee shop; the freedom to visit friends and family in our own home... I consider everything in a new light.

When you start looking, there are so many examples of celebration: Personal thanks; birthdays; the end of a season; the beginning of a season; the start of a project; midway through a project; the end of a project; securing a deal; or a job well done. Whatever it is – whether it's a meal together or a weekend away, celebration is a powerful way to increase team solidarity, efficacy and identity.[142] Celebration is also an incredible way for people to rediscover appreciation and self-motivation. It's opportunity to reflect on accomplishments.

Avoiding a Zero-Sum Game

Make sure you are using the right scoreboard. Author and motivational speaker Simon Sinek writes about finite and infinite games.[143] Leadership is all too often focused on the expedient, on the short-term, on the immediate and on the finite. Infinite games are journeys rather than events.

True celebration understands that the infinite game is about creating and celebrating generational legacy. The infinite game means avoiding a zero-sum game. My win does not have to mean your loss. My success does not have to come at the expense of your failure. There should be no need to feel that, in order to thrive in a highly competitive market, I need to belittle, denigrate and bad-mouth other suppliers.

> Celebration says:
>
> - Thank you.
> - I see you.
> - I appreciate you.

Celebration is intentional and memory-making. Celebration is planned and spontaneous, big and small. Celebration is gratitude and it has an abundance mentality.

Celebration in the Midst of Pain

This year saw a number of firsts. These included an international wave of school goers, school leavers, graduates and postgraduates who were unable to gather together for formal graduation ceremonies as a result of the pandemic. The ingenuity of some institutions was commendable.

The creativity of students was even more remarkable. Imagine my delight when a group of MBA students approached me to conduct an informal virtual commencement ceremony for them. In the midst of a hard lockdown, when we could only leave our homes for essentials, there was an opportunity to celebrate.

Despite the foreboding and general mood, and given that we had not had the opportunity to visit anyone face-to-face for weeks, it was an opportunity to honour a group of people who had achieved a significant milestone. I couldn't access my academic regalia, which I normally hire, but I did put on my tie and a collared shirt and jacket. As we gathered in the virtual hall, each student took their place. From my home office, using my webcam, I had the privilege of honouring them and celebrating their achievement:

"Graduands.

"What a privilege to be able to speak to you today as we hold this virtual celebration of your achievements! Even in the context of a nationwide lockdown, you know that if I address you, then it can only be as leaders.

"Over the last 12 months you have had to navigate completing your MBA as working professionals, all while dealing with the challenges of being parents, spouses, managing children and providing support to so many others. In the middle of all that, you had to negotiate applying for an ethical clearance, conducting your studies and writing up your thesis.

"Now it's time to pause.

"To reflect.

"To celebrate.

"And even to reset.

"This journey through Covid-19 will teach you more about yourself than any MBA. I want to say today: You are acknowledged. You do have a voice and your contribution to the world is noticed.

"People don't remember what you know; they remember how much you cared. Today I want to say: 'What a privilege to share the leadership insights!' But more than anything, I want to you know that I care. We do not know what the rest of 2020 will look like, but always know that you can see this event as a 'standing stone'; as a point of reference.

"May you continue to discover your True North, and may you continue to walk in 'Leadership: The Exponential effect' as you lead you, lead others, lead teams, and lead for results."

Then I read out their names as their photographs appeared one by one, along with the title of their theses. It was a day of mixed emotions. I knew how hard they had worked; how every student looked forward to that moment on stage in front of colleagues, friends and family and how, for this group of students, like many around the world, that moment would be lost forever. Still, we celebrated. We made memories in the midst of the pain, and despite the pain.

I remember a few years ago how, despite grieving the loss of my wife's father, we chose to make his funeral a celebration. In my tribute to this incredible man, I wrote:

"In life, there are a few people who don't just influence, but also shape, impact, redefine and help to chart a course.

"This incredible man was one such person – a man whose role in my life was multifaceted – a rich tapestry woven into the fabric of day-to-day living.

"In marriage, he was my Dad-in-law, in relationship, he was my Dad-in-love, but in heart, he was truly my mentor, my wise counsel, my coach and my confidante. Loss is one thing, but regret is very different. We share the loss, but Dad would not want us to carry regret. He would want us to celebrate!"

As leaders, one of our roles is to look for celebration moments that will help people reframe how they see the world.

Captain Nick Sloane agrees: *"Celebration is really important. I am a strong believer that have to take those opportunities. Every time we had bad weather, we would say: 'Okay, it's time for a braai (barbecue). Let's bring some lamb, some pigs, whatever it takes.' (We know there were) a lot of people there who were going to be frustrated. They have the work wait, so we used it as a team-building exercise – (to) loosen up. You also get to know a little more about people over a braai and a couple of beers.*

"At least three times a week I would have dinner with different team members, just see who they were outside of their work, when they dropped their guard and were more relaxed. I think we learned as much about each other by talking in a more informal atmosphere.

"When we installed the blister tanks, we had a braai; when we did the parbuckling, we had a bigger braai, and when we delivered the ship in Genoa, then we had a really big party.

"But at the same time, we had to respect that obviously there was a tragedy (that had taken place). Thirty-two people lost their lives. It was a crime scene, so we had to respect the state prosecutor's wishes, and there were certain things we were allowed to do on the ship and certain things we weren't allowed to do. You just have to say: ' Well, those are boundaries.'

"But, inside those boundaries, you have to be able to celebrate every milestone that is achieved. If you don't do that, they all start to lose significance. So when you have a global project, don't worry about the detail of the last lap, but when the bell rings for the last lap, celebrate it because you are almost there.

"It's important that every milestone is acknowledged and celebrated. When one team does something great, particularly when they have been struggling with something, then stand up and acknowledge them. Give them a round of applause and let them know that what they have achieved is fantastic. That seemed to make them all feel a lot better. Even tiny challenges... when they overcome them, you let them know that what they have achieved is great!"

Acknowledgement, appreciation and celebration are three often neglected, but vital, elements in the leadership dynamic. Let me repeat what I wrote at the beginning of this chapter: Celebration is an indicator of personal, relational, team and organisational priorities.

12 / EXERCISE

CELEBRATION QUESTIONS

For you to consider:

1. What do you do for fun?
2. What are the small wins that you can celebrate right now?
3. When last did you show acknowledgment and appreciation for others? For whom?
4. Right now, what milestones, no matter how small, provide you with an opportunity to celebrate?
5. How can you avoid celebrating a zero-sum game?
6. Where, even in the midst of loss, disappointment and pain, are your opportunities for gratitude?

AFTERWORD

CONCLUDING THOUGHTS

I began this book by referencing the idea of a leadership crisis. The accounts in this book illustrate that despite this reality, there are, in fact, some phenomenal leaders doing brilliant work; influencing and leading across a broad spectrum of society. But one thing is clear: You can't expect to have public successes without private victories.

Although this book presents 12 leadership principles, I had to be selective and consider those elements that would offer the greatest leverage. Much more needs to be explored, discussed and written about leadership.

There is also an element of maturity involved in this process. Personal victories in terms of character, purpose and identity enhance greater credibility when trying to lead others or teams.

It's also important to commit to developing emotional intelligence, and to understanding the importance of the dynamics involved in building trusting relationships. Many of the principles that apply at the level of self-leadership would be equally applicable in developing others, developing teams and delivering results.

The reverse is also true: You can't have results and solutions without effective teams. You can't have effective teams without good interpersonal relationships. The relationship between these principles is symbiotic, rather than sequential. Your ability to handle one-on-one conflict is naturally going to be a factor in how team conflict is handled, and vice versa.

These leadership principles are timeless. They have been written about before, and they will be covered many more times in the future. As a leader,

I realise that with many, if not all, of these principles, one can only ever demonstrate growing maturity rather than absolute competency, or even complete mastery.

In a recent podcast, I was asked to share advice that I would give my younger self. I was immediately drawn to the pitfalls of comparison, obligation and over-analysis. I really hope that this book will help you to develop the insights and skills to deal with these areas.

I trust that you have found this book insightful. Writing is often a solitary and arduous process, but it also brings tremendous joy as random thoughts crystallise on a page in some semblance of a logical format.

I wish you every success as you continue on your journey of equipping for excellence! I invite you to look at the Personal Leadership Charter made up of 12 key principles taken from the chapters of *Leadership: The Exponential Effect*.

PERSONAL LEADERSHIP CHARTER
LEADERSHIP: THE EXPONENTIAL EFFECT

— 12 KEY PRINCIPLES —

LEADING ME (Developing Myself)

1. Personal **character** is the **hallmark** of high-quality leadership.
2. Individual **purpose** provides the **direction** for personal momentum.
3. **Resilience** is the capability to **endure, bounce back and even thrive** in the face of opposition.

> As a leader, I make a personal commitment to developing my character, defining my purpose and to shaping my resilience.

LEADING THEM (Developing Others)

4. **Trust**: The **currency** of relationship.
5. **Influence**: The most significant forms of **power** are often **independent of position**.
6. **Communication**: The **duplication of ideas** requires understanding, certainty and clarity.

> As a leader, I make a personal commitment to leading others through trust, to positive influence and to clear communication.

LEADING US (Developing Teams)

7. **Team alignment** is best reflected in well-integrated, individual **choices** and **behaviours**, combined into a **single unifying aim**.
8. **Positive conflict** is inherent in **tasks, relationships, processes and status**.
9. **Collaboration** is a dance between **creativity, capability and convergence**.

> As a team member or leader, I make a personal commitment to aligning my choices and behaviours to my team purpose, and to embracing positive conflict and collaboration.

LEADING FOR RESULTS (Delivering Solutions)

10. **Execution** occurs at the sharp end of **incremental gains**.
11. **Accountability** is the scoreboard of **responsibility**.
12. True **celebration** means understanding, recognising and **honouring what really matters**.

> As a leader, I make a personal commitment towards excellence in the execution of results, to responsibility, accountability and to true celebration.

© Dr Andrew J. Brough, www.theexponentialeffect.com

ENDNOTES

1   https://reports.weforum.org/outlook-global-agenda-2015 (Accessed: 13 July 13, 2020)

2   https://reports.weforum.org/outlook-global-agenda-2015 (Accessed: 13 July 2020)

3   *Encyclopedia Britannica*, https://www.britannica.com/science/vacuum-physics (Accessed: 13 July 2020)

4   https://www.edelman.com/research/2015-edelman-trust-barometer (Accessed: 13 July 2020)

Chapter 1

5   Edelman Trust Barometer (2015). https://www.edelman.com/research/2015-edelman-trust-barometer (Accessed: April 4, 2020)

6   Edelman Trust Barometer (2020). https://www.edelman.com/trustbarometer (Accessed: 4 April 2020)

7   *Merriam-Webster Dictionary.* https://www.merriam-webster.com (Accessed: 5 August 2020)

8   https://www.smithsonianmag.com/smart-news/just-twenty-nine-dominoes-could-knock-down-the-empire-state-building-2232941 (Accessed: 4 August 2020)

9   Veldsman, T.H. (2016). The leadership landscape as a meta-framework. In T.H. Veldsman & A.J. Johnson (Eds), *Leadership: Perspectives from the front line*, Randburg, South Africa: KR Publishing.

10   Ulrich, D., Zenger, J., & Smallwood, N. (1999). *Results based leadership.* Boston, MA: Harvard Business School Press.

11   Harter, J. (2018). *Employee engagement on the rise in the US.* https://news.gallup.com/poll/241649/employee-engagement-rise.aspx (Accessed: 20 September 2020)

12   NY Post January, 17, (2012). (Translated into English from the Italian Newspaper *La Repubblica.*)

13   Scharmer, C.O. (2016). *Theory U. Leading from the Future as it Emerges.* Oakland: CA, Berrett-Koehler Publishers.

14   Gini, A. & Green, R.M. (2013). *10 Virtues of outstanding leaders: Leadership and character.* Hoboken: NJ, John Wiley & Son.

15   Edmonds, S.C. (2017). Why real leaders have strong egos (and that's a good thing). https://www.fastcompany.com/3067133/why-real-leaders-have-strong-egos-and-thats-a-good-thing (Accessed: 9 August 2020)

16   Bauman, D. C. (2013). Leadership and the three faces of integrity. *The Leadership Quarterly*, 24(3), pp. 414–426.

17   PWC (2020). Global Economic Crime and Fraud Survey. https://www.pwc.co.za/en/press-room/global-economic-crime-and-fraud-survey-2020.html (Accessed: 30 July 2020)

18   Craig, S.B. & Gustafson, S.B. (1998). Perceived Leader Integrity scale: An instrument for assessing employee perceptions of leader integrity. *The Leadership Quarterly*, 9(2), pp. 127–145.

19   Simons, T.L., Friedman, R., Liu, L.A. & McLean-Parks, J. (2007). Racial differences in sensitivity to behavioral integrity: attitudinal consequences, in-group effects, and 'trickle down' among black and non-black employees. *The Journal of Applied Psychology*, 92(3), pp. 650–665.

20   Giotto Integrity Scale. https://www.getfeedback.net/products/detail/giotto (Accessed: 5 August 2020)

21   Nooyi, I. (2008). The best advice I ever got. https://archive.fortune.com/galleries/2008/fortune/0804/gallery.bestadvice.fortune/7.html (Accessed: 30 July 2020)

22   Zakrzewski, R. (2015). Emotional Intelligence needs a Moral Rudder. https://greatergood.berkeley.edu/article/item/emotional_intelligence_needs_a_moral_rudder (Accessed: 30 July 2020)

23   Goleman, D. (2006). *Social Intelligence: The New Science of Human Relationships*. London: Hutchinson.

24   Goleman, D. (1998). What makes a leader? *Harvard Business Review*, Boston, MA: Harvard Publishing.

25   Eurich, T. (2017). *Insight: The power of self-awareness in a self-deluded world*. New York, New York: Penguin Random House.

26   Shakespeare, W. (1997). Hamlet, Prince of Denmark, Act 1 Scene III, *The Complete Works of William Shakespeare*. UK. Wordsworth.

27   Goleman, D. (2006). *Social Intelligence: The New Science of Human Relationships*. London: Hutchinson.

Chapter 2

28   Carey, B. (2003). William Wilberforce's sentimental rhetoric: Parliamentary reports and the Abolition Speech of 1789. *The Age of Johnson: A Scholarly Annual*, 14, pp. 281–305.

29   Collins, J. and Porras, J. (1994). *Good to great*. New York, New York: Harper Collins.

30   Yukl, G. (2006). *Leadership in Organizations*, 6th ed. Upper Saddle River, NJ: Prentice-Hall.

31   Burns, J. (1978). *Leadership*. New York, New York: Harper & Row.

32   Burke, WW. (2008). *Organizations change. Theory & Practice*. London: Sage Publications.

33 Maak, T.H. and Pless, N.M. (2006). Responsible Leadership: A relational approach, in T.H. Maak and N.M. Pless (Eds), *Responsible Leadership*. London: Routledge.

34 Maak, T. (2007). Responsible Leadership, Stakeholder Engagement, and the Emergence of Social Capital. *Journal of Business Ethics*, 74(4), Ethics in and of Global Organizations: The EBEN 19th Annual Conference in Vienna (Sept, 2007), pp. 329–343.

35 Baumeister, R. (1987). How the self became a problem: A psychological review of historical research. *Psychological Review*, 52(1): pp. 163–176.

36 George, B. (2015). *Discover your True North*. Hoboken New Jersey: Wiley.

37 Fraser-Thill, R. (2020). Want to Stay Healthy? Having purpose is an ideal starting point. https://www.forbes.com/sites/rebeccafraserthill/2020/04/18/need-purpose-pandemic/#53c1db762b5c (Accessed: 30 July 2020)

38 Hedges, K. (2017). 5 Questions to help your employees find their inner purpose. *Harvard Business Review*. Boston, MA: Harvard Publishing.

39 Craig, N. & Snook. S.A. (2014). From purpose to impact. *Harvard Business Review*. Boston, MA: Harvard Publishing.

40 Law, P. (2016). Spiritual leadership. In T.H. Veldsman & A.J. Johnson (Eds), *Leadership: Perspectives from the front line. Randburg*, South Africa: KR Publishing.

41 Schulenberg, S.E., Schnetzer, L.W. & Buchanan, E.M. (2010). The purpose in life test-short form: Development and psychometric support. *Journal of Happiness Studies*, Nov. https://www.aggieerin.com/pubs/schulenberg%2011.pdf (Accessed: 30 July 2020)

42 George, B. (2015). *Discover your True North*. Hoboken New Jersey: Wiley.

43 McCashland, C.R. (2011). Standout Assessment Technical Report. https://www.tmbc.com/portfolio-item/standout-assessment-technical-report (Accessed: 30 July 2020)

44 Garcia, H. & Miralles, F. (2016). *Ikigai – The Japanese secret to a long happy life*. New York, New York: Penguin.

45 Deloitte. (2016). Millennial Survey. Winning Over the Next Generation of Leaders. https://www2.deloitte.com/content/dam/Deloitte/global/Documents/About-Deloitte/gx-millenial-survey-2016-exec-summary.pdf (Accessed: 30 July 2020)

46 Wrzesniewskia, A., Schwartz, B., Congc, X., Kanec, M., Omarc, A. & Kolditz, T. (2014). *Multiple Types of Motives don't Multiply the Motivation of West Point Cadets*. Proceedings of the National Academy of Sciences. https://www.pnas.org/content/pnas/early/2014/06/25/1405298111.full.pdf (Accessed: 4 August 2020)

47 Underwood, C. (2016). Purpose in Leadership. https://www.trainingjournal.com/articles/feature/purpose-leadership (Accessed: 4 August 2020)

48 Law, P. (2016). Spiritual Leadership. In T.H. Veldsman & A.J. Johnson (Eds), *Leadership: Perspectives from the front line*. Randburg, South Africa: KR Publishing.

Chapter 3

49 Manser, R. (2007). *Around Africa on my Bicycle*. Johannesburg, South Africa: Jonathan Ball Publishers.

50 Bennis, W.G. & Thomas, R.J. (2002). Crucibles of Leadership. *Harvard Business Review*. Boston, MA: Harvard Publishing.

51   Everly, G.S., Strouse, D.A., Everly III, G.S. (2010). *The Secrets of Resilient Leadership: When failure is not an option.* New York, NY: Diamedica Publishing.

52   Peterson, C., Craw, M.J., Park, N. & Erwin, M.S. (2011). Resilience and Leadership in Dangerous Contexts, in P.J. Sweeney & M.D. Matthews & P.B. Lester (Eds), *Leadership in Dangerous Situations: A Handbook for the Armed Forces, Emergency Services, and First Responders.* Annapolis, MD: Naval Institute Press, pp. 60–77.

53   Mittlemark, M.M., & Bauer. G.F. (2016). The Meaning of Salutogenesis. In M.B. Mittelmark, S. Shifra, M. Eriksson, G.F. Bauer, J.M. Pelikan, B. Lindström, & G.A. Espnes (Eds), *The Handbook of Salutogenesis.* Springer. https://www.ncbi.nlm.nih.gov/books/NBK435854 (Accessed: 4 August 2020)

54   Machielse, A. Social isolation, meaning in life and resilience. *Innovation in Aging*, 2(S1), 25.

55   Konnikova, M. (2016). How people learn to become resilient. *The New Yorker.* https://www.newyorker.com/science/maria-konnikova/the-secret-formula-for-resilience (Accessed: 30 August 2020)

56   Seligman, M. (2011). Building Resilience. https://hbr.org/2011/04/building-resilience (Accessed: 11 August 2020)

57   Stoltz, P.G. (1997). *The Adversity Quotient.* Canada: John Wiley.

58   https://www.wsj.com/articles/notable-quotable-rejecting-animal-farm-1465338550 (Accessed: 11 August 2020)

59   https://news.stanford.edu/2005/06/14/jobs-061505 (Accessed: 11 August 2020)

60   Lawrence, K. Developing leaders in a VUCA environment. UNC Executive Development. https://www.emergingrnleader.com/wp-content/uploads/2013/02/developing-leaders-in-a-vuca-environment.pdf (Accessed: 11 August 2020)

61   Lawrence, K. Developing leaders in a VUCA environment. UNC Executive Development. https://www.emergingrnleader.com/wp-content/uploads/2013/02/developing-leaders-in-a-vuca-environment.pdf (Accessed: 11 August 2020)

62   Zenger, J. & Folkman, J. (2020). 10 Critical behaviours that improve resiliency. https://zengerfolkman.com/articles/10-critical-behaviors-that-improve-resiliency (Accessed: 12 August 2020)

Chapter 4

63   https://www.bbc.com/news/world-africa-16508829 (Accessed: 11 August 2020)

64   Whitner, E.M., Brodt, S.E., Korsgaard, M.A., & Werner, J.M. (1998). Managers as Initiators of Trust: An Exchange Relationship Framework for Understanding Managerial Trustworthy Behavior. *The Academy of Management Review*, 23(3), (Jul), pp. 513–530.

65   Mayer, R.C, Davis, J.H. (1995). An integrative model of organizational trust. *The Academy of Management Review*, 20(3), (Jul), pp. 709–734.

66   Rosseau, D.M., Sitkin, S.B., Birt, R.S., & Camerer, C. (1998). Not so different after all: A cross discipline view of trust. *The Academy of Management Review*, 23(3), (Jul), pp. 303–404.

67   Borum, R. (2010). The Science of Interpersonal Trust (2010). *Mental Health Law & Policy Faculty Publications*. 574. http://scholarcommons.usf.edu/mhlp_facpub/574 (Accessed: 11 August 2020)

68   Borum, R. (2010). The Science of Interpersonal Trust. *Mental Health Law & Policy Faculty Publications*. 574. http://scholarcommons.usf.edu/mhlp_facpub/574 (Accessed: 11 August 2020)

69   Plutchik, R. (1980). *A General Psycho-evolutionary Theory of Emotion*. New York, NY: Academic Press.

70   Kemp, J. (2018). America's trust deficit. https://www.ipsos.com/sites/default/files/ct/publication/documents/2018-04/18-01-14_trustdeficitfinal.pdf

71   Levine, T. (2019). Five reasons why I am sceptical that indirect or unconscious lies detection is superior to direct deception detection. *Frontiers in Psychology*. https://www.ncbi.nlm.nih.gov/pmc/articles/PMC6706798 (Accessed: 12 August 2020)

72   Edelman, R. (2020). The evolution of trust. https://www.edelman.com/research/evolution-trust (Accessed: 12 August 2020)

73   Swart, T., Chisolm, K., & Brown, P. (2015). *Neuroscience for Leadership: Harnessing the Brain Gain Advantage*. London, UK: Palgrave Macmillan.

74   Barclays fined a record £290m. https://www.ft.com/content/2a4479f8-c030-11e1-9867-00144feabdc0 (Accessed: 18 February 2020)

75   https://reports.weforum.org/outlook-global-agenda-2015 (Accessed: 13 August 2020)

76   Covey, S.M.R. (2006). *The Speed of Trust*. New York, NY: Free Press.

77   Harter, J. (2019). https://info.glintinc.com/uk-state-of-employee-engagement.html?utm_source=google&utm_medium=cpc&utm_campaign=South-Africa_EE&utm_content=NB_employee-engagement&utm_term=388516896919_%2Bemployee%20%2Bengagement&utm_program= wbga18&gclid= Cj0KCQjw7qn1BRD qARIs AKMb HDazArKIYp7JJ q2ZBtEX4vqIkotKt_cFgXeuPorj79QZbjHqt ANvqR8aAq STEALw_wcB (Accessed: 18 February 2020)

78   Zak, P. (2018). The neuroscience of high trust organizations. *American Psychological Association*, 70(1), pp. 45–58.

79   Hall, V. (2009). *The Truth about Trust in Business*. Austin, TX: Emerald Book Company.

Chapter 5

80   Prof Cloete, E. Personal interview, 16 May 2020.

81   Cohen A.R. & Bradford. D.L. (2017). *Influence without Authority*. Hoboken, NJ: Wiley.

82   Cialdini, R.B. (1984). *The Psychology of Influence*. London: Harper Collins.

83   Sharot, T. (2017). *The Influential Mind: What the brain reveals about our power to change others*. London: Little Brown Book.

84   Hadnagy, C. (2011). *Social Engineering: The art of human hacking*. Indianapolis, IN: Wiley Publishing.

85   Ellis, L. Farrington, D.P., & Harrington, A.W. (2019). *Handbook of Crime Correlates* (2nd Edition). Cambridge, MA: Elsevier.

86   Sherman, G., Lee, J.J., Cuddy, A.J.C., Renshon, J., Oveis, C., Gross, J.J. & Lerner. J.S. (2012). Leadership is associated with lower stress levels, *Psychological and Cognitive Sciences*, 109(44), pp. 17903–17907.

87   Anisman, H. Hayley, S. & Kusnecov, A. (2019). *The Immune System and Mental Health*. Cambridge, MA: Academic Press.

88   Zak, P.J. (2017). The Neuroscience of Trust. *Harvard Business Review*. Boston, MA: Harvard Publishing.

89   https://www.wellnessprofessionalsatwork.com/the-magic-of-endorphins   (Accessed: 16 February 2020)

90   https://implicit.harvard.edu/implicit/education.html (Accessed: 14 June 2014)

Chapter 6

91   Block D. (2020). Personal interview, August 8, 2020.

92   P. Pruyn. Continuous partial attention and the demise of discretionary time. https://thesystemsthinker.com/continuous-partial-attention-and-the-demise-of-discretionary-time (Accessed: April 5, 2020)

93   Chandler, D. (n.d). The transmission model of communication. http://visual-memory.co.uk/daniel/Documents/short/trans.html (Accessed: 6 August 2020)

94   Elman, J. (2017). Remote design: How Zapier is building a distributed team. https://zapier.com/blog/remote-design-culture (Accessed: 20 May 2020)

95   Calero, H.H. (2005). *The Power of Non-verbal Communication. How you act is more important than what you say*. Aberdeen, WA: Silver Lakes.

96   O'Toole, J., & Bennis, W. (2009). What's needed next? A culture of candor. *Harvard Business Review*, 87(6), (Jun, 2009), pp. 54–62.

97   Brake, T. (1998). *The Global leader. Critical factors for creating a world class organization*. London: McGraw-Hill.

98   Rackham, N. (1972). Developing negotiating skills. *Industrial and Commercial Training*, 4(6), pp. 266–75.

99   Nelson Mandela Centre of Memory. https://archive.nelsonmandela.org/index.php/za-com-mr-s-16 (Accessed: 7 August 2020)

100 Paulus, D. (2020). Angela Merkel does not use war imagery for Covid. In fact, she hardly uses metaphors. https://theprint.in/world/angela-merkel-doesnt-use-war-imagery-for-covid-in-fact-she-hardly-uses-metaphors/431729 (Accessed: 7 May 2020)

101 Lancaster, S. (2015). *Winning Minds*. London, UK: Palgrave Macmillan.

Chapter 7

102 Kierson, M. (2009). *The Transformational Power of Executive Team Alignment*. Charleston, South Carolina. Advantage Media Group.

Chapter 8

103 Hirshberg, J. (1999). *The Creative Priority: Putting Innovation to Work in Your Business*. New York, NY: Harper Collins.

104 Lederach, J.P. (2014). *The Little Book of Conflict Transformation*. New York, NY: Good Books

105 Bollaert, C. (2019). *Reconciliation and Building a Sustainable Peace: Competing worldviews in South Africa & beyond*. London, UK: Palgrave Macmillan.

106 Suler, J. (2004). The online disinhibition effect. *Cyberpsychology & behavior*, 7(3), pp. 321–326.

107 Katz, D. (1965). Nationalism and strategies of international conflict resolution. In H.C. Kelman (Ed.), *International Behavior: A social psychological analysis*. New York: Holt, Rinehart & Winston. pp. 356–39.

108 Greer, L.& Dannals, J. (2017). Conflict in teams. In E. Salas, R. Rico, & J. Passmore (Eds) *The Wiley Handbook of the Psychology of Teamworking and Collaborative Processes*. Hoboken, NJ: John Wiley & Sons.

109 Mnookin, R.H., Peppet, S.R, & Tulumello, A.S. (2004). *Beyond Winning*. Boston, MA: Belknap Press

110 Fisher, R., & Shapiro, D. (2007). *Building Agreement: Using emotions as you negotiate*. London, UK: Random House.

Chapter 9

111 https://www.igi-global.com/dictionary/collaborative-synergy-leadership-business/4429 (Accessed: 7 August 2020)

112 https://etymology.enacademic.com/34210/synergy (Accessed: 12 February 2020)

113 Salmons, J. & Wilson, L. (2009). *Handbook of Research on Electronic Collaboration and Organizational Synergy* (2 Volumes).

114 Morris, L., Coffman, P., Kaufman, M. & Smethurst, J. (2004). High performance organizations in a wicked problem world. https://www.innovationlabs.com/high_performance.pdf (Accessed: 20 July 2020)

115 Culmsee, P., Kailash, A. (2011). *The Heretic's Guide to Best Practices: The Reality of Managing Complex Problems in Organisations*. iUniverse. Kindle Edition.

116 Elman, J. (2017). Remote design: How Zapier is building a remote design culture. https://zapier.com/blog/remote-design-culture (Accessed: June 3, 2020)

117 Csikszentmihalyi, M. (2003). *Good business. Leadership flow and the making of meaning*. London, UK: Penguin Books.

118 Rosing, K., Bledow, R., Frese, M., Baytalskaya, N., Lascano, J. & Farr, J.L. (2018). The temporal pattern of creativity and implementation in teams. *Journal of Occupational and Organizational Psychology*, 91(4), pp. 798–822.

119 Edmonson, A.C. & Lei, Z. (2014). Psychological safety: The history, renaissance, and future of an interpersonal construct. *Annual Review of Organizational Psychology and Organizational Behavior*, 1, pp. 23–43.

120 Edmondson, A.C. (2019). *The Fearless Organization: Creating psychologically safety in the workplace for learning, innovation and growth.* Hoboken, NJ: John Wiley & Sons.

121 Hill, L., Brandeau, G., Truelove, E., & Lineback, K. (2015). The capabilities your organization needs to sustain innovation. *Harvard Business Review.* https://hbr.org/2015/01/the-capabilities-your-organization-needs-to-sustain-innovation (Accessed: 15 March 2020)

122 Messer, H., Snijder, E., Casali, D., Franzen, A. & Eckstein, J. (2014). How to communicate effectively with a remote team. Lessons learned in offshoring and nearshoring. https://www.amazon.com/How-Communicate-Effectively-Remote-Team-ebook/dp/B00PW4GOJK#reader_B00PW4GOJK (Accessed: 20 June 2020)

Chapter 10

123 Heifetz, R., Grashow, A., & Linsky, M. (2009). *The Practice of Adaptive Leadership.* Boston, MA: Harvard Business Press.

Chapter 11

124 Romzek, B.S. & Dubnick, M.J. (1987). Accountability in the public sector: Lessons from the Challenger tragedy. *Public Administration Review*, [Online]. 47(3), pp. 227–238. Available at: http://www.jstor.org/stable/975901 (Accessed: 15 February 2020)

125 Pless, N. M. (2007). Understanding responsible leadership. Role identity and motivational drivers. *Journal of Business Ethics*, 74, pp. 437–456.

126 Pless, N.M. & Mark, T. (2006). Responsible leadership in a stakeholder society. A relational perspective. *Journal of Business Ethics*, pp. 66, 99–115.

127 Frankl. V.E. (1992). *Man's Search for Meaning*, 4th edition. Boston: Beacon Press, p. 134.

128 SA Bill of Responsibilities. Available from http://www.education.gov.za/LinkClick.aspx?fileticket=QX%2FfCO6lKM0%3D&tabid=454&mid=425 (Accessed: 25July 2020)

129 *Oxford English Dictionary.* http:www.oed.com (Accessed: 3 July 2020)

130 Myatt, M. A crisis of leadership – what's next? *Forbes*, Oct 10, 2013.

131 Wood, J.A., & Winston. B.E. (2005). Toward a new understanding of leader accountability: Defining a critical construct. *Journal of Leadership & Organizational Studies* 11(3), pp. 84–94.

132 Lindberg, S.I. (2009). Accountability – the core concept and its subtypes. Available at http://r4d.dfid.gov.uk/pdf/outputs/appp/appp-wp1.pdf (Accessed: 4 July 4 2020)

133 http://www.news24.com/MyNews24/The-Limpopo-book-crisis-Angie-Motshekga-an-Epic-Failure-20120726 (Accessed: 7 August 7 2020)

134 Wood, J.A. & Winston, B.E. (2005). Towards a new understanding of accountability: Defining a critical construct. *Journal of Leadership and Organizational Studies*, 11(3), pp. 84–94.

135 Taleb, N.N. (2007). *The Black Swan: The impact of the highly improbable.* London, UK: Penguin.

136 Wucker, M. (2016). *The Gray Rhino.* New York, NY: St Martin's Press.

Chapter 12

137 https://edition.cnn.com/2015/05/11/asia/china-france-company-holiday/index.html (Accessed: 12 February 2020)

138 Fogg, B.J. (2019). *Tiny Habits: Small things that change everything.* London, UK: Virgin Books.

139 Amabile, T., & Kramer, S.J. (2015). The power of small wins. Boston, MA: *Harvard Business Review.*

140 https://www.iodsa.co.za/page/DownloadKingIVapp (Accessed: 7 August 2020)

141 Professor Mervyn King, presentation, 22 February 2017.

142 Ross, J.A. (2008). Make your good team great. Boston, MA: *Harvard Business Review.*

143 Sinek, S. (2019). *The Infinite Game.* New York, NY: Penguin Random House.

ABOUT THE AUTHOR

Dr Andrew J. Brough is a global leadership and organisational development and e-learning specialist based in Knysna, South Africa.

Andy is a professional speaker, lecturer, facilitator, executive coach and conference moderator. Starting out in educational broadcasting, Andy went on to become a specialist in adult education and training in four broad areas: leadership and strategy; sales and marketing; high performance teams; and the borderless workplace – preparing leaders for the new world of remote work. He is founder of the Brough Leadership Institute and has worked with thousands of leaders in many Fortune 500 companies and businesses, governments and non-profit organisations in more than 80 countries over the past 25 years.

Andy has a Bachelor of Arts in Education from the University of the Witwatersrand, South Africa, and a Master's degree in Organisational Leadership from Regent University, Virginia, USA. His PhD from the Da Vinci Institute, South Africa, explored the relationship between responsible leadership, corporate reputation and corporate marketing management. Andy is also a registered Chartered Marketer.

As an executive education specialist, he is part of the external faculty for TMA World, leading providers of talent development and global collaboration business training, as well as a number of universities including the Gordon Institute of Business Science, University of Pretoria and Monash University, now IIE MSA.

www.broughleadership.com
admin@broughleadership.com